PRISONERS
OF WAR

PRISONERS OF WAR

Ballykinlar Internment Camp 1920-1921

Liam Ò Duibhir

MERCIER PRESS
IRISH PUBLISHER – IRISH STORY

MERCIER PRESS

Cork

www.mercierpress.ie

© Liam Ó Duibhir, 2013

ISBN: 978 1 78117 041 0

10 9 8 7 6 5 4 3 2 1

A CIP record for this title is available from the British Library

Printed and bound in the EU.

This book is dedicated to the memory of a dear friend
Seamus McCann
1936–2012

Contents

Acknowledgements

This book would not have been written if were not for the various accounts and writings of the men who were interned in the first mass centre for internment in Ireland, Ballykinlar internment camp. The accounts recorded through the Bureau of Military History and the various documents housed in collections of the National Library of Ireland, Kilmainham Gaol Museum, UCD Archives and private collections, formed the basis of this book.

I would like to take this opportunity to thank all of those who assisted, encouraged and helped in many ways throughout the research and writing of this book.

In particular, thank you to Anne-Maire Ryan, Kilmainham Gaol Museum, for all her help when researching and for scanning the various photographs. Many thanks also to Liz Gillis for the copy of the diary of Ted Donohue, which was a valuable insight into the daily events of camp life.

A special word of thanks to Seamus Helferty and the staff at UCD Archives for their help while I was researching the Desmond Fitzgerald and Michael Hayes collections.

The staff members at the Bureau of Military History were, as always, very helpful while I was there and unfailingly prompt in emailing witness statements and other material. I would like to thank Commandant Victor Laing, Noelle, Lisa and Hugh for all their help over the years.

During my research, I was also presented with documents and other material by relatives of the men who were interned in the camp and these were invaluable sources of information. Pat Dawson, Letterkenny, very kindly gave me access to the Ballykinlar papers of his late uncle, Jim Dawson. I would like to thank Pat and his wife Mary for the use of premises where I was able to write this book. Many thanks also to Margaret Carton, Rathmullan, for the transcribed version of the interview of her late father, Michael Sheehy, with Ernie O'Malley (which is part of the Ernie O'Malley Notebooks collection at UCD Archives) and to Kathleen McKenna for access to the various items belonging to her late father, Stephen Carroll, from his time at the camp.

I am grateful to Jack Britton, Donegal town, for the use of a collection of photographs of Ballykinlar camp. This collection of photographs was originally the property of his uncle, Hugh Britton, who was interned for several months at the camp and was killed within a few months of his release.

Thank you to P. J. Dunne, Drumelis and Butlersbridge, County Cavan, for the use of his collection of photographs of the camp and for permission to use information relating to the arrest of Cavan men prior to their internment in the camp. Thanks also to Patrick Tormey for a photograph of his late relative Joseph Tormey, and to Tadhg Galvin, Cork and Brighton, for providing me with a copy of a photo of his late grand-uncle, Tadhg Barry.

I am grateful to all the staff at the National Library for assistance in both the reading room and the main library. Thanks also to the staff at the National Archives of Ireland, the British National Archives and the staff at Galway City Library for all their assistance.

Liam MacElhinney generously allowed the use of an original copy of the *Sinn Fein Rebellion Handbook* and *On My Keeping and in Theirs: a record of experiences on the run, in Derry Gaol, and in Ballykinlar Camp*, written by former internee Louis J. Walsh. I would also like to thank Liam for reading an early version of the manuscript.

The lists of men interned at Ballykinlar camp were compiled from a number of sources, including a copy of the 'Book of Ballykinlar' which was part of the Owen Quinn collection at the National Library. I would like to thank Pádraig Ó Baoighill, Rannafast and Monaghan, for translating the lists for me.

I would also like to thank others who kindly read the manuscript: Dr Fearghal Mac Bhloscaidh, Tyrone and Belfast; Paddy MacIntyre and Helen Salmon, Letterkenny; Wendy Nic Airt, Skerries, County Dublin; and especially Sonya (Black) Keeney, Rathmullan, County Donegal, who read the manuscript and gave me good feedback and helpful suggestions. My gratitude to you all.

I would also like to thank all the staff at Mercier Press and Jenny Laing for editing the book.

To my friends, and particularly my family, who were as always supportive and helpful throughout – thank you all.

Introduction

In December 1920, Ballykinlar internment camp opened its gates to receive hundreds of men suspected of involvement in the IRA or Sinn Féin, organisations proscribed by British law. It was the first centre of mass internment in Ireland and housed up to 2,000 men over a twelve-month period.

Internment in its most naked form is the arrest and imprisonment of individuals based on the mere suspicion of involvement in activities considered a danger to the security of a country or state. They are incarcerated for an indefinite period in a state of idleness, designed to demoralise them to the extent that they will abandon their ideology or aspiration. Once inside the inhospitable barbed wire entanglements of a military camp, such as Ballykinlar, the individuals are classified as internees.

This form of detention was used by the British for centuries, but was only put on a statutory footing following the outbreak of the Great War of 1914–18. It was introduced through the enactment of the Defence of the Realm Act 1914 and subsequent amendments, and was used to counter any threat to the security of British territory. The British were, therefore, able to use internment to suppress opposition to their presence in Ireland in the aftermath of the 1916 Rising. However, the confinement of 1,800 men, many of whom were sent to Frongoch internment camp in North Wales, is now considered to be one of many British blunders in the reaction to the Rising, as this enforced incarceration brought the insurgents together and served as the launch pad for a much more organised assault on the British establishment in Ireland.

The next episode of wholesale arrests and internment occurred in May 1918, following the 'German Plot' saga, when the British claimed that Sinn Féin were involved with the German government in planning an armed insurrection in Ireland. Among those arrested were seventy-three prominent figures within the Sinn Féin organisation, including Éamon de Valera and Arthur Griffith.

The 'German Plot' prisoners were still interned when the Irish War of Independence broke out. The conflict began in January 1919, when a group of IRA men led by Dan Breen and Seán Treacy attacked and killed two RIC men escorting quarry workers with explosives at Soloheadbeg, County Tipperary. From that moment, hostilities between the IRA and the various elements of the British establishment slowly developed.

Initially internment was not used on a large scale in the War of Independence – up to December 1919, only four men were arrested and transported to England for such imprisonment (the Defence of the Realm Act only gave provision for individuals arrested under the act to be detained in England). However, by mid-1920 the war had evolved into a vicious and depraved campaign. Many events during that year heightened the volatile relationship between the Irish people and the British establishment in Ireland, including the murder in March of Tomás MacCurtain, Sinn Féin lord mayor of Cork, by members

of the RIC, and the deaths of another three Cork men –
Terence MacSwiney, Joseph Murphy and Michael Fitzgerald –
on hunger strike in October, and later Conor McElvaney from
County Monaghan. The Restoration of Order in Ireland Act
1920 provided for the death sentence, and the first of twenty-
five executions took place on Monday 1 November 1920, with
the hanging of eighteen-year-old medical student Kevin Barry
at Mountjoy jail for his part in an ambush on British military
in September 1920.

The focus of the IRA's campaign soon turned to the
assassination of senior figures within the RIC and members
of the British intelligence service. The escalation of the conflict
and the breakdown of British administration in the country led
the British establishment to re-evaluate their position, and as a
result much emphasis was put on the internment of suspected
members of the IRA. The Restoration of Order in Ireland Act,
which replaced the Defence of the Realm Act, was passed
on Monday 9 August 1920 and came into force on Friday
13 August. It enabled the British establishment in Ireland to
govern through regulations introduced to counter the threat
from the IRA and Sinn Féin.

On Sunday 21 November 1920, following the assassination
campaign on that day by Michael Collins' Squad, the British
authorities in Dublin Castle ordered wholesale arrests and
internment under the Restoration of Order in Ireland Regulations. This included those suspected of involvement in the
shootings and those generally suspected of membership of the
IRA and Sinn Féin. Many of those killed or injured during

the attacks were British military intelligence, secret service or court-martial officers: the event became a turning point in British policy in Ireland.

The British mounted large-scale arrests the following day and in the months that followed, first in Dublin and subsequently throughout the county. As police barracks, town halls and various other temporary holding centres quickly filled, the British identified a disused military camp, Ballykinlar, at the mouth of Dundrum Bay on the coast of County Down, as an appropriate location that would hold a large number of those arrested. Remote, desolate, surrounded by mountains, the sea, barbed wire and large numbers of British military, Ballykinlar camp was calculated to destroy the ambitions and energies of the men endeavouring to end British rule in Ireland.

Although the use of internment camps was not new to the British, by detaining a cross-section of Irish society they inadvertently established a small community within the barbed wires of Ballykinlar camp. Significantly, twenty-three prisoners in No. 1 compound and forty-nine in No. 2 had previously been at Frongoch, which had become a training ground for resistance fighters. These internees were therefore well-versed in counteracting what was designed to demoralise and destroy, with education, sport, deliberate non-cooperation and varied escape attempts, all of which had a binding effect on the men. Although life in the camp was mostly unpleasant and sometimes dangerous for the internees, the resolve of their British military jailers was also greatly tested.

The British establishment were faced with a dilemma

following the introduction of internment camps in Ireland. To appease certain elements within British politics and the general public, the IRA Volunteers could not be given prisoner-of-war status. General Nevil Macready had prepared a pamphlet addressed to members of the IRA emphasising that on arrest they would not be regarded as prisoners of war. Large numbers of Macready's pamphlet were dropped from an aeroplane over a number of locations, including the town of Millstreet, County Cork, on Tuesday 17 May 1921. It read:

To Members of IRA:
Read this and if you still decide to be led astray by your leaders in the belief that you are 'Soldiers' and entitled to be treated as soldiers, you have only yourself to blame.

Only armed forces who fulfil certain conditions can avail themselves of the rights by the laws and customs of war.
These conditions are:

(1) They must be commanded by a person responsible for his subordinates.

(2) They must wear a fixed distinctive sign or uniform Recognisable at a Distance.

(3) They must carry arms Openly.

(4) They must conduct their operations in accordance with the laws and customs of War.[1]

Publicly British politicians described those arrested and interned with emotive terms such as 'murderers' and 'terrorists', men not deserving of POW status. Yet it was the British military that was charged with detaining and guarding the men, and its soldiers who had the task of daily confrontation with the internees in their challenge to British military authority within the camp. Over time, the military covertly bowed to the resistance of the internees and to some extent capitulated to the demands and protests within the barbed-wire cages.

The story of the Ballykinlar internment camp is on the one hand an account of suffering, death, espionage, murder, mal-treatment and torture. However, from the internees' perspective, it is also a chronicle of survival, comradeship, community, discipline, tuition, celebration and enterprise.

1

Internment –
1916 to 1920

1916

In the aftermath of the 1916 Rising, 3,226 men and seventy-seven women were arrested. A total of 1,862 men and five women were served with internment orders under Regulation 14(b) of the Defence of the Realm Act 1914. They were transferred to Britain and temporarily held in various detention centres in England and Scotland, including Knutsford, Stafford, Wakefield, Wandsworth, Woking, Lewes, Barlinnie prison in Glasgow and Perth.[1] Some of the internees served their terms of detention in English jails, but the vast majority of the male internees were transferred to the Frongoch internment camp, near Bala in North Wales.

Despite the alien environment, the prisoners used their time to plan for a resumption of war against the British establishment in Ireland. Frongoch later received the title 'University of Revolution' as it facilitated the reorganisation of the Irish Volunteers and provided training for men from all over Ireland, who, on their release, were able to use their newly acquired skills in a new phase of the hostilities against Britain. The contacts made in Frongoch formed the blueprint of the intelligence network established during the War of Independence by men from various counties who played prominent roles in that campaign. The internment of such a large number of revolutionaries in one place was a serious mistake on the part of the British, one that would greatly increase the success of the IRA's operations in the years that followed.[2]

1918 – the 'German Plot'

Throughout 1917 the Sinn Féin party reorganised and successfully contested by-elections in four Irish constituencies. At the same time the Irish Volunteers and IRB were also restructuring throughout the country. The success of Sinn Féin in the four by-elections in 1917 concerned the British authorities and they endeavoured to suppress the growing political opposition.

The possible internment of the Sinn Féin leaders was raised at a British cabinet meeting on Friday 19 April 1918. The proposal originated in a memorandum sent to the War Cabinet from the British Home Office and concerned the deportation of the Sinn Féin leaders to England under the Defence of the Realm Regulation No. 14. George N. Barnes, MP for the Gorbals Division, Glasgow, stated that to intern persons under Regulation 14(b) it would first have to be established that they were involved in 'hostile associations' with the enemy, i.e. Germany. Barnes advised that the regulation would have to be amended, as he believed it was doubtful that a connection could be proved between the enemy and most of the Sinn Féin leaders.

The British prime minister, Lloyd George, then read from a letter sent by Lord French, British viceroy and lord lieutenant of Ireland, which concerned a plan to deal with a rebellious outbreak against the introduction of conscription to Ireland. He also read letters from Walter Long, secretary of state at the Colonial Office, and Lieutenant-General Bryan McMahon, British military commander-in-chief in Ireland, who stated that armed resistance was a possible outcome if the Military Service Act which allowed for conscription was introduced in Ireland.

Lloyd George was strongly of the opinion that an amendment should be adopted to counter any insurrection. The War Cabinet decided to amend Regulation 14(b) with the insertion of the following:

> In any area in respect of which the operation of section one of the Defence of the Realm (Amendment) Act, 1915, is for the time being suspended, this regulation shall apply in relation to any person who is suspected of acting or having acted, or of being about to act in a manner prejudicial to the public safety or the defence of the realm, as it applies in relation to persons of hostile origin or association.

This amendment served as the cornerstone of the British government's internment policy in Ireland for the foreseeable future.[3] Barnes stated that he wished his dissension to be placed on record.

The motive for targeting the leaders of Sinn Féin and many others for arrest and internment originated with the large-scale opposition to the threat of conscription being introduced to Ireland in early 1918. The opposition to the Conscription Bill was an embarrassment to the British government and their reaction comprised of a vicious propaganda campaign in Ireland, Britain and America, supporting the bill. The most significant act came on Wednesday 8 May 1918, when *The Times* newspaper published a statement from the Dublin-born unionist politician, Edward Carson, stating that the British government had in their possession the clearest evidence of an alliance between Sinn Féin and Germany. The following week, on Friday 17 May 1918, the British government ordered the arrest and internment of all known and prominent members of Sinn Féin on the premise that they were involved with the German government in a plan to smuggle arms into Ireland. That night, in what became known as the 'German Plot', seventy-three Sinn Féin members were arrested, including Éamon de Valera, Arthur Griffith, William Cosgrave, Countess Markievicz and other prominent figures throughout the country. No charges were preferred and many received their internment orders only while being transported from Dún Laoghaire to Holyhead in Wales on the mail boat. Those arrested were sent to various jails throughout Britain.

The following day the British government issued a press statement giving reasons for the arrests:

In consequence of the knowledge that certain persons in Ireland have entered into treasonable communication with the German enemy, it is the duty of all loyal subjects to assist his Majesty's Government in the suppression of this treasonable conspiracy.[4]

The Sinn Féin leaders had received prior warning of the arrests through Éamon Broy, one of Michael Collins' spies at Dublin Castle, but decided to use the situation to their advantage, allowing the British government to walk into another misguided manoeuvre.[5] Many of the men and women arrested were later selected as candidates for the general election of December 1918, and Sinn Féin effectively used the propaganda of their unjust incarceration to ensure that a number of them would be elected while they were still in British jails.[6]

The issue of releasing the internees was raised at a cabinet meeting in Downing Street on Wednesday 5 February 1919. The British viceroy and lord lieutenant of Ireland, Lord French, thought it advisable to release those interned following the 'German Plot' arrests. The then chief secretary for Ireland, Ian MacPherson, presented the suggestion to the meeting, but some cabinet members felt releasing the prisoners at that point would be perceived as pandering to pressure from Dáil Éireann and Sinn Féin. Winston Churchill, secretary of state for war stated, 'It would be a disastrous sign of weakness to let out the Sinn Féin prisoners.' In contrast, MacPherson voiced the opinion that everybody in Ireland was denouncing the British government for keeping the internees locked up in Britain.[7]

Éamon de Valera, Seán McGarry and Seán Milroy escaped

from Lincoln prison in February 1919, and in March the other men and women interned following the 'German Plot' arrests were released when the British government ordered a general release of all the prisoners.[8]

The War of Independence
and the new internment policy

The Irish War of Independence began in January 1919 and gradually developed into an intense campaign, with the IRA adopting guerrilla war tactics against the superior military machine of the British Army. The arrest and internment of those suspected of involvement in the Irish Volunteers and Sinn Féin continued into 1919 and 1920 with men being transported to various jails throughout England, including Wormwood Scrubs.[9]

From February 1920, the British prison authorities were expressing concerns about the indifference of these Irish internees to the prisons' rules and regulations. In that month seventy internees were being held at Wormwood Scrubs prison. The prison governor, Major Briscoe, had considered the internees to be 'on the whole a respectable body of men ... content to live quietly under the regulations which were approved with much care and thought ... ' until the arrival of Joseph McGrath from Dublin, who had been appointed the officer representing the body of internees. Significantly, Briscoe went on to say that 'few if any complaints were received by the commissioners until the arrival of McGrath'.[10]

The chairman of the prison commissioners, Sir Evelyn Ruggles-Brise, raised the issue of indiscipline among the Irish internees with the British home secretary. He suggested that the use of military camps as centres of internment would be more suitable for the growing number of internees. His proposal was based on the British government's intention of continuing the internment policy as a means of countering the growing threat from the IRA and civilians associated with Sinn Féin. Ruggles-Brise believed the use of military camps in England was the solution, and requested the transfer of internees to the authority of the British military and the War Office.[11]

The small-scale arrest and internment of IRA and Sinn Féin personnel continued in March 1920. Raids targeted prominent members of Sinn Féin and those suspected of membership of the IRA from different parts of the country. The men arrested in the Ulster counties were transferred to Crumlin Road jail in Belfast, where they were held for one week. While there, a large number of the political prisoners went on hunger strike in solidarity with men making a similar protest in Mountjoy jail in Dublin. After a week at Crumlin Road jail the men were removed in lorries to the Belfast docks, where they were subjected to a vicious assault by a unionist mob who threw, amongst other things, nuts, bolts and lumps of coal at them. Many sustained serious injury and were taken to South Wales on a British naval destroyer without receiving medical treatment. They then went by train to London, where they were transferred to Wormwood Scrubs.

Since the British were not prepared for a large number of

men at Wormwood Scrubs continuing hunger strikes to the death, they released them to the care of hospitals in London under the Prisons Temporary Release for Ill Health Act 1913, where they subsequently ended their action. After a few weeks recovering in hospital, they were informed that the British intended to re-arrest them, so they decided to stage a walkout. They made contact with the Irish Self-Determination League in London and arrangements were made to accommodate them with Irish people living in the capital. Their hosts then arrived at the hospital, posing as visitors, and the men walked out with them. All eventually returned to Ireland.[12]

However, the British internment policy continued throughout Ireland and the number of internees was soon to increase dramatically, forcing the British to look for new, larger places to incarcerate their prisoners – the first of these was Ballykinlar.

2

Bloody Sunday

In the latter part of 1920, the British introduced night-time curfews in the Dublin area, which greatly hampered the activities of the Dublin-based IRA and increased the risk of capture. Events escalated on both sides until Sunday 21 November 1920, Bloody Sunday.

In the early hours of Wednesday 10 November 1920, the IRA chief of staff, Richard Mulcahy, had a narrow escape. He was in the house on South Circular Road, Dublin, of Dr Michael Hayes, who lectured in French in Dublin University, when the British military raided it. Mulcahy escaped through a skylight, but in his haste forgot to take with him a briefcase containing the names and addresses of over 200 IRA personnel from various parts of the country.[1] Michael Hayes was arrested and would be one of the first group of a few hundred men to be interned at Ballykinlar internment camp in early December 1920.

The discovery of the briefcase and the information it contained was a significant victory for the British intelligence machine and put considerable pressure on the IRA organisation.

The discovery was communicated to all IRA divisions throughout the country and those whose names were included in the list were warned to vary their routines and stay away from their homes as mass arrests were expected to follow.

About that time, the IRA intelligence department under Michael Collins had been considering an attack on British intelligence by assassinating British secret service agents and court-martial officers living in various addresses around Dublin. Collins summoned his agents in the Dublin Metropolitan Police (DMP), including Éamon Broy, to a meeting at a house in Rathgar. Gearóid O'Sullivan, IRA adjutant general, was also present. The DMP members were asked to monitor the movements of men from certain addresses, particularly during curfew hours.[2]

The man assigned to undertake the overall planning for the assassinations was Dick McKee, OC Dublin Brigade. The operation was to be carried out by the Squad.[3] This special IRA unit, formed by Michael Collins in 1919, was tasked with carrying out the execution of enemy agents, spies and informers. Members of the Squad were always accompanied by one of the intelligence staff during their various assassination operations. They were later supported by an active service unit which was formed to assist in assassination operations and was made up of Volunteers from the four battalions of the Dublin Brigade.[4]

A list of enemy agents and spies was compiled by IRA agents Broy, David Neligan and Jim McNamara, who were all working in the Detective Branch ('G' Division) of the DMP at Dublin

Castle.[5] A network of people was used in the surveillance of the targeted persons and anything suspicious was reported. Maids, house boarders, messengers, waiters and footmen, for example, kept a close eye on anything out of the ordinary. Joseph Dolan, a member of the intelligence staff, visited many of the hotels and boarding houses where the targeted men were living to collect the information gathered by the network, which was then fed back to Collins and the IRA General Headquarters (GHQ) intelligence staff.[6] Intelligence was also gathered on a group of British Secret Service agents known as the 'Cairo Gang' because they frequented the Cairo Café on Grafton Street, Dublin.[7] Charles Dalton, a member of the Squad, was instructed by the intelligence staff to contact a young maid, Maudie, who worked at one of two boarding houses at 28–29 Upper Pembroke Street, where some of these men resided. She provided details of the residents' movements and retrieved torn-up documents and photographs from the waste-paper baskets. When pieced together, the fragments revealed information on Volunteers wanted by the British.[8]

Approximately one week before the planned assassinations, meetings were held by the various battalions around Dublin and they were instructed regarding 'important operations' to take place the following week.[9] They were detailed to cover the units tasked with shooting the selected targets in different parts of the city. Two-man patrols were to cover roads approaching and exiting streets where the British targets were staying. Gerald (Garry) Byrne and Denny O'Brien were instructed to patrol the area from Leonard's Corner to Rialto and to fire shots at any British military or police travelling in the direction of the city centre before 9 a.m. on the morning of the operation. There were other patrols posted at various locations around the city.[10]

On Saturday evening, 20 November, approximately 100 Volunteers from the intelligence staff, the Squad and members of the Dublin battalions assembled in a house on Lower Gardiner Street. The meeting was addressed by Dick McKee, who told them that a major operation had been planned for the following morning, beginning at 9 a.m., with the objective of eliminating a number of British intelligence agents and spies. McKee warned of the dangers involved and emphasised the importance of assassinating the British officers who were residing in hotels and boarding houses around the city centre and were a menace to the IRA. McKee said that he was conscious of the dangers the men would encounter on the day and the repercussions in the days that followed.[11]

The operation hit a slight snag that evening when Dick McKee and Peadar Clancy were arrested at about 10.30 p.m. at a house owned by Seán Fitzpatrick in 36 Lower Gloucester Street.[12] In addition, Conor Clune, an IRA Volunteer from County Clare who was not involved in the operation and had only arrived in Dublin that night, was apprehended. He arrived at Vaughan's Hotel about 1.30 a.m. on 21 November, unaware that the place was likely to be raided: Michael Collins and several others had been there but had been advised to leave as the hotel porter's suspicions had been aroused.[13] McKee, Clancy and Clune were taken to Exchange Court, inside the grounds of Dublin Castle. Michael Collins instructed David

Neligan to search the Bridewell Barracks, but he found no sign of them. A twelve-strong rescue party was waiting in a nearby church.[14]

Despite the setback, the plan to wipe out the Dublin-based British intelligence network began on the Sunday morning.[15] The first target for assassination was Captain Baggally, a British court-martial officer. He was believed to have been one of those involved in the torture of Kevin Barry. Members of the Squad, including Seán Lemass, arrived at Baggally's lodgings, 119 Lower Baggot Street, and parked their car behind a house on the opposite side of the street. Three or four men entered the building while two stood guard outside. The assassination team knew the room in which Baggally was staying and kicked in the door. He attempted to escape through a window, but was shot several times. All the IRA men successfully escaped.[16]

The next to be killed was Colonel Fitzpatrick at 28 Earlsfort Terrace, who was from Tipperary and had a short time earlier been kidnapped by the IRA while stationed in County Clare. He had escaped, suffering a dislocated shoulder in the process, and had been released from hospital in Dublin only a few days before.[17]

Another target was a guest house at 22 Lower Mount Street where two British agents, Mahon and Peel, were staying. Two members of the Squad, James Slattery and Tom Keogh, with six Volunteers from E Company, 2nd Battalion of the Dublin Brigade, arrived at the address shortly before 9 a.m. When a maid admitted them, two men remained at the door to ensure no one entered or left. Another member of the household staff, on realising what was happening, shouted to a group from the RIC Auxiliary Division who were passing. Two went for back-up, while the others approached the building. Billy McLean, one of the IRA men at the front door, opened fire, keeping them at bay for a while, but was injured when they returned fire. Meanwhile Slattery and Keogh shot Mahon. There was a second man in the room, but they had no instructions to shoot him, and only later discovered that he was an 'undesirable character' and should have been killed. On hearing the shots, the other target, Peel, locked his door and managed to escape through a window. The two members of the Auxiliary Division who went for back-up were ambushed and killed by an IRA cover party.[18]

When the IRA men failed to shoot Peel they abandoned the operation. On discovering that the British military were covering their escape route, they left through the rear of the property, engaging in a running battle with the military and Auxiliaries. One of the IRA party, Frank Teeling, was shot and injured. He was subsequently arrested, convicted and sentenced to be hanged, but later escaped from Kilmainham gaol along with Ernie O'Malley and Simon Donnelly. Although wounded, Bill McLean escaped with the help of Tom Keogh. Joseph Dolan and others, who were returning from Ranelagh, picked them up on the road. Dolan and the others had aborted their operation in Ranelagh after discovering that their intended target, Lieutenant Noble, had left his lodgings at 7 a.m.[19]

One British officer and two civilians were assassinated at 117 Morehampton Road: the landlord Thomas Henry Smith and the two men staying with him, Captain McLean and an ex-soldier called J. Caldow, McLean's brother-in-law.

Another court-martial officer, Captain Newbury, was staying at 92 Lower Baggot Street with his wife. IRA men including Bill Stapleton, Jack Stafford, Joe Leonard and Hugo MacNeill, knocked at the front door asking for him. They were shown to the ground-floor rooms where Newbury and his wife were staying. The Volunteers knocked on the front parlour door, but receiving no reply, knocked at the back door, which was opened by Mrs Newbury who, on seeing the men with revolvers drawn, tried to close it. One of the Volunteers jammed his foot in the door and they forced their way in. Newbury and his wife ran into the adjoining room and attempted to barricade the door, but the IRA shot at the door and a bullet passed through hitting the target. The men forced their way in as Newbury was attempting to escape through a window. He was shot a further seven times from inside the room and by those standing guard on the street. He died half in and half out of the window. Newbury's wife was standing in the corner of the room screaming and in a terrified state.[20]

The next address was a boarding house at 28–9 Upper Pembroke Street where six targets were staying. When Charles Dalton, with Paddy Flanagan and several other Volunteers arrived, the hall door was open as the porter was shaking mats on the front steps. Dalton, Flanagan and two other Volunteers went to a room on the top floor occupied by two officers, Major Dowling and Major Rice.[21] The Volunteers pushed the door open and found them awake in bed – both were shot. Captain

Kenlyside was wounded in the arm and was saved by his wife who struggled with the IRA men. Colonel Woodcock was descending the stairs when he came upon the members of the Squad. Woodcock called out to Colonel Montgomery, who was shot in the stomach as he came out of his room. Woodcock was shot as he tried to return to his room to get his weapon. The sixth man, Murray, who was also an officer, was shot and wounded as he was descending the stairs.[22]

A party of IRA men entered 38 Upper Mount Street having been admitted by a servant, Catherine Farrell. She pointed out the rooms of Lieutenant Bennett and Lieutenant Aimes. Bennett was dragged into Aimes' bedroom and both men were shot dead.

The last operation of that morning took place at the Gresham Hotel on Sackville Street (now O'Connell Street). The IRA party split into two groups with one going to room 14 occupied by Lieutenant L. E. Wilde, who was shot when he opened the door. The other party went to room 24 and shot ex-captain Patrick McCormack five times as he sat in bed reading a newspaper.[23]

The British reaction to the Sunday morning events was both swift and brutal. Large numbers of military, Auxiliary cadets, Black and Tans and RIC converged on the streets of the city as part of a large-scale security operation. The city was already a hive of activity as crowds were arriving for the Gaelic football match due to take place at Croke Park that afternoon between Dublin and Tipperary. The match attracted up to 15,000 men, women and children, and was to become the target of a vicious British reprisal. The combined British forces entered Croke Park at approximately 3 p.m. while the game was in progress and began indiscriminately shooting into the crowd, killing fourteen and injuring many others.[24] The victims were John Scott, aged fourteen, James Mathews, Jeremiah O'Leary aged ten, Patrick O'Dowd, Jane Boyle, William Robinson, Thomas Hogan, James Burke, Michael Feery, James Teehan, Joseph Traynor, Thomas Ryan, Michael Hogan and Daniel Carroll.[25]

The three IRA men who had been arrested on the previous night, Dick McKee, Peadar Clancy and Conor Clune, were tortured and murdered in Dublin Castle by members of the Auxiliary Division that night. This caused a lot of anger among the Volunteers of the Dublin Brigade and the Squad. Michael Collins was in a bad way over their deaths and tried to identify the informer who had betrayed McKee and Clancy to the British. Every member of the Squad wanted to deal personally with the person responsible for their capture.[26]

Michael Collins made it clear that the methods of the British military would be met with harsh retribution:

My one intention was the destruction of the undesirables who continued to make miserable the lives of ordinary citizens. I have proof enough to assure myself of the atrocities which this gang of spies and informers have committed. If I had a second motive it was no more than a feeling such as I would have for a dangerous reptile. By their destruction the very air is made sweeter. For myself, my conscience is clear. There is no crime in detecting in wartime the spy and the informer. They have destroyed without trial. I have paid them back in their own coin.[27]

Widespread raids throughout the city resulted in over a hundred arrests that night. The events of the previous day sent shockwaves through the British establishment, in both Ireland and England. David Neligan was at breakfast in Dublin Castle that morning and later described the scene:

> In the Castle, pandemonium reigned. An officer, whose pals had been wiped out, shot himself in his room. The tragedy was hushed up … A long string of cars and baggage choked the Castle gate all day. Officers, Secret Service men and their wives were flying to protection and a room could not be found in the Castle for love nor money. A British officer wounded himself in the D.B.C. café in Dame Street and then put up a tale of being attacked and received compensation …[28]

In the days that followed, a hotel was commandeered for officers' quarters and was heavily guarded by the military, as was City Hall.[29]

As well as the immediate, violent reaction by British forces on Bloody Sunday, the killings by the IRA on that day would force the British government into large-scale action that would lead to a massive surge in the numbers of interned men.

3

The Internment Round-Up

The long-term reaction to the events of Sunday 21 November 1920, which became known as Bloody Sunday, was not confined to Dublin. On Sunday evening, 21 November, a party of the Auxiliary forces attached to the RIC raided Bruree, County Limerick, arresting two men, John Driscoll and Patrick Murphy. Both were taken to Macroom Castle in County Cork and on the journey one of the Auxiliaries told them that they would be very lucky if they were alive in the morning. They were held at Macroom Castle for several days and on Monday 29 November they heard a lorry pull up in the castle yard and a soldier say that sixteen Auxiliary cadets had been killed in an ambush the previous day at Kilmichael, County Cork. A short time later two Auxiliary cadets entered the men's cell and asked for the adjutant of the Third Cork Brigade. The men replied that they were not aware who was in the IRA, let alone who the adjutant was. They were subjected to verbal abuse and told to have their prayers said by the time the Auxiliary forces returned as they were about to travel to Kilmichael to retrieve the bodies of their comrades. One of the cadets said, 'When we come back we will do you in.'

The cadets returned a few hours later and forced John Driscoll from the cell, marching him to a room where the sixteen bodies were laid out. Driscoll later said he could not see the wounds or any signs of mutilation described in subsequent reports from the British military. A cadet asked him if he was afraid and if he had anything to say for himself. Driscoll replied that he had nothing to do with what had happened and knew nothing about it. He informed the cadet that he had been arrested a week before the ambush, but the reply was that it did not matter and that Driscoll's comrades were responsible.

Later that day a further two men were put into the cell: Patrick Coughlin and a man called Murray. The following morning at 8.30 the four were taken from the cell and made to wash the room where the dead had been the day before. They were also ordered to wash the lorry that had taken the bodies to the castle and, afterwards, to burn the uniforms that had been removed from the corpses. They worked until 6 p.m. and throughout the day a party of military, who had arrived at the castle that morning, repeatedly beat them and fired several shots striking the ground within yards of them. The Auxiliary cadets did not take part in the beatings or shooting, but did nothing to protect the four men. Patrick Coughlin was in his mid-fifties and complained of a bad heart, but this only gave another reason for beating him severely. He was barely able to walk, but the soldiers fired shots at him and threw empty buckets at his head.

The four men were kept at Macroom Castle for another two weeks and were subjected to regular thrashings while carrying out heavy work for the military and cadets. The food they received was so bad that they could not eat it most of the time.[1]

***

The decision was made on Monday 22 November to initiate large-scale arrests for internment of what Hamar Greenwood described as '2,000 of the most active gunmen'. Some arrests were made based on information contained in captured documents, while others were based on data given by loyalists and informers all over the country. The new powers came under the Restoration of Order in Ireland Regulations and set the scene for a vicious assault on the general population with raids throughout the country. At Clonmel, County Tipperary, nine men were arrested, as were twenty men at Cobh in County Cork. Over twenty were taken into custody in County Galway and six at Dungarvan, County Waterford. At Omagh, County Tyrone, a solicitor who was a prominent member of Sinn Féin was seized. The courthouse at Nenagh in County Tipperary was raided and arrests made, while two young men were apprehended at Listowel, County Kerry. Seven men were detained following raids in Athlone town in County Westmeath.

Many other counties were visited by military and police on that day, including Kilkenny, Longford, Wicklow, Leitrim, Clare, Wexford and Donegal, and a lot of the men taken would find themselves residents of the newly opened Ballykinlar internment camp.[2]

The first batch of internees, between eighty and ninety, was transferred to Ballykinlar camp in late November and had to endure a ten-and-a-half-hour sea journey in gale force winds with a constant downpour to which they were exposed. Held on deck for the journey, they were refused permission to relieve the call of nature. The wind was so strong that the men's blankets and baggage were washed overboard.

They first arrived in Belfast, where they were handcuffed together in pairs and taken by lorry across the city to the County Down Railway Station. There they were put on a special train destined for the railway station at Tullmurry, known as the Ballykinlar Halt, approximately three miles from Ballykinlar camp. The men were threatened by the officer in charge, who said that anyone who lowered the windows or attempted to escape would be shot. He pointed out several times that he was offering a great opportunity for any man who wanted to die for Ireland.[3] These men would soon be joined by many others.

In County Clare the military converged on the town of Ennis, and arrested Art O'Donnell at the courthouse. He was transferred to the local military barracks and held there for several weeks, during which time up to sixty men were seized and taken there. In mid-December all prisoners were transferred to Cork jail and after a few hours were taken to a boat at Cork docks and thence to Belfast, en route to Ballykinlar.[4]

In County Wexford James Quinn was arrested by a party of military and police while working near his home at Camolin Park in the north of the county. He was not even given time to put on his coat and was marched to the military lorry approximately three miles away. As they walked along the road the military continuously jabbed him with bayonets. Quinn collapsed about 100 yards from the lorry and was verbally abused and ordered to keep his hands raised above his head. One of the soldiers told Quinn that he was to be shot and asked if he wanted to see anyone before he died. Quinn replied he would like to see his mother and a priest. He was then put onto the back of the lorry with another prisoner, William Kavanagh. The vehicle set off to Ferns where another two men, John Reilly and John Kavanagh, were arrested. They continued to Enniscorthy, with the military repeatedly jabbing at them with bayonets. Reilly had a bayonet put into his mouth, so that if the lorry had jolted in any way he could have been killed. At Enniscorthy they were taken to the courthouse where they received a severe beating from a party of military before being put into a cell. They were given further thrashings in the cell, which continued for several hours, and one soldier threatened to shoot Kavanagh. The military forced them to sing 'God Save the King', kiss the Union Jack and to dance on a republican flag lying on the floor. They were held at Enniscorthy for several weeks before being transferred to Kilworth camp in County Cork, thence to Cork jail and, on Monday 31 January, by sea to Ballykinlar.[5]

On Tuesday morning, 23 November, Thomas Treacy was arrested at his business in Parliament Street, Kilkenny, and taken to the local military barracks. James Lalor, Thomas Nolan and Michael Loughnan were also arrested later that night. All four were held in Kilkenny for one week before being moved to Clonmel military barracks and later to Kilworth camp in Cork.

In the early hours of Thursday 9 December, approximately 250 prisoners were removed to the docks in Cork and were put on board a ship bound for Belfast.[6]

Thomas Whelan from Clifden, County Galway, was arrested at his lodgings, 14 Barrow Street, Dublin, in the early hours of Wednesday 24 November. He was held in Portobello Barracks for several hours before being transferred to Arbour Hill prison. While there, on Wednesday 1 December 1920, he was ordered to take part in two identity parades, during the second of which he was identified by a witness as having been part of the group involved in killing Captain Baggally. The following evening, Thursday 2 December, Whelan was mistakenly removed from Arbour Hill and transported with a group of prisoners to the North Wall (on the River Liffey adjacent to Dublin Port). There they boarded the British Naval gunship *Sea Wolf*, which a short time later set sail for Belfast.[7]

Another Volunteer who was transferred to Ballykinlar on the *Sea Wolf* was Gerald (Garry) Byrne from Crumlin in Dublin. Byrne had been advised not to sleep at home (his parents' house) following the capture of Richard Mulcahy's briefcase in early November. He and other local Volunteers organised a billet at Marrowbone Lane Distillery where they slept and ate. One night Byrne thought it would be safe to visit his parents, but mistakenly stayed past the curfew hour. Considering it safer to remain indoors, he decided to stay the night, but the house was raided in the early hours of Thursday 25 November. Byrne and his father were arrested and taken to Wellington Barracks. A few days later, along with 200 others, they were transferred to

Arbour Hill prison. While there, they were ordered to take part in an identity parade where members of the DMP 'G' Division inspected them. On Thursday evening, 2 December, they were taken to the North Wall, put onto the *Sea Wolf* for the journey to Belfast and from there they were sent to Ballykinlar by train, arriving the following day at approximately 3 p.m.[8]

The RIC and British military based in Killarney town, County Kerry, carried out raids on the morning of Thursday 25 November and arrested local cattle dealer Chris Courtney at his home on College Street. They took him to the Great Southern Hotel, which was being used as a military barracks at the time. A British military officer called Sherwood asked Courtney if he held the rank of officer in the IRA, saying that if he did, he would receive special treatment. Courtney replied, 'I will have to miss that treatment.' He was moved to the local RIC barracks later that day and, with four others, was put into a twelve-foot by six-foot cell with one fixed plank bed. They were kept there for three weeks before Courtney was returned to the hotel and placed in a cellar with seven other men, where he remained for a further three weeks.

On Thursday 21 December, Courtney and another prisoner were taken from the basement and informed that they would accompany the military on patrol as hostages: if the IRA attacked the lorry, they would be used as human shields. The officer in charge ignored Courtney's protests. As they were driving along the road, an RIC man said, 'You will have to take your chances.' The patrol was out from 1 p.m. to 7 p.m. and the two men were handcuffed the entire time. The patrol fired at one young boy working in a field and subsequently arrested him. They raided a number of houses and fired at several buildings for no apparent reason. Chris Courtney and about twenty other prisoners were transferred to Cork jail on Tuesday 28 January and held there until they were transferred to Ballykinlar camp in mid-February.[9]

James Duignan, a student, was arrested in late November at Slath, Rooskey, County Roscommon. A party of military arrived at his home in the afternoon and handed him over to the local RIC constable, who was with a group of Black and Tans. They took Duignan to a nearby pigsty and forced him down on his knees in the filth and mud. One of the policemen put a revolver to his head, threatening that if he did not disclose information about the local IRA he would be shot. Duignan refused to speak and was struck on the back of the head with the butt of the revolver. He was then taken to Rooskey RIC Barracks where he was interrogated in a first-floor room by three Black and Tans. Two stood either side of him poking him in the ribs with revolvers as the third questioned him. When Duignan refused to answer they took him downstairs, tripping him halfway down, causing him to fall to the bottom. They took him to the yard at the rear of the barracks and, pushing him against the wall, said that he was going to be shot if he did not answer their questions. One counted down from twenty. An RIC man came out into the yard and struck Duignan in the stomach with the butt of his rifle. Later that evening Duignan was handed over to the military and taken to the old jail at Carrick-on-Shannon, where he was placed in a cell that was wet and cold as there was no glass in the windows. He was held in solitary confinement for several days before being removed to Athlone from where, on Thursday 10 February 1921, he was transferred to Ballykinlar.[10]

Michael Carroll was arrested on Friday 26 November at his home in Tubber, Gort, County Galway. A party of military and Auxiliary cadets stopped their lorry a short distance from his home, having passed him as he stood at his front door. Two cadets jumped from the truck and ran back towards Carroll's house with revolvers drawn, shouting at him to raise his hands. They called him a wanted man and made him run to the lorry. When he was on the back of it, two of the military started to punch him in the face. Three of them threw him off the vehicle, but his coat became caught up and he was left hanging from the back. One of the Auxiliary cadets freed him, so he fell to the ground. Three soldiers jumped from the lorry and grabbed his arms and legs, throwing him back on. There were two other prisoners on the lorry at the time, brothers Harry and Patrick Loughnane from Shanaglish, who had been arrested while working on the family farm.

The truck had travelled about two miles when the military stopped and smashed their way through another house, but they returned having failed to find anyone to arrest. They ordered the prisoners off the vehicle and gave them a severe beating. They eventually reached Gort RIC Barracks and were marched into the dayroom where Michael Carroll was again beaten. The military tried to knock the Loughnane brothers to the ground, but they were too strong for them and resisted the attempts to hit them. The three men were then searched and questioned by an RIC man and put in a cell. About an hour later, a head constable and two constables took them out to a dayroom. Almost immediately, Michael Carroll was returned to the cell, while the Loughnane brothers were left in the dayroom. Carroll did not hear any voices, but was aware of a lorry driving away a few moments later. He did not see the Loughnane brothers after that.[11]

It seems that Patrick and Harry were removed from the barracks by members of the Auxiliaries and were not heard of again until Sunday 5 December, when their bodies were found in a pond at Owenbristy, about a mile from Drumhasna. It was stated at the time that a relative of theirs had dreamed for several nights after their disappearance that their corpses had been dumped in a pond at that location. A search party was organised and the grim discovery was made on the Sunday afternoon. Both bodies were badly charred, having been set on fire. The corpses were subsequently taken to Kinvara, where coffins were provided before they were brought to their home at Shanaglish. The funeral mass was held on Tuesday 7 December at Shanaglish chapel, but was interrupted by a party of two RIC, two military officers and two members of the Auxiliary Division accompanied by Dr James Sandys of Gort. They removed the coffin lids and Dr Sandys examined the bodies. The priests conducting the funeral, Fr J. Nagle and Fr John Garvin were in tears. Fr Nagle repeatedly asked one of the military officers to look at the remains and say if it was possible for such a horrid thing to happen in a Christian country in the twentieth century. 'I have been through the African War and I have been everywhere a soul required my services and a worse thing than this I never saw.' The RIC sergeant replied, 'We are not responsible and no one regrets this more than the police.' The military and police then left the chapel and the funeral continued. The remains were taken the 200 yards to the local graveyard where the brothers were laid to rest side by side. There were emotional scenes at the graveside with both women and men crying. Three volleys of shots were then fired over the grave.[12]

The man arrested on the same day as the Loughnane brothers, Michael Carroll, was taken to Earl's Island, Galway on Saturday 27 November, where a British intelligence officer questioned him. The officer's revolver lay on the table and he threatened Carroll that he would shoot him if he did not answer his questions about certain people in Gort. Carroll did not speak and was repeatedly punched and kicked. The following day he was transferred to Galway Town Hall and some weeks later taken to Ballykinlar.[13]

The internment round-up continued in County Cork, with the arrest of Maurice ('Mossie') Donegan, who had been 'on the run' for some time in the Bantry area. On the morning of Sunday 28 November he attended mass in Durrus along with three other Volunteers. As they were driving away from the chapel they realised that the whole area had been saturated with British military, whom they tried to avoid by staying away from main roads. However, the British had all roads covered and the Volunteers drove into a party of military. They abandoned the car and ran through the fields but were fired at and had to throw themselves on the ground to avoid being hit. They were arrested and taken to the military barracks at Bantry workhouse. Maurice Donegan gave a false name (Thomas Fitzpatrick) when arrested, as he feared he would face trial and execution for his activities. They were later taken to Cobh in a cruiser before being transferred to a smaller craft and taken upriver to Cork city. A large number of prisoners were then put on a British naval destroyer and sailed to Belfast docks.[14]

Michael Ryan, County Longford, was injured in late October while preparing landmines at a house in Kilnacarrow. One of the mines accidentally exploded, causing injury to his left hip and leg. After some time spent recuperating, he wanted to visit his wife to assure her that he was not badly injured. He had only been at home for a short time when military and police surrounded the house. He was taken to the local barracks and then transferred to Athlone. Some time later he was transferred to Mountjoy jail in Dublin. On Sunday 28 November he was moved, with approximately ninety other prisoners, to the docks in Dublin and put on board a British naval destroyer. A dense fog descended as they sailed from Dublin and the destroyer did not arrive at Belfast docks until midday on Wednesday 1 December. The prisoners, who did not know where they were going, had not received any food and were kept on the deck of the destroyer, handcuffed together in pairs. They were given a very hostile reception by the dock workers and a unionist mob at Belfast docks.[15]

Seán Kennedy was arrested on Thursday 2 December at

his home, 22 Parnell Street, Dublin, some time after curfew, and was held at the North Dublin Union for a fortnight before being taken to Belfast by sea. On arrival at the Belfast docks Kennedy and the prisoners with him could see the hostile unionist mob awaiting them and a British officer remarked, 'If you want to die for Ireland, now is your opportunity.' One of the prisoners shouted, 'Up Dublin', and another replied, 'Up the Republic.' This incensed the unionist mob and soon nuts, bolts and scrap metal began raining down on the prisoners as they stood on the deck. The British officer in charge ordered the crowd to disperse and directed his men to be prepared to open fire if necessary. This subdued the rabble and the prisoners were marched to the County Down Railway Station where they boarded a train and travelled under heavy armed guard to Tullmurry Station.[16]

IRA personnel all over the country generally adhered to the November directive from GHQ to stay away from their homes and to be more vigilant in their local areas. However, some found it necessary to return at times. James McMonagle went home late on Sunday 5 December and stayed the night. The military and police carried out extensive raids in Letterkenny and, at 5 a.m. the following morning, McMonagle's home was targeted. He was arrested and taken to the No. 2 police barrack, beside the courthouse. McMonagle had known for some time that he was a target for arrest by the RIC, since his home at Castle Street was often raided. He often hid in the bell tower of St Eunan's Cathedral, which overlooked the houses on Castle Street; this enabled him to watch as the British and RIC raided his family home. On his arrival at the No. 2 barracks he found James Dawson, battalion commandant, and a civilian, Hugh Deery, already there. Hugh Deery was not a member of the IRA and was most likely arrested in error, but was later commended for his silence and for serving several months interned, as his arrest was said to have prevented the arrest of another Volunteer. The residence of Dr J. P. McGinley was also raided that morning, but he was not at home.[17]

In the east of County Donegal a large-scale arrest operation was carried out on 6 December. A Volunteer officer, Michael Doherty, was working on his land when he spotted a carload of RIC and military in a lorry approaching his house. They surrounded the house and asked his father his whereabouts. As they drove away they stopped another Volunteer, Thomas McGlynn, on the road and arrested him. They also seized John James Kelly, J. D. McLaughlin, Edward McBrearty, James McCarron and John O'Flaherty, all members of the IRA.[18] All the prisoners were removed to Derry jail and held for a number of days before being transferred to Belfast by train. They were met at the County Down Railway Station by a hostile unionist mob shouting in a very aggressive manner, 'You bastards, you are not behind a stone wall in Donegal now.' The military escort had to clear the station platform and keep the men in the waiting room until their train to Ballykinlar arrived. While waiting they noticed lorry loads of prisoners arriving from the docks, having been shipped from various counties in the west and the south. Nearly all the approximately 200 men showed signs of assault, with cuts and bleeding about the head and face.[19]

The village of Butlersbridge, County Cavan, was raided on Wednesday 8 December. A party of military, police and Black and Tans arrived from Cavan town in the early hours of the morning. Many houses in the village and surrounding areas were raided and seven men were arrested, including Mick and Tommy Foynes, Jimmy McPhilips, Mick McGerty and Bernard Emmo. They were taken to the local hall in the village and later moved to the military barracks in Cavan town where many others were being held. Local people brought the men breakfast and refreshments before they were removed from the barracks. They were later transferred to Belfast by train en route to Ballykinlar camp.[20]

Meanwhile, in the west of the country over fifty men were taken under heavy escort from the Town Hall, Galway, on Monday 13 December, to the Galway docks. They were placed on HM Sloop *Leamington*, which sailed around the coast making its way to the docks in Belfast.[21]

As the internment round-up intensified, General Nevil Macready made a request during a British cabinet meeting held on Thursday 9 December 1920, for two additional vessels capable of carrying at least 100 men with escorts. One vessel was to be based in the west of Ireland and the other in the Cork area: they were to be used to convey hundreds of men arrested in the raids in Connacht and Munster.

Macready also requested two other vessels be made available, with one to be based at Cobh (then known as Queenstown) and the other to be sent to Dublin to transfer sixty men to Portland prison in England. The British Admiralty informed the War

Office that their ships were unsuitable for conveying large detachments of prisoners and that they were only prepared to make vessels available as a last resort; they suggested the use of mercantile transport instead.[22]

At the same meeting, the British cabinet discussed introducing martial law in Munster, such was the scale of the IRA's assault on the British military and police.[23] The military and police in Munster were being overwhelmed by the success of IRA actions. A proclamation was issued by Dublin Castle on Friday 10 December declaring martial law in four of the Munster counties: Cork (County and city), Limerick (County and city), Kerry and Tipperary. It suppressed the whole fabric of civil law, with the British military under General Nevil Macready taking over governance in the proclaimed areas.[24] On Thursday 30 December, the British cabinet (at the request of the British generals in Ireland – Macready, Strickland, Boyd and Tudor) authorised the extension of the martial law areas to Counties Clare, Kilkenny, Wexford and Waterford, which came into effect in early January 1921.[25]

The volume of arrests was so great that additional internment camps had to be established later at Collinstown, County Dublin, at Bere Island and Spike Island, County Cork, and at the Curragh in County Kildare.[26]

***

A British naval destroyer, the *Valorous* arrived in Dublin on Thursday evening, 2 December 1920, and between 10 and

11 p.m. on Sunday 5 December up to 200 men in two batches were convoyed in military lorries from Arbour Hill prison in Dublin to the North Wall. They were marched on board the naval destroyer, which proceeded to sea shortly afterwards. The voyage was horrendous on that particular night, with gales of up to seventy-one miles per hour until they docked at Belfast. The majority of the passengers were seasick as they were forced to sit for the entire journey.[27]

The following week orders for internment were issued for 278 men and in the early hours of Saturday 11 December large numbers of prisoners were removed from other places of detention in Dublin and transferred to the North Wall. They were placed on board another British naval destroyer, the *Malcolm*, which then sailed to Belfast docks.[28]

On Tuesday night, 28 December 1920, the RIC in Sligo town carried out a number of raids and arrested, among others, Michael Gallagher, at his home on Bridge Street. He was taken to the local RIC barracks in the town where he was questioned and searched by an RIC sergeant called Lavelle. Gallagher's answers obviously did not impress and one constable said, 'Take the bastard outside and shoot him.' Another sergeant chastised the constable: 'Don't be using that language. There is no need for that.' But this failed to deter the man – when the sergeant left the dayroom he told Gallagher that he would be shot at dawn, and continued to use abusive language. Gallagher was then put into a cell. Next morning he shouted through the hole in the door asking if he was to receive breakfast. The RIC asked him if he had any money. The men in the adjoining cells shouted to Gallagher that the food being brought into the barracks by friends was being exchanged by the RIC for the food cooked in the barracks as the food being sent in was much better. That evening Gallagher and two other prisoners, John O'Donnell and James Cahill, were transferred to Sligo jail, where they were held for five to six weeks before being transferred to Derry jail. They had been there only a few days when, along with a large number of others, they were put on a train to Belfast en route to Ballykinlar camp.

While on the train, Michael Gallagher spoke to the military sergeant of the guard about what he had heard of the treatment meted out to the other prisoners on arrival at Belfast. The military escort was from the Dorset Regiment and the sergeant replied, 'You are our prisoners and every man of us has 100 rounds each and I will guarantee that nothing will happen to you.' On arrival at Belfast the men were taken to Victoria Barracks, where they were held until the next train was due to depart from the County Down Railway Station for Tullmurry. A couple of hours later they were taken out of the barracks and confronted by a large, belligerent unionist mob. The military sergeant ordered the crowd to disperse but when they did not comply, he instructed his men to fix bayonets and advance towards them: the mob quickly dispersed. The men were then taken to the County Down Railway Station and travelled to Tullmurry Station.[29]

The prisoners from the west and south of Ireland did not have the option of train travel or in most cases the protection of their escort. The sailing from the west and south of Ireland to

Belfast docks took two to four days and as it was winter the sea was very choppy. Many of the men suffered from seasickness. On arrival at Belfast the men were put onto lorries at the docks and were greeted by a very hostile unionist mob. The Belfast shipyard workers showered them with missiles of scrap metal, stone, nuts and bolts, and cries of, 'What will de Valera do for you now?' The prisoners were then transferred across the city to the County Down Railway Station by lorry, from there to entrain to Tullmurry.

On arrival at Tullmurry the prisoners had to walk to the camp handcuffed together in pairs and carrying their belongings. Many were barely able to walk the three miles following the long journey by boat and train and, in many cases, suffering from serious and untreated injuries sustained at Belfast dock.[30] For example, Dan Faher from Dungarvan, County Waterford, was nearly seventy and suffered greatly from the sea journey. He almost collapsed as he walked to the camp, but was forced to continue by a junior officer who shouted at him, 'If you were behind a ditch you would be active enough.'[31]

***

The mass round-ups continued throughout the latter part of 1920 and into 1921, with arrests in all areas of the country. Many men were also arrested in England and transported to Ireland for internment in Ballykinlar and the other camps. In many cases they were held in barracks throughout the country for several months without charge or trial. One young man spoke to a reporter from *The Freeman's Journal* shortly after his release after four months' detention. He said he only had two baths over the period and that hygiene conditions were far from ideal, with many suffering from scabies, a very serious and contagious skin disease.

Families and friends had no contact with their loved ones until they arrived at Ballykinlar camp, as it was only then that they could write and send letters. The predicament of one woman, Annie McGrath, who was searching for her husband, was brought to light in a letter published by *The Freeman's Journal* in March 1921. Seán McGrath had been arrested at his office at Shaftesbury Avenue, London, on Monday 21 February 1921. He was held in Cannon Row police station until the following morning, when he was transferred to Ireland. Annie and his solicitor were both refused permission to see him.

As McGrath was being transferred from Holyhead in Wales, a party of Black and Tans preparing to make the crossing to Dublin asked that he be handed over to them, but the escort party said they would deliver the prisoner to Dublin themselves. On Tuesday 1 March Annie McGrath received a telegram, purporting to be from her husband, saying that he was being held at Arbour Hill prison, Dublin. She immediately went to Ireland, arriving in Dublin the following day. At Arbour Hill she asked about her husband's whereabouts and was told he was there, but that she would need to make a request for a visitation order to Dublin Castle. At the castle she was informed she must either write to or phone the assistant provost marshal, the assistant head of the military police, to request permission to see her husband. She tried several times, but the phone was not answered. She then made her way back to Arbour Hill, arriving at approximately 1.30 p.m., and was told that her husband had been removed from the prison at about 12.30 p.m. The prison authorities would not tell her where he had been taken.

In a letter to *The Freeman's Journal*, Annie McGrath wrote:

> Since his arrest on February 21st I have not been able to ascertain any definite information of the whereabouts of my husband. I have tried every possible means to do so. I cannot but feel that the authorities at Arbour Hill and Dublin Castle were simply sending me on a wild goose chase while they spirited him away. There is no charge whatever against my husband.

It turned out that he had been transferred from Arbour Hill prison on Wednesday 2 March to Ballykinlar camp, where he was held in the No. 1 compound.[32]

***

The status of the internees was raised in Westminster on 30 November 1920, when a question was put to Hamar Greenwood, the chief secretary for Ireland. Hamar Greenwood stated that the intention was to intern the men and accord them treatment similar to that normally given to prisoners of war, although that did not imply the recognition of the men as prisoners of war or the grant to them of that status. Indeed in May 1921 when General Macready suggested the use of the then vacant

Portland prison in Dorset, England, as a possible venue to accommodate the growing number of internees, Winston Churchill stressed that although the internees had been treated, for the purposes of rations and discipline, as prisoners of war, it was 'important to make it clear that they are not prisoners of war'. He suggested that the additional internees could be transferred to a large British military camp at Catterick in north Yorkshire as an alternative to Portland prison.[33]

The lack of clarity on this issue gives some indication of the British government's reluctance to recognise the hostilities in Ireland as a war. It is also an indication of the haste with which the internment policy was implemented and the change from transportation and incarceration in British jails to camps in Ireland. While internment had been considered as a means of suppressing the activities of the IRA and Sinn Féin previous to that day, the events of Sunday 21 November 1920 forced the British government based at Dublin Castle into a spontaneous reaction – one for which they were not fully prepared, as could be seen by the lack of suitable facilities ready for the increasing numbers of internees.[34] The former British military training camp at Ballykinlar, having been identified as the most appropriate location, became the first mass internment camp in Ireland.

4

Ballykinlar Camp

Ballykinlar (from the Irish *Baile an Choinnleora* – town of the candelabrum or *Baile-Caindlera*) is so called because from the twelfth century the parish had been the property of Christchurch Cathedral in Dublin, granted to it by John de Courcy, and the tithes collected in the parish or townland of Ballykinlar were allocated to the cathedral for the supply of candles. According to local tradition, St Patrick landed at Ballykinlar strand when he was taken to Ireland as a slave.[1]

In 1920 the mention of internment camps was normally associated with the imprisonment of foreign nationals from a country at war with the native country. At Ballykinlar the occupants were not hostile foreigners, they were Irish.

Ballykinlar camp was located on a ten-acre site at the mouth of Dundrum Bay, situated approximately three miles from Dundrum village between Downpatrick and Newcastle, County Down. Located in the parish of Tyrella and Dundrum, it had previously been used as a training camp for the Ulster Division of the British Army during the summer months.[2] Far off to the south-east a faint glimpse of the blue sea can be seen at

Dundrum Bay as it merges into a distant misty horizon. Away to the south rises Slieve Donard mountain with its attendant chain of hills, the Mountains of Mourne, no less beautiful, stretching far away to the west. The spectacle of this natural beauty surrounding the Ballykinlar camp merely reminded its inhabitants of their past freedom. This beauty seemed within touching distance, yet was out of reach, nestled beyond the barbed-wire entanglements of the camp.[3]

Covering approximately ten acres, the camp was built practically at sea level on a bleak, wind-swept peninsula. It was made up of a number of compounds, large areas of which throughout the winter, during and after heavy rains, were flooded, making it almost impossible for the internees to take a walk or exercise without collecting a mass of mud on their boots and getting their feet wet. During the summer months the rain and mud were replaced by sand blowing from the nearby beach covering everything exposed to it, including food.[4]

Travelling by road, the first glimpse of the compounds could be seen from a rising on the road, inside what was termed the 'prohibited area', a radius of a few miles around the complex. People living inside that area had to have permits and a number of farmhouses were close to the outer barbed wire. The local people lived in anxiety since, if they appeared outside their homes after dark, they could be challenged by an armed sentry and faced the prospect of being shot if they failed to hear or reply. The front portion of the camp contained what was known as the Extended Camp, which consisted of the commandant's accommodation as well as the soldiers' quarters and all the necessary facilities including administration offices, hospital, stores, post office, cookhouse, dining halls and washrooms. This was the first introduction to the camp for the internees. They would then have had to walk less than a quarter of a mile to the first compound where they would be imprisoned. Before entering the compound the men were held in a building resembling a stable.

The weather was generally wet and windy, with the result that the roads were broken and churned into one deep mess of mud and watery pools.[5] The prisoners' compounds were surrounded by two rows of barbed wire entanglements about ten feet high with a thick canvas screen on the outer perimeter. The screen stretched to the height of the huts with the result that the internees could not look out and the local residents could not look in. The outer row of barbed wire was about two yards from the inner one. There were five sentry boxes in each compound, one at each corner and one in the centre. The sentry boxes were approximately twenty feet above the ground, overlooking the compound, with armed soldiers watching the area day and night. Inside the compound ran a road which was wide enough for two lorries to pass, as would often happen as they transported equipment and other items.[6]

On their arrival in the camp, the first batch of internees were placed for two to three hours in horse stalls where conditions were wet and bitterly cold.[7] They were then taken into an office and asked a number of questions: name, address, marital status, etc. Their physical features were recorded: colour of eyes, height, etc. Each man was then assigned a hut and sent into

No. 1 compound (known to the internees as 'the cage') for the first time.[8]

According to the British Army Medical Service regulations, the space per head within camps for prisoners of war was 500 cubic feet and the cost per head per annum was £60 3s 4d.[9] The No. 1 compound consisted of four lines of ten huts, each of which accommodated up to twenty-five men. Two huts were used as punishment cells, a third was used as offices and a fourth was a store. Half of a fifth hut was used as a post office and later on two other huts were used as a dispensary and washhouse. That left thirty-three huts, with one being used as an isolation hut for contagious diseases and the rest occupied by internees. All the buildings were made of wood and sheeted on the outside with galvanised iron. The floors were made of wood and the boards forming the sides were badly jointed and in many cases the chinks were stuffed with paper or covered with cardboard nailed to the back. Besides the door in use, there were two others in each hut, permanently locked. The wind, which blew constantly as the camp was located on the coast, came through the chinks and doors, making the huts cold, especially at night, and unhealthy. There was a small cell, boarded off at the end of each hut, used as a night latrine or toilet. Each hut was twenty yards (sixty feet) long and six yards (eighteen feet) wide. Each bed consisted of two wooden trestles about eight inches high, with three bed boards. Each hut had a long table, three or four forms or benches, a stove, and some buckets, a couple of which were always filled with sand in case of fire. Conditions in the camp in the early days were very bad.[10]

In some huts the internees had to sweep the water from the floors and endure the pungent smell of dampness. For the first week there was no fire and the men had to put on damp clothing in the morning and many could not put on underclothing as it was too wet to wear. The huts were always cold and many suffered from colds, influenza or pneumonia during the winter months. In the first couple of months in the camp each hut served as a living-room, a kitchen, a laundry, a recreation hall and a dormitory. During the rainy days of winter the internees had the choice of remaining in the huts all day or getting soaked to the skin and covered in mud if they went out into the compound.[11]

The first days of camp life were very strict and the internees' day started with reveille, the military waking signal, at 7.15 a.m., after which they had to be out of bed by 7.30 a.m. Washing was at 8 a.m., followed by a breakfast of bread, butter and tea. Dinner was at 1 p.m. and tea was at 4.30 p.m. In the beginning the men spent the remainder of the day strolling around the camp and passing the time as best they could. They had to be back in the huts for lock-up at 5.30 p.m. and until lights out at 9 p.m. they passed the evening with stories, songs and any other forms of entertainment they could muster. The rosary was recited last thing every night.[12]

Such was the haste of the internment round-up that when the first batch of internees arrived in early December they were received by Lieutenant Sangley, who admitted that he had no instructions about what to do with them and that he had neither beds nor food to give them. Sangley, accompanied by two soldiers and an internee named Robert Lynch from Bantry, County Cork, went to the British military canteen, where they prepared tea with no milk and hard biscuits for the men. On the first night the internees were forced to sleep on the bare floors.[13] The daily diet for the first few weeks was biscuits and tea or coffee and a stew for dinner, but following protests the variety of food improved, although the quality was poor most of the time.[14]

The morning after the first internees arrived, the first British commanding officer, Colonel Hely-Hutchinson, addressed the detainees, as he continued to do with every new batch on arrival:

> Now men, I understand that you are soldiers, and I intend to deal with you as such and to treat you as prisoners of war. It is my wish that your time here should be pleasant as possible in the circumstances: and if you play the game with me I'll play the game with you. If you observe certain rules and regulations in regard to the camp and carry out certain duties, which are necessary for your own health and well-being, you will have no trouble from us.

It was not long before the men gave Hely-Hutchinson the nickname 'play the game'.[15]

The internees were then ordered to march to a big shed outside the compound filled with stacks of straw. They were given large bags and told to fill them with straw and that these would be their mattresses until proper bedding and blankets were arranged. The straw was pressed and very damp. When they eventually received their blankets, these were old and threadbare. A number of weeks later a scabies epidemic spread through the compound and the internees' doctors believed that the blankets were the source. They suspected that they had been used by the British military during the previous war and had not been properly washed.

Later that day the internees realised that they were in for some grim treatment when they were ordered to empty the toilet facilities. This meant taking the latrine buckets outside the compound to be emptied into a large pit.

Several days passed before coal was supplied and the prisoners had to carry it from outside the compound to heat the stoves in the huts. They were handcuffed to the buckets each time they went to collect it. The military filled the pails and the men carried them back to the compound. The coal supply was insufficient to keep the stoves lit during the winter months, and they produced inadequate heat. Some men moved the stoves from the wall to the centre of the huts, but the military compelled them to return them to their original positions. The men resented having to carry out such duties and, as other internees arrived on a daily basis, they grew in strength and confidence, subsequently refusing to do so. When the British would not accept this, the internees retaliated by burning the bed boards to heat the huts.[16]

In the early days of the camp the men were issued with internment orders upon arrival at the camp. The basis of their confinement was provided for under Regulation 14(b) of the Defence of the Realm Act and Restoration of Order in Ireland Regulations as follows:

Anyone whose behaviour is of such a nature as to give reasonable grounds for suspecting that he has acted, or is acting, or about to act in a manner prejudicial to the public safety or the defence of the realm.[17]

The first arrivals at the camp included a large number of Dublin men arrested in the aftermath of the Bloody Sunday killings, as well as many who were not aligned to the IRA or Sinn Féin and were considered by the IRA Volunteers an undisciplined bunch. The IRA personnel immediately established a policy of identifying all officers and Volunteers, and drafted a roll listing the members. In the early days of the camp, a meeting was held at which a provisional camp commandant, staff and a provisional camp council were elected, with each province being equally represented on the council. Patrick Colgan, Dublin, was appointed commandant, Dominick Mackey, Tipperary, was appointed vice-commandant, Seamus Ward, Donegal, was adjutant and Tom Meldon, Dublin, was quartermaster. The other members of the provisional council were Dr T. F. O'Higgins, Carlow/Laois, Art O'Donnell, Clare, Seamus Ward, Donegal, and Paddy Hogan, Galway. The council issued instructions to the internees to elect a leader in each hut to represent the internees and raise concerns with the camp commandant. A camp staff or panel of officers was also appointed to cater for the general everyday running of the compound. Dr Richard Hayes and Dr T. F. O'Higgins were appointed medical officers. Michael Hassett, Wexford, was appointed provost marshal, while Sam Holt and Andy Mooney, Leitrim, were appointed as post office workers. Henry Dixon, Dublin, was appointed chairman of the education committee and various other committees were also formed.

When the camp council was satisfied with the competence of those appointed, a delegation met with the British military authorities and demanded they be recognised as prisoners of war with their own officers and staff to control the compound.[18] This infuriated Colonel Hely-Hutchinson, who, although initially agreeing to treat the men as prisoners of war, did not like being told what to do, and the demand was initially refused. The British soon realised that it would be a difficult task to subdue the internees and impose their authority, as it would be resisted by organised protests, refusal to obey military orders and simple things such as declining to answer at roll call.

The British military adjutant, Captain Newton, spent much of his time liaising with the internees' representatives to resolve the various disputes and was credited with advising Colonel Hely-Hutchinson to see the benefits of the internees' demands. A short time later, Newton informed Patrick Colgan that the demands were granted and that the military would not interfere within the compound, apart from inspections, roll call and opening in the morning at 7.30 a.m. They also agreed to delay lock-up from 5.30 p.m. to 9.30 p.m.[19]

The No. 1 compound was filled to capacity by mid-December and the British were busy preparing the second compound. The second enclosure had a similar layout and facilities as No. 1 compound, except that there was no hospital. Having elected camp staff, the internees in No. 1 compound held another conference to elect permanent officers in order to introduce a structure to organise the entire compound. Patrick Colgan was elected compound commandant, Thomas Fitzpatrick (Maurice 'Mossie' Donegan), Cork, vice-commandant, Tom Meldon, Dublin, quartermaster and Seamus Ward, Donegal, adjutant. Other positions were also filled, including provost marshal, postmaster and court-martial judges. There were four internee companies, one for each line of huts in No. 1 compound: Companies A, B, C and D. Each company had a line captain elected by the men of the line. Over the twelve months of the camp's existence the line captains were as follows – A Company: Michael Nolan, Dublin, and J. McGuill, Louth; B Company: J. Fitzgerald, Kildare, and F. Crowley, Cork; C Company: P. C. O'Mahony, Waterford, J. Murtagh, Dublin, and F. Ruane, Mayo; D Company: John (J. P.) Cooney, Tipperary.[20]

Despite assurances that they would not interfere within the compound after lock-up, the British regularly carried out night raids on the huts to identify men wanted for various activities against the police and military before their internment: they were always accompanied by RIC detectives. The internees' commandant, Patrick Colgan, met with Captain Newton to request that the night patrols be discontinued and that the military only enter the compound in the morning for opening and at night for lock-up. The British paid little attention to this request: the patrols continued and the military carried out surprise raids, accompanied by RIC detectives and at times members of the British Secret Service. The soldiers flashed lights in the faces of the internees while RIC detectives or British Secret Service tried to identify the men.

The camp filled with such speed that the internees became suspicious that some men were deliberately being sent to the camp to mingle with them and gather scraps of information for British intelligence. To counter this threat, Patrick Colgan established an intelligence group to verify the authenticity of all the men in the compound. If anyone was considered suspicious, or was not known by other men from his area, he would be questioned on various aspects of his background and his associations with the republican movement. If there were any doubts about an internee, other men from the same area would be asked to identify him and corroborate his credentials.[21]

Despite the significance of the discovery of Richard Mulcahy's briefcase, British intelligence exhibited a certain level of incompetence in the general round-up of suspects, who included a mix of the very young and very old, with the ages of internees ranging from seventeen to over seventy. There were men from all walks of life, many with little or no connection to Sinn Féin or the IRA. One such example was John Graham from Belfast, who had received the Mons Star for his service in the British Army and was arrested in December 1920 when he was working for the Belfast Tramway Service.[22] The military called at his home in the early hours and when he opened the door they rushed in, pushing him against the wall. An officer asked if he was James Graham, to which he said, 'No, I'm not. I am John Graham.' They ignored his answer and ordered him onto the lorry. He was first taken to Holywood Barracks in County Down and some weeks later was transferred to Ballykinlar camp, where he was handed his internment order with the name James Graham on it. He brought the mistake to the attention of a British military officer. The officer simply took the internment order, scored out the name 'James', wrote 'John' above it and handed it back.

Internment orders were issued against many men who had no connection with the republican movement, yet they found themselves serving several months of internment. One man who was obviously not involved in any political or other activity was a member of the Plymouth Brethren, an evangelical religious group. He was mistakenly arrested in the first few weeks of the round-ups and found himself caged in Ballykinlar. When he arrived with a new batch of internees, he spoke to Colonel Hely-Hutchinson who, on delivering his usual speech to the arrivals, added:

Of course, there may be individual cases of hardship amongst you. Perhaps some men are here who should not be here. But, if on the one hand you are soldiers of the Irish Republic you will be prepared to suffer for the cause to which you have devoted yourselves, whilst, on the other hand, if you are loyal subjects of the British Empire you will also be willing to put up with the inconvenience of being here, knowing that this round-up has been deemed necessary by those responsible for the safety of the Empire.

The member of the Plymouth Brethren shouted: 'I am neither a soldier of the Irish Republic nor do I bear allegiance to earthly empires or monarchs. I only serve one master and the only army to which I belong is the army of God!' Another internee shouted, 'Well, you're a devilish long way from your barracks here.' This comment elicited a burst of hearty laughter from the colonel, who was unable to continue addressing the new arrivals and walked away laughing.[23]

Many others were mistakenly interned and the majority joined the ranks of the IRA and put their incarceration to good use by receiving military training and availing themselves of the various educational opportunities they would otherwise never have had.

The internment order given to each prisoner on arrival in the camp included a provision for appealing against it. The matter of men mistakenly arrested during the round-ups was addressed by the British through an advisory committee. It was set up in early January 1921 under Regulation 14(b) of the Restoration of Order in Ireland Act to deal with applications by internees who considered themselves wrongly imprisoned. The committee was composed of Justice John Ross (chairman), Justice Robert J. Doyle KC, recorder of Galway, and William Sullivan, resident magistrate. The applicants were to address all correspondence to the chief secretary's office in Dublin Castle. The committee visited Ballykinlar in late January 1921 to hear almost forty appeals, though they lacked the power to order the men's release and had to give a report on each case to the British military authorities. Seventeen men were released on Monday 2 February 1921.[24]

Initially, the number of men who appealed their internment was lower than might be expected. The internees' camp
commandants issued a policy of non-cooperation regarding the
appeals process. Despite the fact that about one-fifth of the
men interned had no prior involvement with the IRA or Sinn
Féin, the policy was largely observed. However, later the appeals
process was viewed as a good opportunity to secure the release
of valuable IRA personnel, so a decision was taken that some
Volunteers who held important positions within their brigade
areas should appeal against their internment. This decision was
not communicated to all the detainees and only concerned
a small number of men who were subsequently released and
returned to their units to take an active part in the war. Some
of the Volunteers who successfully appealed included Patrick
O'Daly and Mick Love from Dublin and James McCarron
from Donegal.[25] McCarron was killed in June 1921, during
an ambush on British soldiers at Trusk Lough near Ballybofey,
County Donegal.[26]

In early January seven men were arrested in England and
transferred to Ballykinlar camp. A report from the directorate
of intelligence presented to the British cabinet on Thursday 13
January 1921 stated:

Seven of the most dangerous Sinn Féiners in Lancashire have
been removed to Ireland for internment under the Restoration of
Order in Ireland Regulations. The news of this action on the part
of the government has had a very sobering effect upon the English
Sinn Féiners throughout the country.[27]

Between January and May 1921, twenty-two men were transferred to Ballykinlar following their arrest in various parts of England.

Despite the intentions of the British government and military to intern, as Hamar Greenwood put it, 'two thousand of the most active gunmen', in reality most of those captured posed little or no threat to 'the Realm'. To highlight the foolishness of many of the internment orders, Dr T. F. O'Higgins from County Laois conducted a survey of the internee population of both compounds. It identified the following: 'Men over 45 years of age – 100; Men permanently disabled owing to various deformities and injuries etc. – 40; Men suffering from permanent serious illnesses such as heart and lung complaints – 40.'[28] Moreover, a large percentage of the internees who had been active workers for Sinn Féin on the political front had no connection with the IRA. Their detention, however, aided the IRA campaign, as it took several hundred British military to guard them and cost the British Exchequer a considerable sum of money each week.[29]

On seeing the conditions in which they were to live, the first thoughts of one man from County Cork were 'Lloyd George is going to win this time.'[30] However, the men soon saw through the British plan and various activities were organised to exercise the prisoners both physically and mentally as a means of countering the effects of their forced imprisonment.

One incident that showed the folly of the internment policy, and the British military in general, occurred on Thursday 20 October 1921. A small ceremony was held for the presentation of the Mons Star (also known as the 1914 Star) to an internee at Ballykinlar camp, John Pilkington of Sligo. This British military campaign medal was for service in the 1914–18 war.[31] There were 365,622 Mons Star medals issued to officers and men who had served in France or Belgium between 5 August and midnight on 22/23 November 1914.[32] Pilkington was informed of his award on Thursday morning, 20 October, and that afternoon one of the senior British officers in the camp entered the No. 2 compound and carried out the ceremony. In typical fashion, the internees themselves could not resist holding a mock ceremony and the Mons Star was awarded to John Pilkington a second time, but this time he had the honour of receiving his medal from the 'lord mayor of Ballykinlar', Chris Mullins of Dublin. The irony was not lost on the recipient, who wore the medal (which has a red, white and blue ribbon) every day and at night pinned it to his blanket.[33]

While the plight of the internees was in the hands of the British military, their families were, in some respects, abandoned following the arrests of their male relatives. The Irish Republican Prisoners Dependants' Fund instructed groups in each county 'to organise local committees to cater for the needs of families of prisoners and internees'. On Wednesday 23 December 1920, Lieutenant-Commander Joseph Kenworthy, MP for Kingston upon Hull Central, asked Hamar Greenwood in the House of Commons whether provision was being made for the wives and children of the men who were being interned in Ireland without trial on suspicion of being members of illegal organisations, or whether they would be left to starve. Hamar Greenwood simply replied, 'No, sir.'[34]

Camp authority

The Duke of Cornwall's Light Infantry were responsible for the administration of Ballykinlar camp, while the King's Royal Rifles (KRR) provided the camp guards and sentries. The Cornwalls had most contact with the internees, with a lieutenant and a sergeant being in charge of each of the four internee companies or lines. The internees considered the Cornwalls to be considerate and had a fairly good relationship with them, whereas the KRRs were extremely hostile to them. Colonel Hely-Hutchinson, later replaced by Major General Cameron, GOC Northern Command, had overall authority of the camp. During the short period of its existence, three British commandants were responsible for camp administration and had direct contact with the internees: Colonel Little, Colonel Ennis and then Colonel Browne, who remained until the camp closed.[35]

The senior ranking British military officers at the camp were for the most part professional and conducted themselves as soldiers, whereas the officers of lesser rank often acted like glorified bully-boys when not on the leash of their superiors. The subordinate officers possessed an air of self-importance and there was an obvious division, almost a class division, between them and the soldiers. Colonel Ennis had a healthy contempt for the nastiness often portrayed by the lieutenants and sergeants towards the detainees. However, the internees enjoyed watching the subordinate officers trotting behind Colonel Ennis when they entered the compound for inspection. The internees were often subjected to the wrath of the over-zealous minions when they entered the compound accompanied by soldiers.

On one occasion, as the internee fire detail was attending to a small conflagration in No. 2 compound, a British lieutenant accompanied by two soldiers approached the internee in charge, James McInerney from County Limerick, telling him to take his hands out of his pockets and help the others. McInerney promptly told him where to go and was immediately arrested and taken to the cells. After a few days he was taken before Colonel Ennis and the subordinate officer made his charge. When Colonel Ennis asked him what he had to say for himself, McInerney replied: 'Oh, I have nothing to say for myself, but I do want to put in a word for this young man,' pointing to the lieutenant, who had a look of astonishment on his face. 'He's young, colonel, and he may have never seen a fire before, and so lost his head … but he'll come all right, colonel, he'll come all right. Don't punish him.'

Colonel Ennis looked at the subordinate officer with a smile in his eyes and ordered him to escort McInerney back to the compound.[36]

The families of internees attempted to attract national attention to highlight the hardships endured by their loved ones at Ballykinlar through the publication of letters in national and regional newspapers. In late January the then British camp commandant, Lieutenant Colonel C. Little, received a newspaper cutting from a resident of County Cork, which referred to the treatment of the internees. He responded in a letter to the *Irish Independent*, saying the statements were a distortion of the facts. In an obvious propagandist reply he stated, 'The prisoners receive fuel on a larger scale than the troops there … they have the same bedding, bed-boards, straw mattresses, pillow and four blankets. Visits are not allowed, newspapers, as chosen by the internees are received daily.' He even suggested that the internees' rations were considerably larger than the soldiers'.

In fact, the internees did not receive any newspapers and were forced on occasion to burn bed boards and any other wood that could be scavenged to heat the huts in winter. As for the rations, if it had not been for the parcels of food sent into the camp from families and friends, the internees would have experienced near starvation.[37]

In general the internees enjoyed a certain level of control regarding management within the compound, but this was often interrupted by military interference, whether through official policy or vindictiveness. Despite the British military having overall authority in the camp, the establishment of the internees' own authority within the compounds inevitably created friction between the internees and the military. The camp council arranged a meeting with the military authority requesting permission to appoint their own personnel for the administration of the compounds, including the appointment of cooks and other routine arrangements regarding the supply of food. After some consultation this was agreed, and over time the internees established their own government under the authority of the camp council, which replaced the provisional council.

The new camp or compound council comprised a commandant, vice-commandant, line captains and four others appointed by all internees in the compound. In the interest of fair representation, the four additional members were taken from each of the four provinces. In No. 1 compound these were Dr T. F. O'Higgins, Leinster; Art O'Donnell, Munster; Seamus Ward, Ulster; and Patrick Hogan, Connaught. Each compound was under the authority of a commandant with the assistance of a vice-commandant, and both were chosen by the internees and approved by the camp council. The commandants, line captains and hut leaders were responsible for maintaining discipline and ensuring that routine orders and standing orders were adhered to.[38]

The most important officers for the thirty-two huts in each compound were the line captains. Each line or company consisted of ten huts, eight of which were for accommodation. These held up to twenty-five men, so, when fully occupied, could house approximately 200. The line captain was responsible for the discipline of his company or line and for ensuring that the hut leaders carried out their duties. The hut leaders were elected by the men in each hut and were responsible for making sure that the buildings were kept in a proper state of cleanliness both inside and in the area immediately around them. They had to ensure that each hut was swept daily, all beds were made up, ashes removed from the stove and that refuse was disposed of correctly.

The internee line captain worked closely with the British line captain in the day-to-day governance of the compound and accompanied him when he carried out the daily inspection of the huts. The internee line captain also escorted the camp commandants and the British commandants on periodic inspections. All requests and complaints were passed to the internees' line captains and then on to the commandant of the compound, who would subsequently pass them on to the military authority. In certain exceptional circumstances the line captain took requests or complaints directly to the military officer assigned to each line, and was also responsible for passing all mail to the postmaster, who handed it to and received it from the British military censor.[39]

The internees at Ballykinlar camp came from all walks of life, and included accountants, architects, bankers, barbers, carpenters, chefs, dentists, doctors, electricians, engineers, farmers, journalists, politicians, post office staff, schoolteachers, shopkeepers, solicitors, tailors, university professors and clergy. The internment policy had unwittingly established a small community within the barbed wire confines. With such a diverse collection of professions, the internees were better qualified to carry out the administration of the camp than the British military, and it was as much of a learning curve for the British military as it was for the internees. The internees seemed to adapt to life in the camp much more quickly than their captors.[40]

Ballykinlar cuisine

The first example of Ballykinlar 'cuisine' was the hard biscuits and black tea given to the first internees on their arrival, and the first (and last) proper meal served at Ballykinlar camp was the one prepared by the internees in No. 1 compound on Christmas Day 1920, after their families and members of Cumann na mBan had sent gifts of turkeys and hams.[41] T. K. Walsh of County Cavan wrote to his wife about the preparations for Christmas dinner, explaining that all internees were asking family and friends for turkeys, cakes, etc. and informing them that they had to be posted on Tuesday 21 December to ensure delivery by Christmas Day.[42]

Patrick Colgan, then No. 1 compound commandant, approached one of the internee cooks, Thomas Meldon from Dublin, and told him that turkeys and hams had been sent to the camp: if he could cook a Christmas dinner, they could accept the food. Meldon asked the British quartermaster for the ingredients to make stuffing, including twelve loaves, onions, sage, thyme, etc. A couple of days later the British quartermaster took a sack to the compound cookhouse and said to Meldon, 'I think that is what you asked for, but you must return the loaves after Christmas.' Meldon thanked the officer and wished him a Happy Christmas.

A request by Meldon to the military to leave the cookhouse open on Christmas Eve was refused, but he and his assistants were allowed to remain in the hut overnight and a successful dinner was served the following day. Some of the men were so grateful for the feast that they presented Meldon with a couple of cigars. He retired to his hut that night and, lying back, lit up and allowed his mind to drift to the sound of surf on the shingled beach of Killiney in County Dublin.[43]

The general diet did not improve much, but the military insisted the internees received 'soldiers' rations'. According to the British Ministry of Defence, the daily ration of food per man was: bread (one pound), potatoes (ten ounces), vegetables (four ounces), rice (two ounces), tea (half ounce), oatmeal (two ounces), sugar (half ounce), margarine or dripping (half ounce), milk (half pint), meat (ten ounces). Once a week they were permitted bacon (eight ounces) and fish (twelve ounces).[44]

From the beginning of December to the middle of January the actual meat ration was five ounces per day, which included bone, gristle and inferior parts. The low quality of the meat meant it was usually only suitable for stewing, but the vegetables were also of poor quality, potatoes being the exception. They also received twelve ounces of milk per 100 men, which was not even sufficient to colour the tea. The military eventually recognised that the rations were insufficient for the large number of men and agreed to seven and a half ounces of meat which was later increased to eight ounces, but still included bone, gristle and inferior parts. There were three rations of bacon per week, but the quality was so bad that it was inedible. Eventually the bacon ration was reduced to one day a week.[45]

The beef supplied to the internees was usually very tough and on many occasions badly tainted. The meat supplied on Tuesday 29 March was refused as it was contaminated with tuberculosis. The bacon supplied as a replacement was also condemned and the camp councils made formal complaints to the British to supply no more bacon unless it was fit for human consumption. The internees were generally cautious before accepting fresh meat, since it was often suspected of causing widespread sickness in the compounds. On more than one occasion over half the men were struck down with illness attributed to bad meat. In early February 1921 so many men were sick that the daily parade was cancelled. This problem continued regularly throughout the year and on many occasions the meat was not replaced.[46]

The internees received financial assistance from organisations outside the camp. The Chicago-based Celtic Cross Association had been formed following the burning of Cork city by British forces in December 1920, to provide relief for the local population who subsequently suffered privation. In March 1921 the association forwarded $500 for the purchase of clothing and food for the internees. The association's official account of this decision was that 'Many of the young men "on the run" in Ireland have not been in their own homes for two years, and consequently have not been able to procure adequate clothing.' The money sent by the Celtic Cross Association was soon followed by a consignment of American tinned food, which arrived in the camp on Saturday 16 April to the delight of the internees. It was distributed to both compounds and was greatly appreciated as a nice break from the usual excuse for food.[47]

The 342 lbs of meat supplied to the camp on Tuesday 4 October 1921 were so bad that the matter was reported to the camp doctor, Dr Moore. He informed the Royal Army Medical Corps (RAMC) officer who, after inspecting it, condemned it as unfit for human consumption and reported the matter to his superiors, requesting a fresh consignment, although the men had to go without that day.

The fish supplied on Fridays was often very stale and on many occasions was so bad that most of the men could not eat it. Those brave enough to consume it were inevitably on the sick list that evening and had to request the services of the camp doctors. The internees never received butter, only margarine, which was so badly tainted that it was inedible.[48]

The bread supplied to the men was usually blue-moulded and on one occasion some 200 loaves were pronounced unfit for use, representing a day's bread rations for over 400 men. The head cook, John Kane of Donegal, complained to the British commandant. The loaves were left in the dining room until they were replaced, but in the end they had to be dumped as they had lain rotting for several days.

Even the tea supplied to the camp was of an inferior quality.[49] The only foodstuffs that were of consistently good quality were potatoes and rice (when it was supplied), but the rations were not always sufficient for the large numbers of internees.[50]

The internees could not survive on the rations and were dependent on the food parcels and purchases from the canteen, which included bread, tea and sugar. An average of 250 loaves was purchased from the canteen each week.[51] On several occasions when the internees were in dispute with the British military, the latter would refuse to collect parcels from the railway station with the result that the internees experienced semi-starvation.

Ballykinlar camp canteens

The demand by the internees for the basic necessities of life, such as razors, toothbrushes and cigarettes, was addressed by the opening of canteens in both compounds. In traditional Ballykinlar fashion the internees formed a canteen board in the respective compounds, consisting of chairperson, staff and secretaries. The canteen eventually supplied cigarettes, tobacco, sweets, jams, stationery, fruit, butter, bacon, sausages, eggs, razors, toothbrushes, bootlaces, etc. Initially the conditions for establishing the canteens were that all products be supplied directly from the British military stores – this meant that they would come from English manufacturers. If the weekly purchases for the individual canteens totalled £100 there would be a rebate of two-and-a-half per cent. As a business proposition the internees considered this very unfair. On the outside, they would have been boycotting English products, yet in Ballykinlar camp they would be promoting their sale. As members of the army or citizens of the Irish Republic the internees considered it their duty to support Irish products and due to their confinement they were being forced to assist the economic growth of their enemy. They considered refusing all canteen privileges unless they were permitted to manage canteen affairs as they saw fit. The other option was to beat the British strategically by pretending to comply with routine orders while secretly establishing a system of trading with leading Irish manufacturers through IRA contacts.

After discussions between the officers of both compounds,

the internees opted for the latter course of action, beginning with tobacco products. Before long they had secured a regular supply of cigarettes and tobacco by post, with parcels addressed to individual internees. By the end of March 1921 the canteen was selling cigarettes, tobacco, sweets, jams, stationery, fruit and butter supplied by Irish firms at cost price.[52] This provided a substantial camp fund as the canteen profits were approximately £10 per week on cigarette and tobacco sales alone. The new scheme provided free cigarettes to internees permanently employed in the compounds, including cooks, barbers, tailors and boot repairers. Later on, the canteens began selling eggs, supplied by a grocer in nearby Downpatrick, and there was also a regular supply of bacon and sausages. The sale of items such as tea, sugar and condensed milk enabled the internees to prepare supper in their huts at night. The canteen profits also provided an allowance of 2/6d per week to internees who had no money of their own.[53]

The new enterprise worked well for the first month until the British became suspicious when the weekly order from the canteen stores dropped to £8. They scrutinised all letters to determine the source of the canteen supply and concluded that there was indiscriminate trading and that this should cease immediately. The British issued an order stating that all supplies had to be purchased through the military stores. This was communicated to the camp councils in both compounds and an agreement was reached whereby the camp canteens could source cigarettes and tobacco products, but all other products were to be purchased from the military stores. The

British said that the military stores would supply Irish products where possible and that the rebate would increase to five per cent. Despite the agreement, the internees continued to source various products on a reduced scale. However, the British held the upper hand and when disputes arose they refused to collect parcels and consignments from Tullmurry Railway Station. Many packages containing perishable goods rotted in the railway stores. When the disputes were resolved, the canteens returned to normal service.[54]

Camp currency

The internees were not permitted to have British currency while in the camp, mainly to prevent them from bribing the honest and trustworthy soldiers of the crown. On arrival at the camp all money belonging to the internees was confiscated and exchanged for 'chits' or coupons, which were initially slips of paper with the value of various coins printed on them.[55] Internees who did not want their money exchanged for coupons had to state the fact in writing to their line captains and this was held on record until their release.[56] The special currency was printed on coloured paper for small denominations (1d to 2/6d). The larger denominations were typed on white paper: 10/– to £1.[57]

The camp currency enabled the internees to purchase various items from the canteens. In September 1921 the British camp commandant ordered a check of the amount of camp money in circulation, so all currency was recalled and it was discovered that more camp money had been handed back than was originally issued. This could have been an error on the part of the British, but a more likely explanation was that some of it was forged. The British commandant refused to issue any more camp money, but after a long period of protest by the internees, the British did agree to allow the camp council to issue its own currency. This scheme involved prisoners signing a document to have their money transferred from the care of the British commandant to the internees' commandant. The scheme worked quite well.

In the early days of the camp the chits were handwritten and copied on a small duplicator. To prevent forgeries the camp money was checked and renewed at regular intervals. The paper used was of inferior quality and easily torn. In September 1921 enquires were made about having the currency professionally printed. Contact was made with Colm Ó Lochlainn of O'Loughlin, Murphy and O'Brien Printers, Dublin, who agreed to provide printed money free of charge. It was nicely designed circular 'coins', printed on thin hard cardboard in two sizes, ranging in value from 1d to £1.[58]

Camp hospital

The camp hospital was located in No. 1 compound in a large purpose-built hut that was longer than the accommodation huts and partitioned off into two wards containing up to forty beds. The hospital was fairly well equipped and supplied with the necessary medicines and supplies to treat minor ailments.[59]

However, the number of beds was inadequate for the amount of imprisoned men and on many occasions the internees from the No. 2 compound had to be sent back to their huts due to the lack of hospital accommodation.[60]

During the summer it was a suitable place for treating trivial complaints, but during the winter it was not, as it was very cold, wet and miserable. Even if the camp hospital had been the best equipped and constructed building imaginable, it would never have been a suitable location for serious cases so long as it remained inside the barbed wire cages of Ballykinlar. That environment was unsuitable for convalescence and could easily give rise to serious depression when the physical condition of an internee was low.[61] When the British military were ill they were immediately transferred to a hospital in Belfast, but the internees had to remain in the unhealthy surroundings of the camp. If an internee was very seriously ill and a request was made to have him transferred to a hospital, the request would not be processed for at least six weeks.

There were a few cases of men whose health broke down so completely that they were confirmed invalids incapable of the slightest physical work. They were recommended for release by the Royal Army Medical Corps (RAMC) doctor attached to the hospital and were taken out of the camp to the offices of the British military authority, with their bags packed. They were presented with a form, which was a comprehensive repudiation of the IRA, Sinn Féin and Gaelic League. If they refused to sign they would be returned to the camp.[62]

Over the twelve months that most of the internees spent

behind the barbed-wire cages of Ballykinlar, several men developed psychiatric illness, partly due to the conditions they were forced to live in. The methods adopted by the British military to find out information from the prisoners were certainly a contributing factor. Maurice 'Mossie' Donegan, a.k.a. Thomas Fitzpatrick, outlined the extent of the espionage methods in a letter to the *Irish Independent*. He maintained that when listening devices were found hidden under some of the huts, some of the internees developed mental illness. The men had to exercise caution, as they feared the mention of a name in any conversation might result in their arrest; this naturally told on the nerves of the more highly strung, and the tensions led to insanity.[63]

In early October 1921, four men were suffering from severe neurasthenia, a weakness of the nervous system characterised by general lassitude, irritability, lack of concentration, worry and hypochondria. The condition is usually triggered by stress and anxiety. Three were so badly affected they were admitted to the camp hospital. One had completely lost his reason and the condition of the other two gradually worsened. The camp doctors felt powerless when treating patients whose mental health had completely broken down. In the case of the fourth man, Dr Moore requested that he be released, and waited for a number of weeks in hope. As the internee's delusions became more pronounced, Dr Moore began to consider that treating him in such unsuitable surroundings was counter-productive, and that by undertaking to treat the men in Ballykinlar he was making himself part of the system.

In a move to put pressure on the British, Dr Moore refused to take any further responsibility for the patient. He hoped that this move would secure the internee's release where there would be some hope of recovery in the care of his family. However, the British removed him to the guardroom where he was kept for over four weeks.[64] He was eventually released when he became too much of a burden. A telegram had been sent to his family in early September stating that he was to be released, but that a fee of £6 was to be forwarded to the camp for the purchase of a railway ticket. Unfortunately, his release came too late and his family had to admit him to the Richmond psychiatric hospital in Dublin within days.[65] It was the opinion of the various interned doctors that British military policy was to hold men suffering from psychiatric illness until they had lost all reason.

In a letter to *The Freeman's Journal*, Dr T. F. O'Higgins expressed this concern:

> During my internment I noticed that the most hopeless and most depressing cases were those who were mentally deranged. These cases were hopeless and depressing because in every case, although the symptoms were recognised in the early stages, it was apparent that it was the cold and deliberate policy of our custodians to keep the unfortunate sufferer in captivity until he was a hopeless, raving lunatic and then release him in order that his case might terrorise others.

Dr O'Higgins said that what depressed him most as a doctor was the fact that he knew that the men who had suffered psychiatric illness could have been treated had they been removed to more suitable surroundings. He believed that the intense espionage policy of the British military and other terror tactics were responsible for the mental health of so many men breaking down.[66]

Internees who became seriously ill had to remain in the camp hospital until they were released as broken men or removed in coffins. The Royal Army Medical Corps officer often did his best to recommend seriously ill men for release when he considered it absolutely necessary.[67] Some internees died because of the inadequate facilities and failure by the British camp authorities to have them transferred to a better equipped hospital. They included Patrick O'Toole, Carlow, who died of pneumonia due to ill-treatment on Tuesday 8 February 1921; Maurice Galvin, Waterford, who died of Bright's Disease, a chronic inflammation of the kidneys, on Saturday 9 April 1921; John O'Sullivan, Kildare, who died of haemorrhage as a result of ill-treatment on Thursday 5 May 1921; Maurice Quinn, Cork, who died of consumption (more commonly known as tuberculosis) on Tuesday 7 June 1921; and Edward Healy, Waterford, who died of pneumonia on Thursday 23 June 1921.[68]

The death of Maurice Galvin highlighted the callous nature of the British military. His remains were removed from the camp hospital on Sunday 10 April at midday and a guard of honour was formed by the internees in No. 1 and No. 2 compounds as they were transferred to the No. 2 chapel compound. A volunteer guard stayed with the body, which was held until his family had forwarded the cost of transferring it to County Waterford. His remains were eventually removed from the camp following mass on Tuesday 12 April and were carried to the main gates by his comrades. The internees formed a guard of honour and the corpse was placed on a Red Cross lorry for the journey to Dublin before being transferred to Tallow, County Waterford, by train.[69]

The circumstances following Galvin's death were raised at the House of Commons on Thursday 2 June 1921 to the embarrassment of the British government. Galvin was seventeen years old when he was arrested and interned at Ballykinlar camp: the British maintained he was a lieutenant in the IRA. Commander Joseph Kenworthy, MP for Kingston upon Hull, asked Hamar Greenwood, chief secretary for Ireland, if he was aware that the military authorities had sent a bill for £34 4s to Maurice Galvin's mother for the cost of conveying the body of her son from Ballykinlar to County Waterford. Greenwood replied that the relatives, on being notified about Maurice's death, telegraphed the commandant at Ballykinlar camp requesting him to send the remains to Tallow. Greenwood said that the military authorities had complied with the wishes of the family but they had no power to defray expenses in cases of that kind. Kenworthy asked Greenwood if he would consider altering that state of affairs, but Greenwood avoided answering the question, citing lack of time and the large number of questions on the paper.[70]

The death of John O'Sullivan, Kildare, on the morning of Thursday 5 May was also not without controversy. He died in the camp hospital and his remains were transferred to the No. 2 compound that evening. A guard of honour lined the route from the hospital through the gates to the chapel in the other compound. His comrades maintained a guard over the body throughout the night. John O'Sullivan's relatives arrived at the camp on Friday morning with a coffin and claimed his remains. The Tricolour was draped over the coffin while in the hospital, but removed in the afternoon as the remains were carried through the compound to the front gates. A guard of honour was also formed along the route through the camp. The internees accompanying and carrying the body were surrounded and searched at the main gate. The military hunted in vain for the Tricolour, but instead discovered a camera on Leo Henderson, the No. 2 compound OC. He was subsequently removed to the guardroom, which sparked protests by the No. 2 compound internees who refused to answer to their names at lock-up that night. They even began storing food and water in their quarters in anticipation of a siege. This continued until Henderson's release on Saturday 7 May.[71]

One example of the lack of concern on the part of the British authorities for the wellbeing of internees was the case of Patrick McKeown from County Longford. He was admitted to the hospital on Wednesday 17 August 1921 suffering from pleurisy. After a couple of days, Dr P. M. Moore found that McKeown's condition was extremely serious and he brought it to the attention of the RAMC officer attached to the hospital, who recommended the sick man's immediate release to his superiors. However, the recommendation, which usually involved a request from the British military authority in the camp to Dublin Castle, was held up by a 'higher authority'. McKeown's condition deteriorated to the extent that a telegram was sent to his wife for her to arrange a visit to the camp. The RAMC officer made a second request to his superiors and recommended his release to the military hospital in Belfast. This appeal was sanctioned, but McKeown refused to be removed to the hospital in Belfast. His condition deteriorated further and he was unconditionally released into the care of his family.

The camp doctors were also worried that they did not have suitable facilities to carry out emergency procedures if an internee required immediate surgery. They would have to make an application through the command structures in the camp, and then permission could only be granted by the British authorities at Dublin Castle or in some cases by the military GHQ at Park Gate, Dublin. They were frustrated by the red tape associated with requests to have seriously ill patients removed from that debilitating and harmful environment, and because the RAMC authority in the camp could not sanction a release – that decision had to be made by the 'hidden hand gang' in Dublin Castle, who the doctors felt had little or no regard for the plight of the internees.[72] They worked tirelessly in their care of the patients and tried to have many men released or moved from the confines of the unsavoury surroundings of the camp when they felt it would be beneficial to their recovery.

On one occasion, in mid-October, the RAMC officer informed Dr Moore that his superiors had sanctioned the transfer of three seriously ill internees to the military hospital in Belfast. Based on the assumption that it would benefit their recovery, Moore advised the three to accept the transfer. One of the men was diagnosed as having a stone in the bladder and possibly a kidney stone. The palliative treatment was rest and light diet. The second patient was suffering from exophthalmic goitre with commencing nervous symptoms, also known as 'Graves' Disease', an autoimmune disease where the thyroid is overactive and produces excessive amounts of hormones. The third man was suffering from the early stages of psychiatric illness and Dr Moore felt his removal from the camp would assist his recovery.

Moore believed that the men would be removed from the camp in an ambulance. To his horror, on Wednesday morning, 19 October, they were handcuffed and, wearing only light, ragged clothing, marched through the compound in a heavy downpour to the main gates where they were bundled onto the back of an open lorry, surrounded by a party of armed military. They were then driven the thirty-two miles to Belfast in heavy rain. Dr Moore was greatly dismayed at their treatment and felt he was somehow responsible, as he had advised them to accept the offer to move to better facilities.[73]

Art O'Donnell, Clare, was admitted to the camp infirmary with suspected tuberculosis. At that time the hospital was crudely equipped, but having spring beds it was considered fairly comfortable except for the cold. During his stay another patient, Seamus Hoey from Bray, County Wicklow, was admitted suffering from pneumonia and in very bad health. He spent a long time in the hospital and was eventually released due to his very delicate state, but died shortly after his release. Hoey had also been interned in Frongoch internment camp in 1916.[74]

In April 1921 a Press Association representative was given access to the camp. Throughout his tour he was accompanied by the then No. 1 compound commandant, Joseph McGrath, and a British military officer. He reported that, 'The hospital is certainly bare and cheerless and there are not the facilities which should be at hand in a well-equipped hospital', and argued that for seriously ill patients a hospital should have been provided outside the compound, one properly equipped with medical and nursing staff. However, following publication of his article, British military headquarters stated that the hospital was similarly equipped in every particular to that of a military hospital and where necessary men were sent to other medical facilities. Clearly this was not the case.[75]

Several men in the camp suffered from asthma and the conditions within the camp, the sandstorms and sea air, were very detrimental to their ailments. A letter published in *The Freeman's Journal* was also given to the British military commandant in the camp:

> We demand unconditional release, or removal to some gaol, for the following reasons: There are five of us suffering from chronic asthma. The climate conditions on this wind-swept peninsula are particularly unsuited for our complaint.
>
> The continuous sandstorms, the dusty huts and the all-pervading dampness, are highly detrimental to our health, and if

continued during the winter months must result in permanent injury to all concerned. Under the present conditions each man is laid up about three days out of every week, and with the advance of winter worse may be expected. The internees' medical officer has already recommended our release, but no action has been taken. In the circumstances we would prefer prison conditions, with those drawbacks. We have all had experience of prison conditions, and are quite aware of what this decision entails. If this demand is not acceded to within seven days we shall be obliged to take further action. Signed by: Matthew Patrick Higgins, Frank McKay, Francis Carney, Peter Murphy and M. Ross.[76]

The internee's doctors considered one of the British medical officers, Major Kyle, inexperienced and insensitive. He seemed to delight in tramping around the hospital in ordinary military footgear even though the RAMC regulations were that all staff working in the hospital should wear the slippers provided. The military also walked into the hospital wearing their boots, often at all hours of the day and night for the flimsiest of reasons, regardless of the conditions of the patients.[77]

One internee, who was released shortly after the Truce of July 1921, described the conditions in the camp hospital in a letter to *The Freeman's Journal*. Seán Breathnach from Maghera in County Derry criticised the continued incarceration of elderly and seriously ill internees:

Had they [British military] been possessed of the instincts of soldiers and statesmen instead of those of shopkeepers and

> gombeenmen, they would have begun the creation of the desired
> atmosphere by setting free all men aged forty years and upwards,
> as well as those others who are victims of disease or other physical
> disablement, as in the following cases: One public man was in
> hospital during the entire six months that I spent in camp.
> Another poor fellow is so badly crippled with rheumatism that
> he has to be wheeled around in a bath chair. A third is a nervous
> wreck: while yet another is the subject of a serious form of heart
> disease ...[78]

The hospital wasn't only used to treat sick internees. It was often
used for meetings between the officers of the two compounds
when it was necessary to discuss important issues of policy, for
example. An officer or reliable person from No. 2 compound
would feign illness to gain admission. The infirmary was also
used to hide or transfer wanted men from one compound to
another. If an internee was sought by the British authorities he
would be admitted to the hospital under an assumed name and
would exchange identities with another patient and transfer
from No. 1 to No. 2 compound or vice versa.[79]

Religion and faith at Ballykinlar

The vast majority of the internees were greatly devoted to their
faith, and it was said that the saving of them was 'first their
religion and then their sense of patriotism'.[80] The camp chaplain,
Fr John McLister, was on hand to attend to spiritual needs and
help in many other ways during their captivity.[81] The priest, a

native of Torr Head in County Antrim, was appointed shortly after the internees' arrival in December 1920.[82] 'Ballykinlar camp – The Bearer, Reverend John McLister, has permission to enter the cage as Chaplain to internees. Signed – C. Little, Col., OC, Ballykinlar camp – Dated December 18, 1920.'[83] Fr McLister was the Catholic curate in nearby Dundrum and his appointment was approved by Joseph McRory, Bishop of Down and Connor.[84]

Fr McLister was highly respected and a friend to all the prisoners, being present in the camp every morning to say mass at 10 a.m. He spread his time between the two compounds for the first two months until the beginning of February 1921, when Fr Thomas Burbage arrived in No. 2 compound as an internee.[85] Burbage was born in Mountmellick, County Offaly, in 1889 and ordained a priest in 1904. He was a member of the Irish Volunteers and curate in the village of Geashill, also in County Offaly, at the time of his arrest on Saturday 15 January 1921. He was first taken to the Curragh camp in County Kildare and then to Arbour Hill prison.[86] With approximately 100 other men, he was removed from Arbour Hill and transferred to the North Wall in Dublin. They were put on board a British naval destroyer and forced to sit side by side on the deck. They were not allowed to move or stand throughout the voyage and suffered greatly as it was a bitterly cold night. On their arrival at Belfast docks the following morning, they received the usual hostile reception from the unionist mobs working at the Belfast shipyards. Fr Burbage received special attention as he was dressed in his clerical clothing. The venomous mob spat in his face and kicked and punched him repeatedly shouting, 'To hell with the Pope.' The military guard tried to protect the men, but were overpowered. Patrick O'Daly, from Inchicore in Dublin, was walking behind the priest and as one unionist made another attempt to spit at him, O'Daly stepped forward and struck him with all his force. The unionist was knocked to the ground and the angry crowd erupted. A tall soldier got hold of O'Daly and threw him and Fr Burbage onto the back of a lorry. He then shouted to the driver to move off even though the lorry was only half full. The soldier said to O'Daly, 'You are an awful mad-man. That was an awful blow you gave the swine. I would love to do the same but I dare not. I'm a Roman Catholic too.' The men were forced to lie down on the lorry as the missiles of nuts, bolts, metal and other items rained down on them. They were taken to Victoria Barracks before being transferred to Ballykinlar by train later that day.[87]

The internees arrived at Ballykinlar camp on Wednesday 2 February and initially Fr Burbage was known for wearing his cloth cap and hobnailed boots, choosing to be treated the same as all the others.[88] Fr McLister had received a letter from Bishop McRory on that day, informing him that Fr Burbage was an internee in No. 2 compound: 'I gladly give the same faculties to Fr Burbage as I gave to you. I remember him well and am glad to know that he is in good form. Please tell him so, and give him my good wishes.' Fr McLister made a point of visiting Fr Burbage, told him of Bishop McRory's letter and appointed him as No. 2 compound chaplain. Fr Burbage immediately took over religious duties there, allowing Fr McLister the freedom to focus on the internees in No. 1 compound.[89]

The internees attended mass every morning at 10 a.m. apart from a few occasions when the British military prevented Fr McLister from entering the compound as a punishment during the many protests and disputes. The rosary was said in the huts every night and confessions were heard every Saturday.[90]

When the Truce was announced in July 1921 the internees thought release would follow soon after and a large number of those in the No. 1 compound expressed a desire to travel to Lough Derg to do the pilgrimage at St Patrick's Purgatory. Lough Derg is approximately four miles north of Pettigo on the Donegal/Fermanagh border, but as the weeks passed and with no sign of a release date in sight they decided to hold the 'pilgrimage' in the No. 1 compound.[91] It started with the participants beginning the fast from midnight on Thursday 11 August until after midnight on Sunday 14 August. The 'pilgrims' were allowed one meal a day of black tea, oat bread and Lough Derg soup, which consisted of hot water, salt and pepper. There was no sleep on the first night, nor until 10 p.m. the following night. Over the three-day 'pilgrimage' the men attended mass each morning at 8 a.m. and then the devotions, the Stations of the Cross, and the rosary and litany at 8.30 p.m. Confessions were heard on Saturday between 11.15 a.m. and 12 noon, 12.30 p.m. and 1 p.m., and 3 p.m. and 6 p.m. Over 270 internees from No. 1 compound took part: they were from counties all across the country and one man was from London.[92]

The St Vincent de Paul society

One of the most interesting features of the camp was the creation of a branch or conference of the St Vincent de Paul Society. This Catholic voluntary organisation is dedicated to tackling poverty and disadvantage by providing direct practical assistance to anyone in need. There were many captives in Ballykinlar whose families could not afford the cost of weekly parcels and the St Vincent de Paul Society was seen as a means of assisting these men. One of the first actions of the Ballykinlar branch was to carry out a collection among the prisoners to purchase essential items for those most in need. Many of the internees were members of the society before their arrest and in ordinary life devoted some of their leisure time to the relief of the poor.

As they could not visit the underprivileged, which was the principal work of the society, they adopted certain spiritual exercises for the general good of the members in the camp. They established the Adoration of the Blessed Sacrament and all the members of the camp carried this out in turn. They also distributed prayer beads, prayer books, scapulars and Catholic literature to the internees. On Christmas morning 1920 they organised mass and planned for all Catholic members of the camp to receive Holy Communion: there were close to 900 communicants that morning. The Ballykinlar branch was named after the three patron saints of Ireland – St Patrick, St Brigid and St Colmcille.[93]

Hygiene, laundry and unsanitary conditions

The general conditions of the camp were terrible and great efforts were required to make living conditions tolerable. The water supply during the winter months was so derisory that the internees were forced to ration the water to wash each morning. Sometimes the men were compelled to collect rainwater from the hut roofs. The supply deteriorated during the drier weather and water was so scarce that it was only turned on three times a day: from 9 a.m. to 12 noon, from 2 p.m. to 5 p.m., and from 6 p.m. to 7 a.m. the next morning. If any man could not get to a tap to wash in the morning he had to wait until midday or even until late afternoon just to wash his face.[94] The men did not get sufficient baths and found it difficult to arrange one bath per week. The water supply was so bad during the months of August and September that they could not bathe at all.[95]

The lack of adequate water supply during the dry periods posed serious hygiene problems, and many men contracted scabies and had to be confined to the isolation hut. The British military attempted to address this problem by sinking pumps into the ground of the compounds to draw water to the surface. However, the water obtained from the pumps was so contaminated that it had to be mixed with a disinfectant for basic scrubbing purposes and was not suitable for drinking or washing.[96]

The camp councils tried to ensure that hygiene was a priority for the internees and issued very strict orders for the upkeep of the huts and compounds. Dumping refuse underneath the huts was prohibited and rubbish that could not be burned had to be deposited in a pit near the gates, which was emptied by the military each day. All beds were to be made up first thing each morning, with the huts being swept by 9.30 a.m. and the ashes from the stoves removed by 10 a.m.[97] Despite the internees' best efforts to keep the buildings clean, during the winter months the compounds were awash with mud, and water gathered in large puddles in many parts of the waterlogged camp. The British dug a number of trenches in an attempt to drain off the water around the compounds, but these simply filled with stagnant water, the stench of which was so bad that the men had difficulty finding a place in the camp to breathe pure fresh air.[98]

The laundries or washrooms consisted of four sheds measuring approximately thirty feet in length, open at both ends with four windows on each side. Inside, supply pipes fed eight taps with a zinc ledge and trough or sink below each. The laundry was poorly constructed and the tap water poured onto the zinc ledge instead of into the troughs, wetting everyone and everything in the immediate area. A fifteen-gallon boiler at the end of each trough supplied the hot-water taps. Behind the boilers were zinc tanks, holding approximately 400 gallons of water, each about five feet long by about three feet wide and three feet deep sitting on top of scaffolding planks about six feet from the ground. The water was pumped into the tank by a double-handled pump, which drew water from a well sunk just outside the compounds. It was murky and most of the time emitted an offensive smell and was not fit for washing clothes.

The safest use of this water was for cleaning hut floors, but even that gave off an unpleasant stench.

When the camp was experiencing a water shortage, which was a regular occurrence during the summer months, laundry days were restricted to one day per week for each company line (up to 200 men) and the internees experienced all sorts of personal hygiene problems. As the sheds doubled up as laundries and washrooms, great care had to be taken to ensure the troughs were properly cleaned after laundry day to prevent diseases spreading. Cups, plates and other items were also washed in the huts, so proper organisation was required to ensure that individual needs for bathing, laundry or doing the dishes were efficiently catered for.

When the washing was completed the men carried their clothes to the drying rooms in the centre of the compounds, which were approximately eighteen feet square. There were two small closed stoves in each drying room, with bars running across to hang clothes on. The stoves generated sufficient heat in the confined areas to dry the material, but the soot from the boiler fell over the washed garments and most of the men preferred to dry their clothes in their huts. The time allocated for laundry was one day each week per two huts, with use of one of the drying rooms for that day until eleven o'clock the following morning. However, with the insufficient supply of coal and the absence of several panes of glass in the windows, the men who did use the drying rooms would usually have to take their clothes to their own huts to complete the process.[99]

British reaction to internment

By 1921 the internment situation was attracting a lot of attention in Ireland and Britain, prompting a series of questions in the British House of Commons. During one debate, on Thursday 14 April 1921, a series of questions were raised regarding internees: William John, MP for Rhondda West, asked about the total number of uncharged and untried persons in custody in Ireland up to that date. In the absence of Hamar Greenwood, the question was taken by Denis Henry, MP for South Derry, who was attached to the attorney general's office. He explained that at that time 2,208 were interned and a further 1,250 were in custody awaiting internment. At the same sitting, Joseph Kenworthy, MP, asked what steps had been taken to address complaints about conditions in the camps in view of the fact that the internees had not been tried. Denis Henry replied that judging by the reports in the press the internees were having the time of their lives.[100]

The plight of the internees was again raised at the sitting of Thursday 21 April 1921. Francis Acland, MP, asked what arrangements were being made regarding the inspection of Irish prisons and internment camps in light of statements concerning the unsanitary conditions and the hardships inflicted on the internees, many of whom were untried and uncharged. This was followed by a similar question from Henry Cavendish-Bentinck, MP. The questions were again taken by Denis Henry standing in for Hamar Greenwood, who stated that military places of detention and internment camps were regularly inspected by senior military officers and medical officers, and that an inspector of military prisons and internment camps had been appointed. Henry pointed out that eight complaints of ill-treatment had been made in the previous three months and had been carefully investigated. He added that in each case the conditions complained of were not of the nature alleged. Henry also added that many internees had written to friends and family speaking highly of the good treatment they were receiving.[101] This statement was undoubtedly biased given the camp censors' eagerness in cutting any unsavoury comments about the conditions or the treatment by the military from letters leaving the camps. Any reference by the internees to the food being good was an indication of their sense of humour, rather than a statement of fact, as the food was generally of inferior quality and the men relied mainly on food parcels from home.

By June 1921 the number of those interned had reached 3,252. The majority of these were in Ballykinlar, the Curragh, Spike Island and Bere Island, although others were held at barracks and jails throughout the country.[102] Further pressure came from British MPs concerning the methods employed in the arrests of suspected men in Ireland and the avenues open to them to appeal the internment orders. The issue was raised at the sitting of Wednesday 22 June 1921 by Frank Briant, MP, who asked the British home secretary if the internees had been informed of the precise grounds for their internment and, if not, what opportunities were available to them to rebut the charge against them. John Baird, under-secretary of state, answered that due to the dangers to persons providing information against the accused, the military were not in a position to provide internees with a formal statement of evidence against them. He said that the advisory committee at the camps heard all applications in person and the evidence against the internee was given as far as possible.[103]

5

Protecting Wanted Men

The haste with which the British internment policy was implemented following the events of late November 1920 meant some men who had been suspected of involvement in the assassinations of the British secret service personnel on 21 November were mistakenly transferred to Ballykinlar, as were many who had been 'on the run' before their arrest. The British were anxious to locate anyone who had been involved in major incidents throughout the country, including the Bloody Sunday assassinations in Dublin. Ballykinlar, the first major centre for internment, housed men from all thirty-two counties of Ireland and the British believed it presented them with a unique opportunity not only to gather information, but to identify people who had previously been wanted for various IRA activities. The camp military received visits from various elements of the British military and police including the Secret Service and RIC detectives, seeking such men. Anyone identified would inevitably be arrested and removed to face prosecution, a long prison sentence and possible death.

The principal method of safeguarding wanted men in the

camp was to get them to change identities with other internees and where possible with men who resembled them. In some instances the wanted man was ordered to change identity with another internee, move to a different hut, shave his head or grow a beard.

In January 1921 a British sergeant was escorting an internee, Hubert Wilson of Longford, into the No. 1 compound. He recognised another internee, James McMonagle (from Letterkenny, County Donegal) as having been involved in a train raid at a railway station in County Donegal when he had been a member of a British military escort party. He told Wilson that he recognised McMonagle from the raid in which he and three soldiers were disarmed, and that he intended to report his presence to his superiors. Wilson began signalling to McMonagle, who at first could not understand the reason for it, but taking no chances moved away. Wilson had a long conversation with the sergeant and he realised that the man had been conscripted into the army and was due to leave, having almost served his time. Wilson persuaded him not to make the report, but next day visited McMonagle in his hut, explained to him that he was the one who had been signalling to him the previous day and told him that he believed he had persuaded the sergeant not to report the matter to his superiors. Patrick Colgan was made aware of the incident and as a precaution ordered McMonagle to cut his hair, shave his head, move hut and change names with another internee.[1]

In some cases a double identity exchange was made: A became B, B became C, and C became A. Another way was to move men from one compound to another, which was usually done through the camp hospital. If a man from No. 2 compound was sick and hospitalised, a wanted man from No. 1 compound would return to the other compound, assuming his identity.[2] In an effort to conceal the identities of wanted men, the then No. 1 compound commandant, Patrick Colgan, instructed the intelligence staff to locate men who were 'on the run' before arrest or had been mistakenly sent to the camp from various prisons while awaiting trial or sentence.

Some men erroneously sent to Ballykinlar camp had switched identities with other prisoners when being held in a prison or detention centre.[3] For example Henry McGowan from Ballybofey, County Donegal, was wrongly sent to Ballykinlar camp. He had been arrested in June 1921 following a raid on an IRA dugout on the Donegal/Tyrone border. He was facing the prospect of charges relating to a raid on an RIC barracks in County Tyrone in which an RIC constable was killed, and for an attack on a party of British military in Donegal, as well as possession of weapons and ammunition found at the time of his arrest. McGowan could have faced capital charges and possible execution. When he arrived at Derry jail the day after his arrest he met his brother Patrick who had been arrested in April. Patrick was due to be transferred to Ballykinlar camp the following day and the two changed places, so when Patrick McGowan was called out the following day for transfer to Ballykinlar, Henry went in his place. On arrival at Ballykinlar, Henry reported to the then No. 1 compound commandant, Joseph McGrath, and informed him about his situation.

McGrath said he would arrange to lose him in the camp should the military ask about him.

At the trial in Derry against McGowan, an RIC constable giving evidence said that the man before the court was not Henry McGowan, and the charge against his brother Patrick was struck out. Henry McGowan thought he was off the hook until a few weeks later, when the British military caught him out in a counter ruse. A British intelligence officer, Sergeant Williams, entered the compound, called out Patrick McGowan's name, saying that he was to be unconditionally released. Henry presented himself to the sergeant and was escorted to the guardroom where he was informed that he was being sought in relation to a charge for possession of weapons and was being transferred to Derry jail. He was subsequently convicted.[4]

Some of the men involved in the operations on 21 November in Dublin were identified by intelligence staff; they included a number of Dublin men: Patrick O'Daly, Seán Lemass, Aidan Corri and Thomas Whelan, who was from Clifden, County Galway, but living in Dublin at the time of his arrest. Two Cork men also being hunted by the British were Maurice 'Mossie' Donegan, who had been using the name Thomas Fitzpatrick, and Mick Crowley, who had been using the name Paddy O'Sullivan from the time of their arrests. Patrick Colgan interviewed the four Dublin men separately and instructed each not to make himself known to any member of the military. There was little threat to the two Cork men, but the capture of Aidan Corri and Thomas Whelan was a priority for the military. Colgan arranged for Corri and Whelan to change identities and huts with other internees, but Whelan refused as he considered he had no charge to answer. Whelan told Colgan that he had not been involved in the operations on Bloody Sunday and that he had witnesses to prove it. Colgan approached friends of Whelan's to try to persuade him to agree to the arrangement.

Some time later Sergeant Williams entered No. 1 compound and called Thomas Whelan's name. Colgan approached the officer to ask what he wanted with Whelan and was told that he was to be released. Colgan told Michael Nolan, line captain, to inform Whelan he was being sought and to make a last desperate appeal to him not to identify himself, but the man was adamant that he had no charge to answer and when Colgan approached him Whelan bade him goodbye.[5]

Whelan was removed from the camp on Wednesday 22 December and taken to Victoria Barracks in Belfast. He was held there for one night, before being transferred to Kilmainham gaol, Dublin, arriving in the early hours of Thursday 23 December. He was put in an identity parade on Tuesday 30 December 1920 and on Thursday 6 January was taken to Dublin Castle, where he was charged with carrying firearms not under effective military control under Regulation 9 AA of the Defence of the Realm Regulations. He was then taken to a room and identified by a man who claimed that Whelan had held him at gunpoint on the morning of 21 November 1920 at 22 Lower Baggot Street. He was again taken to Dublin Castle on Monday 10 January 1921 and identified by another man as being among a party of armed men running down from Upper Mount Street. The witness said that some of the men had pointed revolvers at him and ordered him to leave the area. Whelan was put in another identity parade on Tuesday 11 January 1921.

Michael Noyk, solicitor and legal adviser to Michael Collins and Arthur Griffith, was instructed to act for Thomas Whelan and five others accused of involvement in the killings of Sunday 21 November 1920. Noyk described Whelan as a soft country boy, very talkative and with a beautiful character. He visited his clients at Kilmainham and was greatly alarmed when speaking to Whelan and his cellmate James Boyce, as during their discussions a military officer entered the cell and said, 'Won't you do everything you can for poor Whelan as he is so nice.' Noyk being suspicious of the officer's comment asked Whelan if he had been talking to the officer. Whelan said he had. He said the officer told him, 'I admire you as one soldier to another and am interested to know what battalion you belong to?' Whelan had excitedly and proudly replied, 'I belong to "C" Company of the 3rd Battalion, Dublin Brigade.'

Noyk knew at that point that Whelan had fallen into the trap and had incriminated himself. At his trial, despite having several witnesses who put him at mass in Ringsend chapel at the time of the shootings, Whelan was convicted of murder and sentenced. He was hanged on Monday 14 March at Mountjoy jail.[6]

Following Thomas Whelan's removal from Ballykinlar, Patrick Colgan anticipated a ruse by the British to apprehend Aiden Corri. To prevent this happening Corri agreed to change identities with another internee, Owen Slowey from Drogheda,

County Louth. Some weeks later Sergeant Williams again entered the compound looking for Aiden Corri and Colgan again asked why he was being sought. Sergeant Williams used the same story and Colgan replied, 'I will give Corri for release. If he is not released I will not produce any other man.' The officer gave his word and Colgan called Aiden Corri's name. Owen Slowey stepped forward and was removed from the camp. He was first taken to Arbour Hill prison in Dublin for an identification parade and then to Dublin Castle, where he was subjected to terrible treatment during interrogation, including half-hanging, cold-water hosing, cold baths, severe beatings and other forms of torture which continued over a number of days, but he did not reveal his true identity. He was held for over a month and was eventually identified by an RIC detective from Drogheda. Shortly after that he was returned to Ballykinlar.

On the day after Slowey's true identity was revealed, Aiden Corri was summoned, removed from the camp and taken to Dublin. This time a man from Galway played the role and was instructed by Colgan to reveal his identity when he arrived in Dublin. This process continued until the British seemed to abandon their efforts to identify the wanted man. However, when the British military informed Patrick Colgan a short time later that they required one of the huts for use as a post office, and that the occupants of that hut were to be transferred to No. 2 compound, Colgan took the opportunity to transfer Aiden Corri to the other compound. Another internee exchanged his identity with Corri and the transfer was made.

Leo Henderson, commandant of No. 2 compound, concealed Aiden Corri in that compound.[7]

One morning in early February 1921, the British military entered the compounds, fully equipped as for battle with bayonets fixed to their rifles. All men were ordered to return to their huts and while doing so were subjected to a fusillade of profanity, obscenity and threats of being shot if they did not hurry. The British line officer conducted an inspection and roll call before the doors were locked at 11 a.m. A couple of hours later the officer returned and, opening the doors of the huts, ordered all men to form a single line. The usual profanities and threats were heard from the soldiers as internees were ordered to march towards the main gate where officers in warlike attire and men in plain clothes were standing. The prisoners were instructed to produce their internment orders and those who had not received theirs were asked to step aside and give their serial number, name and home address.

The men were paraded in front of a hut, which had one window painted white, with a spy hole. Inside were RIC detectives and members of the British Secret Service. The whole charade was to locate Aiden Corri, who by that time was among the internees of No. 2 compound. Patrick Colgan, who was also a resident of No. 2 compound at that time, realised what was taking place and felt confident that, as he was a prominent figure in the camp, the British would not be focused on anyone near him on the identity parade. He instructed Corri to walk behind him and the ruse apparently worked, as the mysterious eyes behind the spy hole failed to identify the wanted man. The men were paraded to the new recreation ground, which was surrounded by soldiers under the command of a brutish-looking officer, who hit the men with a heavy cane if they did not move quickly enough. He struck Patrick Domican from Kells, County Kildare, across the neck and back, but Domican marched on without flinching. The men were held in the recreation ground until late that evening without food or water and later found that their huts had been ransacked by the military and various items were broken or thrown out into the compound.[8]

A few days after the identification parade, Patrick Colgan was summoned to the British commandant's office to meet with the new GOC Northern Command, Major General Cameron. The two men had a general conversation and smoked a few cigarettes and then Cameron said to Colgan, 'I am being made a damn fool in the eyes of my superiors. I have 1,000 men in Ballykinlar and I can identify anyone but the prisoner Corri. I give you my word of honour as an officer if you produce Corri he will not be taken away.' Cameron tried to induce Colgan to give up the wanted man, but he refused and Aiden Corri was never discovered.[9]

6

The Murders of Joseph Tormey and Patrick Sloane

The opening of the second compound at Ballykinlar camp presented the British military with a problem, as the men in No. 1 compound wanted to communicate with those in No. 2 compound. Part of No. 1 compound ran parallel to No. 2 compound, but was separated from it by two high rows of barbed wire. Between the barbed wire and the first huts in No. 1 compound was a strip of grass approximately forty feet wide, and then a road wide enough for two lorries to pass each other. The men met to talk with those in No. 2 compound at the corner of the hospital hut in No. 1 compound.[1]

The British military issued a warning to the internees to remain a certain distance from the wire. The men adhered to this as under camp regulations they would face fourteen days in the cells if they disobeyed, but they were at the mercy of the sentries over what constituted the appropriate distance from the wire. One of the sentry boxes in No. 1 compound overlooked the spot where the men met to have a chat, but the lookout did not have a view of the men from No. 2 compound. One morning James Lalor and Thomas Treacy, both from Kilkenny, left the chapel after mass and as they walked along the road inside the compound near the hospital hut a sentry fired a shot without warning. The bullet narrowly missed them, although they were over seven yards from the restricted area. It was only after the shot was fired that the sentry issued the warning 'Get away from the wires.'[2]

The No. 1 compound commandant at that time, Patrick Colgan, complained to the then British commandant, Colonel Little, who was dismissive and suggested that the shot was only a warning and not intended to hit anyone. Colgan put it to Colonel Little that if the men were not permitted to walk along the path adjacent to the wire then an official order should have been issued. Colonel Little said he did not wish that and said if the internees did not approach within three feet of the wire there would be no problem. This reassurance rang hollow and within days other internees narrowly escaped being shot by a sentry without provocation or warning.[3]

On the opening of the second compound, the camp intelligence staff, under the command of Maurice Horgan of Kerry, had been tasked with verifying the credentials of certain people. As with the opening of the first compound, the second filled rapidly with the daily arrivals of internees. Maurice Horgan was instructed by Patrick Colgan to interview a man from Killarney, County Kerry, named James Coffey. He had arrived in early January 1921 and raised the suspicions of some in No. 2

compound. The job was made more difficult with the restrictions on communications between the two compounds and the threat of being shot by a sentry.

On Monday 17 January 1921, Maurice Horgan arranged for the internee to be taken to the location in No. 2 compound near the wire used for inter-compound communication, to be interviewed. Fred Crowley of Cork and Joseph Tormey and Patrick Sloane both from Westmeath accompanied Horgan. Coffey was accompanied by another internee from Killarney and after a brief interview his credentials were verified. Horgan and the others were standing beside the hospital hut, sheltered from the sentry's view. Each time Horgan stepped out into view the sentry shouted at him to get away from the wire. When the inquiry was concluded, Horgan walked towards the main compound to report to Patrick Colgan, while Joseph Tormey, Patrick Sloane and Fred Crowley went towards their huts. As they walked along beside the road, the sentry fired a shot without warning: it struck Joseph Tormey in the head, passed through him and hit Patrick Sloane in the neck. Sloane fell into the arms of Fred Crowley and Joseph Tormey fell beside him. Crowley instantly went to fetch Dr O'Higgins, who was working in the hospital hut.[4] News of the shooting quickly reached Patrick Colgan, who immediately made his way to the scene. By the time he got there, other internees had gathered, but were being prevented from approaching the dying men by the sentry who had fired the fatal shot. Patrick Colgan walked towards the two men and the sentry ordered him to stop, raising his rifle and aiming it at him. The OC ignored the threat and knelt down beside the two men. He had a crucifix with a plenary indulgence, which he held to the two men's hands and recited an Act of Contrition.[5] Before long practically all the internees in No. 1 compound had gathered at the scene and the sight of the two men lying there created a highly charged and emotional state of affairs. All were on their knees reciting the rosary, when a British sergeant and two privates stepped into the ring of praying men.

Their attitude enraged the internees, but Patrick Colgan stood up and said, 'Boys there are enough men outside to avenge this, all we can do now is to pray for the souls of the deceased.' Colgan and other officers showed great leadership and brought calm to the very volatile situation: some men even suggested that in revenge the British camp commandant should be captured and killed.[6]

The camp chaplain, Fr McLister, who was in the compound, came to administer the last rites. Dr O'Higgins and Major Kyle, the RAMC officer, were both quickly on the scene. The two men were removed on stretchers to the hospital where they were pronounced dead.[7] Patrick Sloane was twenty-nine years old and Joseph Tormey was twenty-two. Both were from the Moate district of County Westmeath. Tormey lived with his brother and sister at a place called Hall and was employed as an agricultural labourer at the time of his arrest. Patrick Sloane, who had been married only four days before his arrest, lived approximately five miles away in Legan.[8]

The remains of the two men were removed from Ballykinlar late on Thursday evening, 20 January, and were carried to the gates by their comrades. The internees in both camps paraded and stood to attention as the bodies were driven away from the camp.[9] The cortège then travelled to Westmeath for burial, arriving at Moate by train on Saturday afternoon. The remains of the two men were taken to their respective homes at Legan and Hall. The burials took place the following morning, with Joseph Tormey's funeral taking place at St Patrick's church, Hall.

The funeral of Patrick Sloane took place at Mount Temple parish church on Saturday morning, where requiem mass was celebrated by Fr F. Skelly. The funeral attracted a large number of military, who were actively looking for an older brother of Patrick Sloane. Following the funeral mass the cortège of over 200 made its way to Drumraney and, as it passed the large military presence, the coffin was saluted. The military had an armoured car and two lorries, one driving in front of the cortège and the other following. Drumraney graveyard was surrounded by the military and a large number of men were held up and searched after the burial.[10]

Joseph Tormey's body lay overnight in St Patrick's church and the funeral took place there on Sunday morning. As with the funeral of his friend, the British military were present in large numbers. The grief of his young wife, parents and family was increased when Joseph Tormey's younger brother David, aged sixteen, was arrested just before the funeral mass. The coffin was draped in a Tricolour. At Mount Temple graveyard the large British presence did not interfere with the mourners.[11]

Meanwhile, back at Ballykinlar the internees' camp council requested a meeting with the commandant to demand an inquest into the killings. Telegrams were prepared for despatch to the kinsfolk of the deceased. A telegram was also prepared for legal representation for the families and was addressed to T. M. Healy, barrister, who was an uncle of Dr T. F. O'Higgins. Patrick (P. J.) Hogan, a solicitor interned in the camp, was nominated as solicitor to act on behalf of the families and internees. Patrick Colgan issued three telegrams, but they were not passed on by the British military censor, so the families were not represented at the inquiry.[12]

It was obvious that the military authorities at Ballykinlar were determined to cover up the circumstances of the killings. To achieve this they issued a press release to the *Belfast Telegraph* stating that the men had been shot for getting too close to the restricted area and had been suspected of attempting to escape. The military authority refused the internees' request for an inquest, on the grounds that the Restoration of Order in Ireland Act suspended coroner inquests. However, the six north-eastern counties had not been included in the martial law area. Because the military had not sent the telegrams issued by Patrick Colgan, the camp council refused to take any part in the military court of inquiry, opting instead to conduct their own inquiry. The official report issued by Dublin Castle was published in the daily newspapers on Wednesday 9 February. It made no mention of the earlier false story of the attempted escape:

A Court of Inquiry, in lieu of an inquest prohibited by Regulation 81 Defence of the Realm Regulations, assembled at Ballykinlar camp on the bodies of Patrick Sloane and Joseph Tormey, who were killed on 17 January 1921. Several military witnesses deposed to the fact that a number of men in two adjoining cages persisted in communicating with each other, despite the repeated warning of a sentry. They eventually dispersed, only to collect after short intervals and to continue to disobey the orders given by the sentry, who considered himself forced to fire one round in the execution of his duty in order to ensure their dispersal.

Medical evidence showed that the bullet hit Tormey on the right side of the head and passing through hit Sloane in the neck. The court found Joseph Tormey and Patrick Sloane died from shock and haemorrhage caused by gunshot wounds inflicted by a sentry in the execution of his duty, and was a case of justifiable homicide. Every facility was extended to any of the internees who desired to give evidence before the court, but none availed themselves of the opportunity. Upon the inquiry as to how one shot killed the two prisoners, it was stated that the bullet passed through the base of the head of Joseph Tormey and then pierced the throat of Patrick Sloane, who was behind the former.[13]

The incident was later raised in the House of Commons in London on Wednesday 16 February 1921, where a question was put to the chief secretary for Ireland by Jeremiah MacVeagh, MP for South Down: 'Has any action been taken in the case of the soldier who shot dead two interned prisoners in the Ballykinlar camp?'

Chief Secretary Hamar Greenwood replied that the military inquiry held in lieu of the inquest found that no blame attached to the soldier, who fired in the execution of his duty. MacVeagh asked if it were not a fact that Colonel Little, the commanding officer, agreed that the prisoners should be allowed to converse with the prisoners in the adjoining camp provided that they did not approach the wire entanglements, and that the two men were shot dead by the soldier, without any order from the officer, while they were forty feet away from the wire entanglements. Greenwood said that he had no information regarding that issue.

MacVeagh then asked if the soldier was put on trial and if he was court-martialled, to which Greenwood replied again that no blame attached to the soldier. He also said that every opportunity was given to the internees to give evidence at the inquest, but no one responded. MacVeagh suggested that the reason the internees did not respond was because they did not have confidence in the impartiality of the tribunal as the inquiry was conducted by the officers of the man who had committed the two murders.[14]

During a later sitting of the British parliament another MP, Albert Parkinson, asked Hamar Greenwood if another court of inquiry would have described as 'justifiable homicide' the action of a sentry who fired on a group of men who had received express permission to converse with those in the adjoining camp, provided they did not approach within a certain distance of the wire. Greenwood replied that Parkinson 'was entirely mistaken in thinking that permission had been given for internees in one camp to communicate with those in another. On the contrary it had been expressly forbidden in published orders.' He strongly repudiated the suggestion that a military court of inquiry did not conduct their proceedings impartially or fairly.[15]

The IRA inquiry

In light of the suspicions held by the internees regarding the British military's inquiry, the IRA authority in the camp decided to hold their own investigation into the circumstances surrounding the deaths of the two men. Patrick Colgan arranged for evidence to be taken under oath from all internees who witnessed the shooting. A message was sent to No. 2 compound to carry out a similar inquiry, which was immediately acceded to, and a Commission of Inquiry was established in both compounds. A competent draughtsman drew up a map of the scene and a list of the witnesses' names was prepared. The Commission of Inquiry consisted of a chairman, secretary, devil's advocate and an orderly, who was tasked with identifying the witnesses so that the work of the inquiry could be carried out expeditiously.

A room beside the chapel hut in No. 1 compound was used and evidence was collected over a number of days. Each internee was put in front of the commission separately and cautioned about the importance of the inquiry and the necessity for accuracy and relevance in their evidence. A full statement was first taken and then each man was fully examined and cross-examined on various aspects of his evidence to ascertain the accuracy of the statement and whether anything could be contradicted later. This process was very thorough and any point that was considered unreliable was eliminated. When the examination was complete the witness was warned to keep to himself the evidence he had given and questions he had been asked, and not to discuss anything with any other witnesses to ensure accuracy.

M. J. Sheridan then prepared a transcript of all the evidence. The commission then recalled each witness and the text of his evidence was read over to him and amended if necessary. Each internee was again cross-examined on the various points to ascertain that no aspect of the statement was flawed and was then asked to swear to the truth of his statement, which was then signed. At the conclusion of this process, the commission believed that they had obtained a just, reliable and accurate account of the tragic occurrence. The evidence was then collated and a report was prepared before being passed to the camp council. The report concluded that the shooting of the two young men was an act of callous and deliberate murder and could not be justified on any grounds. The men were over six feet from the wire when shot and were not in breach of any military regulations.[16]

The camp council believed it was essential to have the report smuggled out to IRA headquarters in Dublin. Joseph Considine of Dublin devised an ingenious method of doing this: he wrote the statement on a linen handkerchief which he sewed to another layer of linen, obscuring the writing. Henry Dixon then requested to see his son Joe, a solicitor in Dublin, concerning personal legal business. The visit was granted and Henry Dixon was able to pass the handkerchief to his son without the military censor, Captain Newton, noticing. Joe Dixon then passed the handkerchief to the IRA and the statement appeared in the *Irish Bulletin* which was published by Sinn Féin.[17]

Another shooting occurred in No. 1 compound on Sunday morning, 29 May 1921, on the pretext that internees were interfering with the wires. On the north side of No. 1 compound the huts ran parallel to the wires; the sides of the huts being separated from the wires by a walkway approximately four feet wide. One of these huts was the canteen and the door was less than two yards from the wires. Another nearby hut was used as a tailors' and boot-repair shop. A side door on this hut was a similar distance from the wire. The walkway between the huts and the wires on the north side, besides being the only way to the canteen, was used regularly by the prisoners for exercise.

Michael O'Brien, Dublin, Edmond Barry, Cork, and James Buckley, Tipperary, stopped off at the canteen while walking around the compound. Buckley entered while the other two waited at the door. Michael O'Brien was standing with one foot on the doorstep and the other on the walkway, with Edmond Barry standing beside him. After a few minutes, without warning, a sentry fired a shot in their direction. The sentry box was located at the north-west corner of the No. 1 compound and commanded a clear view of the north side from end to end, so the guard had a full view of everyone using the walkway or going into the canteen. Patrick Roe of Dublin and another internee were sitting nearby when they noticed the rifle being levelled and the shot fired in their direction. It was unclear at whom the sentry was actually aiming. Michael O'Brien and Edmond Barry, who were standing outside the canteen, heard the bullet pass very close to them. Peadar Lane, Wexford, on hearing the shot, ran out of his hut towards the sentry box. As he was standing close to the sentry box, a sergeant climbed into the box and asked the soldier, 'Did you hit anyone?'

'No, I missed.'

After a few minutes other internees arrived and Michael Nolan of Dublin, and James McGuill and William Atkinson, both from Louth, were standing under the sentry box when the guard, who appeared to be very excited, turned towards them and, aiming his rifle, said, 'Get back you bastards or I'll plug one or two more of you.'

It was suspected that the shooting incident was retaliation for the compound commandant, Joseph McGrath, reporting the strange behaviour of a sentry some days before, resulting in the soldier being removed from his post and being put under arrest. The British commandant told McGrath that the man would be taken before a military court, but it was not known if he was actually tried.

In response to the shooting on Sunday 29 May, the British commandant informed Joseph McGrath that the sentry fired after giving warning to men interfering with the wire. McGrath presented the internees' version of the incident, but the British military insisted that the sentry was telling the truth and said he would face no further action.[18]

7

Camp Intelligence and Communications

Military-style training and manoeuvres were prohibited in Ballykinlar and meetings or debates were closely monitored. The British established an extensive intelligence system to monitor the camp. The first and most obvious method of gathering information was through censoring the incoming and outgoing mail. In addition, some British intelligence officers actively induced internees to divulge information about their comrades, while in the first few months the internees observed that the most primitive means of intelligence gathering used by the British military was listening at the windows of and crawling under the huts at night, hoping to overhear conversations.

To counter this, the internees established their own network composed of senior IRA officers and those who had been intelligence officers before their arrest. An intelligence officer was appointed to each company and one for each hut: they were expected to become fully acquainted with the men. They discreetly questioned all the prisoners about their past history, events that occurred in their area and the people of their area, etc. The internee intelligence staff also removed the post box from the canteen so they could inspect the letters of suspected individuals to see if these were being sent to the police, military or anyone suspected of being loyal to the British outside the camp.

The internee intelligence staff also received information from fellow internees about their suspicions of men entering the camp. One man, James McCabe, came to their attention in No. 2 compound after some of the Cork internees reported him as being of questionable character. His mail was checked on a regular basis and was found to contain derogatory statements about Sinn Féin, the IRA, camp council and officers. The military censor frequently called him out of the compound and requested information about internee activity and backgrounds. He was told that if he helped he would be released and, to prevent suspicions being aroused by his frequent visits to the censor, the military would occasionally arrest him and remove him from the compound. They also told him that they would use invisible ink in all letters from them or Dublin Castle to him.

It was suspected that the British censor had read his letters condemning the republican movement and, based on that, approached him to work for them. The word spread around the compound and McCabe was given the cold shoulder by other internees. If he entered a hut he was asked to leave. Unnerved, he consulted the No. 2 compound intelligence officer. He admitted that he had been approached to work for the British, but said that he gave them no information. McCabe even offered to allow the compound intelligence officer to read all his outgoing and incoming mail. He was suspected of working for the British for some time and was observed handing notes to the military, but he was obviously desperate to redeem himself. When the British realised he was under suspicion they removed him from the camp one night and he was subsequently released.

Another Cork man, John Devereaux, an ex-British soldier, was considered suspicious before his arrival in the camp. Other Cork internees reported him to the intelligence staff and he was immediately put under observation. Devereaux was seen approaching the military post officer without the consent of the compound commandant and when the intelligence staff confronted him, he said that he was making enquiries about his pension. One of the intelligence staff considered Devereaux to be more cunning and more intelligent than McCabe and to have the potential to be a British spy. He was kept under strict observation up to the time of his release.

Another suspected agent was ex-British soldier James Browne from Dublin, who arrived in the camp with Paddy Daly from Monaghan. Daly was suspicious of Browne from the time of their arrest and during the journey from Dublin to the camp. Browne was immediately put under observation. He was considered an 'ignorant fool', but a competent liar. On one occasion as the men were preparing for bed an internee called Browne 'Cash', which was his wife's maiden name, and he flew into a rage saying, 'Don't call me that name – that will get me into trouble.' Some members of his wife's family had served with the British during the Great War and had been suspected of working as informers in Dublin. Browne was also observed handing a note or letter to a British officer who was heard to call him Commandant Browne. When confronted he initially denied that he had handed anything over, but was obviously unnerved by this and a short time later approached Joseph McGrath, the No. 1 compound commandant, confessing that he had passed a note to the military.

On another occasion, when Browne was a patient in the camp hospital, he was summoned to the British administration office. A military intelligence officer was present with other unidentified men in plain clothes. Browne was asked to sign a form which would secure his release on condition that he worked for British intelligence and reported anything he discovered following his release. Browne feared that this would guarantee a death sentence and refused to sign. When he was returned to the hospital he requested to see Joseph McGrath and reported the incident to him.[1]

The British military's most sophisticated method of gathering information was the use of listening devices or dictaphones. The listening devices had been installed around late February or early March and it was around that time that the internees noticed that the military were either receiving information from men within the compound or had in some other way received prior notice of their plans. The No. 1 compound camp council regularly held their meetings in the commandant's hut, which was also known as the 'Black Hut', as it was black while all other huts were maroon. The internees were suspicious for some time, as they began to notice that some of their plans to disrupt the British administration of the camp were being frustrated or prevented. The camp council were very concerned about the leak of information and suspicions were being cast at the internees attending the meetings.

Thomas Treacy, Kilkenny, was the first to suspect that the British were using some sort of listening devices. He informed the camp council that before his arrest he had read an article about an electrical invention called a dictaphone. He was convinced that this was how the British were getting the information and asked the camp council for permission to conduct a search of the huts. Although they considered his suspicions far-fetched, they agreed, so he summoned a number of internees and carried out a search of the huts, but failed to find anything.

The internees in No. 1 compound had planned to com-memorate the anniversary of the 1916 Rising on Easter Sunday 1921 by burning the huts. However, the evening before the planned operation the British military entered the compound in large numbers and surrounded all buildings. They remained there until lock-up the following evening and it was obvious that they were anticipating something. This convinced the No. 1 compound officers that information was being leaked, but they could not discover the source.

Thomas Treacy argued for a second search of the huts. The camp council saw it as a futile, but Treacy was persistent and asked for the assistance of Tom Hickey, a carpenter by trade, to organise all other carpenters to remove and replace every board in the huts starting with the 'Black Hut'. This had to be done discreetly with minimal noise and using improvised tools. Within half an hour, having removed a number of boards in the 'Black Hut', they discovered a dictaphone about three feet above the ground and two feet from the heating stove. They immediately sent for Joseph McGrath, Maurice Donegan and the other members of the camp council. They were rendered speechless when Thomas Treacy produced the listening devices. No doubt the members of the council were recalling the various discussions during meetings and the general conversations around the stove at night.

They continued searching the 'Black Hut' and discovered another three devices in the timber lining. Devices were found in other huts located around the stoves, where the men generally sat and talked at night. The wires for the 'bugs' had been hidden in trenches leading from the British military quarters outside the compound to the huts, a task made easy by the soft sandy ground. The internees traced and cut the wires. For a time it was obvious that the British were sneaking into the compound at night and replacing the wires.[2] Thomas Treacy was instructed by Joseph McGrath to check for fresh tracks every morning and accordingly he walked around the compound inspecting the ground, so the British soon abandoned their endeavours.

Following the discovery of the recording devices, the British military had to revert back to more primitive means of intelligence gathering. The internees had to exercise extreme caution, because even the mention of men from their local areas could result in the capture or execution of a comrade. The reference to a name might even have seen an innocent man arrested.[3]

Throughout the War of Independence the British did not allow visitors to many jails or internment camps. Visitors were only allowed in very exceptional circumstances, so the internees had to devise clever methods of communication between the camp and IRA GHQ in Dublin. They initially attempted to communicate via the normal postal system using cryptic messages in letters. However, the strict censorship of letters prevented this line from developing. The British censors at Ballykinlar rejected any letter considered suspicious or in their view containing hidden messages. The communication dilemma was resolved in early January 1921 when Paddy Lane, an internee from Dún Laoghaire, introduced the then No. 1 compound commandant, Patrick Colgan, to a British officer, Sergeant Love, who was from County Louth. He offered to act as courier between the camp and the IRA GHQ in Dublin.[4] Sergeant Love's duties included acquisition of supplies for and supervision of the camp canteens and workshops, including the barbers, tailors and boot repairers, so he was perfectly placed to receive messages from both compounds as he had to spend much of his time there and would not raise the suspicions of his superiors.[5]

Sergeant Love told Patrick Colgan to be wary of all other ranks having contact with the internees, as they were members of the British intelligence branch. Love lived at Castlewellan, County Down, and never asked for or accepted any money for his services: all despatches from the camp to the IRA GHQ and vice versa arrived safely. To cover Sergeant Love's role as courier, Patrick Colgan gave him personal letters from internees, which Love then passed on to the military intelligence officers. This gave the impression that all letters given to him were passed to the military intelligence officers. Love smuggled the despatches out of the camp sewn under the soles of his boots and always kept a second pair at the camp for this purpose. Jack Fitzgerald, from County Kildare, who worked in the boot repair workshop, was responsible for the concealment. A member of the IRA based at Castlewellan did the sewing on the outside.

The British eventually became suspicious of the sergeant, who was held up and searched on several occasions by the RIC between the camp and Castlewellan. Twice, he was taken to Castlewellan RIC Barracks and strip-searched. Shortly after Patrick Colgan was transferred to No. 2 compound in early February, Sergeant Love was transferred out of the camp.[6] He was replaced by a quartermaster sergeant called Farrell who was from County Cavan. Farrell was very friendly to the internees and gave the impression that he could be trusted. During a conversation with an internee from County Meath, Patrick Bartley, Farrell hinted that he would be willing to smuggle despatches from the camp to the IRA GHQ. This was passed on to the new No. 1 compound commandant, Joseph McGrath. The two men were introduced and McGrath was satisfied that Farrell was genuine and agreed to the arrangement. However, Farrell considered the role of courier as high risk and requested payment for his troubles. He was given £1 per week, an expense shared between both compounds.[7] The No. 1 compound vice-commandant, Maurice Donegan, was not convinced of Farrell's sincerity or trustworthiness and raised his concerns with Joseph McGrath, who thought he was being foolish and laughed it off.[8]

Thomas Treacy was responsible for the safe-keeping of all despatches from GHQ and copies of despatches sent to GHQ as well as other camp council documents. All despatches from the IRA GHQ were in the handwriting of the then IRA director of intelligence, Michael Collins.[9]

Following the deaths of Joseph Tormey and Patrick Sloane in January 1921, a new system of communication was devised between the compounds and simply involved tying a despatch or message to a stone. An internee with a long and accurate throw would hurl it into the neighbouring compound where it would be quickly collected.[10]

8

Letters, Parcels and the Ballykinlar Post Office

There were few things more important to the internees than their letters, parcels of food and other comforts from home. The paucity and low quality of the camp food made contributions from home an absolute necessity, with the internees' very survival depending on the arrival of the weekly delivery. The camp post office played a pivotal role in the lives of the internees, with distribution of over 1,500 packages every week.[1]

In the early days the parcels were pilfered and damaged by the British: some were never received. The mother of one internee wrote to a friend that her son had not received, 'a single one of the many parcels we have sent him, and the letters do not appear to be given to him either – perhaps because the parcels are mentioned in them. Isn't it cruel?'[2] The internee commandants reported incidents of lost or damaged parcels to the British commandant and requested that the internees be involved in the post office. Soon afterwards, a postmaster was appointed in both compounds to take charge of all incoming mail. The No. 1 compound postmasters were Sam Holt and later Andrew Mooney, both from County Leitrim, and the No. 2 compound postmaster was Patrick C. O'Mahony from Waterford. The postmasters accompanied the British officers each afternoon to the post office to take possession of all registered and unregistered post. They would check everything to ensure the goods were intact, refusing to take delivery of any damaged parcel and making a claim for compensation. In the beginning many parcels were damaged, but following a number of reports and compensation claims, that figure was drastically reduced. When the postmasters were satisfied that all post had been received, the British transported it on wagons to the compounds, where it was handed over to the postmaster. The mail was re-checked to ensure the numbers were correct and no letters had blown away in transit.

The sorting office in each compound consisted of six tables, twelve feet by four feet, forming a triangle so that postal staff and military censors would be facing each other. It was locked and made secure by the British military until 9.30 a.m. the following morning, when three or four military censors would begin opening, censoring, sorting and distributing the mail in the presence of the internee postmaster and eight other internee postal staff. The military censors checked the packages for forbidden items including coins, explosives, firearms, alcohol, hacksaws, hatchets and hammers. Two members of the postal staff were responsible for re-labelling the parcels after the censor had read the letters and inspected the parcels. Another was responsible for distributing the now-censored parcels to the other five internees to check the contents. The parcels would always contain a list of contents to ensure all items arrived safely, but the military would sometimes steal objects from them, and the internees would draw attention to any missing items. When all parcels had been checked, the military would leave and the internee postal staff would sort them for the different huts. The hut leaders were then informed and, having signed for the parcels, they would take them to the huts for delivery to the internees.[3]

Incoming letters arrived after completion of the parcel process, as they were censored by the military with no internee representatives present: all references to the British or British forces, to the camp or the treatment within the camp were cut out. The members of the internees' post office staff were merely distributing agents, but this was still a job of the utmost importance, as the letters arrived opened in the sorting section and privacy was imperative. Only two trustworthy internees dealt with sorting and delivering letters, under the supervision of the postmaster. The despatch of letters was straightforward, with all mail being placed in letter boxes in the compound canteens.

The postmaster had to be present when the military post sergeant cleared the boxes on Mondays and Thursdays.[4] The internees were allowed to write only one personal letter per week for the first few months in the camp. This rule was changed in March 1921 when they were permitted to write two letters of two pages each, with the proviso that they be enclosed in one envelope and addressed to one person.

The internees were permitted to write one business letter per week, which had to be strictly confined to business matters. However, the British military censors' interpretation of the term 'business' was such that very few internees could avail of this privilege.[5]

Camp regulations stated that all letters could only be written on one side of the paper and had to be handed in with the envelope unsealed. Stamps were purchased at the canteen. The internee's serial number, hut number, company number and number of his compound had to be written at the top of the first page and on the inside flap of the envelope. All letters were put into a post box in the compound canteen. All outgoing letters were examined by the British military censor and if they contained any information relating to ill-treatment or criticism of the British, they were not forwarded.[6] Letters which stated, for example, that water was scarce, that the officers were ill-mannered, that Monday's dinner of rotten pig was returned untouched or that medical supplies were insufficient, were cut.[7] The internees often discovered that outgoing letters were not delivered, while it could take five or six days for incoming letters to arrive in the camp.

However, despite the diligence of the censors, some letters were missed. An extract from a letter written by an unnamed internee was later published in *The Freeman's Journal* on Monday 7 March 1921: 'I'm well now, thank God – at least, I'm as well as can be expected under the circumstances. There are a big lot sick here. The accommodation is very unhealthy and uncomfortable. Of course, if we are here for the summer it will be worse, as the camp is wholly unsanitary.' On another occasion, a military censor cut a long extract from an incoming letter which contained a number of cryptic references. He accidentally dropped the extracted portions into the envelope and it was passed on. The British military authority was made aware of the error and the censor was later reprimanded.

An example of the type of information cut from outgoing letters was: 'We have Black and Tans for breakfast, for dinner and for tea.' Another example of the vigilance of the censor can be seen when an incoming letter contained information that was cut and later sent on to Dublin Castle. The extract said: 'Jack is staying with the Sasanach since 13 March ...'

The receipt and despatch of telegrams was another important and confidential function of the internee postmaster. All outgoing telegrams were received by the postmaster and then forwarded to the military post sergeant for daily despatch at 2.30 p.m. and 4.30 p.m. All incoming telegrams were received and immediately distributed to the addressees. Telegrams were sent from the camp and received only in times of family crisis or in cases of urgent business matters; however, telegrams were also a luxury restricted to those who could afford them, as the cost was much more than postage.

The efficiency and professionalism with which the Ballykinlar post office was managed can be attributed to the internees who worked there under the guidance of the postmaster. The members of the post office staff were sensitive to the privacy and care of their comrades' letters and parcels and strove to ensure that no loss or damage was caused.[8]

9

Education, GAA, Drama and Other Recreation

Education

The principal aim of the British internment policy was to demoralise those in the 'cages'. The system was designed to convert the most optimistic and energetic men into lazy, spiritless human beings. However, twenty-three men at Ballykinlar had also been interned at Frongoch in North Wales in 1916, and recognised the need to organise various recreational and educational activities. Henry Dixon, interned at both camps, knew that engaging in educational pursuits countered the effects of internment. Before the opening of Ballykinlar, the camp had not been inhabited for some time and the grass was long and wild, the ground was waterlogged and huts were damp and smelling of mould. It was imperative to counteract the effect of such surroundings on the men's mental and physical health.[1]

When Henry Dixon was first appointed as chairman of the education committee, No. 1 compound, the camp council was indifferent and gave him little support, but his enthusiasm soon led to an extensive educational curriculum being established. Initially much emphasis was put on the teaching of Irish and classes were provided for all levels, from beginners to advanced students. They endeavoured to accommodate the internees from the different provinces but could only cater for three of the four dialects, as there was no one capable of teaching the Ulster dialect, even though the camp was based in that province. Before long Dixon had established other classes in shorthand, bookkeeping, French and the Classics. Unfortunately no reading room was made available for the men and it was almost impossible to study in a crowded hut, but Dixon was often seen walking around the compound, with notebook in hand, recruiting men for some new class. Later on classes were organised for singing, fiddle/violin and piano.[2] Martin Walton of Dublin formed the Ballykinlar Violin Orchestra and one of his students was Peadar Kearney, author of 'The Soldier's Song', later adopted as the Irish national anthem, 'Amhrán na bhFiann'. The Ballykinlar Violin Orchestra played for many of the dramatic performances and musical events organised in the camp. Martin Walton composed a piece of music called 'The Ballykinlar March', and this was often played. Peadar Kearney also wrote words for that piece.[3]

The educational activities in No. 2 compound soon became more advanced than in No. 1 compound, with the camp staff establishing a board of education. Dr Michael Hayes, Assistant Professor in French at University College Dublin before his internment, was appointed to the board in February 1921 and was given a directive to draw up an educational scheme including classes, lectures and debates. He was to compile a list of capable teachers and allocate them to the different subjects. The educational activities in No. 2 compound were very proactive: Irish classes were obligatory and held in every hut for half an hour each night.

Participation in the Irish classes in No. 1 compound was not obligatory, although the hut leaders were ordered to maintain silence and discipline while they were being held. Daytime classes were held four days per week for three-quarters of an hour. Advanced classes in Irish were held daily between 3 p.m. and 5 p.m.[4] In a letter to a friend in London in March 1921, Seán McGrath said that ninety-five per cent of the internees in No. 1 compound were studying Irish and that many were hoping to qualify for the 'Fáinne' in the coming months.[5]

As the classes developed, other subjects were added to the curriculum, including mathematics, taught by Martin Ryan, and surveying, taught by James Quigley, who had been employed as county engineer with Meath Council. Examinations were held and certificates were issued at the conclusion of some courses. The validity of the certificates was recognised long after the camp had closed; Joe McRickland secured a job as land commission inspector in 1923 when he produced a Ballykinlar certificate as evidence of his qualifications.[6]

In addition to the formal classes, lectures, debates and discussions were held on a regular basis on a range of topics including the future of Irish agriculture; milk for cities and towns; rural labour problems; the history of Ireland in the nineteenth century; the history of Ireland from 1800 to 1848; the knockout blow; personal experiences in the French Foreign Legion; personal experiences in South America; prison experiences; cottage industries; violin making; and the Irish Republic in 1940 (a lecture and discussion on what Ireland would be or should be twenty years after independence). Other lectures were on local government in Ireland; Irish coal mines; commercial Ireland; St Enda's school; the fishing industry; Irish communications; banking finance; the national land bank; hygiene; and roads and road making. Lectures were held on Wednesday afternoons and were always well attended.[7] The No. 2 compound board of education also acquired a small space for a library, which was stocked with books dealing with Irish history, biography and works of fiction; books on engineering, law and some on military matters were also acquired.

The books were sourced by University College Cork, which had formed a society for procuring and distributing books to Ballykinlar and other internment camps. The Dublin-based Society of Friends (Quakers) were also very active in obtaining books for the internees. The Quakers sent any books requested, no matter how expensive, to the camp. The librarian in No. 2 compound library was Denis McCullough from Belfast. The library room was small and was not used as much as had been hoped. During the summer months some internees would try to find a quiet space in the compound to read or study, although with several hundred men in a confined space this proved difficult.[8] The Ballykinlar boards of education left great impressions on the minds and characters of the men brought together within the barbed-wire cages of Ballykinlar camp.[9] The education curriculum also helped to ease the boredom and monotony of the long dreary days spent on the shores of Dundrum Bay.

Ballykinlar GAA and athletics

Recreational and sporting activities were varied and, apart from the daily camp duties, the internees were under no obligation to take part. The general camp rule was that the mornings were devoted to camp duties and educational classes, while the afternoons were taken up with outdoor recreation, but inclement weather was obviously a factor. Sports committees were formed to organise various activities, including football, boxing or, for the less athletic, chess and card games.[10] In one case a particular sport – handball – became vital as camouflage for escape plans.

In March 1921 Henry Dixon presented Leo Henderson, the then No. 2 compound commanding officer, with nine medals to be used for chess tournaments. A meeting was held on Friday 18 March to organise chess tournaments and elect a committee. The No. 2 compound chess club held nine tournaments beginning on Sunday 20 March, which continued until Monday 29 August 1921. The chess tournaments generated great interest in No. 2 compound, with many taking part and a large number expressing an interest in learning the game.[11]

In October 1921 Charles Steinmayer, an internee in No. 1 compound, forwarded a letter to *The Freeman's Journal* to publicise the success of the Ballykinlar Chess Club, giving an account of the competitions:

> Sir, Thinking it would be of interest to your readers, the committee of the Ballykinlar Chess Club have directed me to send you the results of the first chess competition held here. The club has been formed with the idea of providing the internees with a means of passing a few of the many monotonous hours pleasantly. The interest and enthusiasm shown by men who already had a good knowledge of the game induced many to learn, and the promoters of the club feel confident that their venture to keep the club in existence when all have been released, will meet with success. The first of a series of monthly competitions has been won by Kane Harley, Hut 34, A Company, No. 1 camp, who thus becomes the holder of a splendid gold medal presented by Messrs Hopkins and Hopkins, O'Connell Street, Dublin to the club. The medal is suitably inscribed and becomes the property of the member who wins the greatest number of times by the time we are released. – I am, yours faithfully – Charles J. Steinmayer, Sec. No. 849, Hut 7, D Company, Ballykinlar camp No. 1, October 11, 1921.[12]

There was no designated recreation ground for the first few months in the camp, so the men made the most of what limited space there was and some games were organised. Gaelic football teams were formed and the internees raised money to purchase footballs by putting a levy of five shillings on each hut. In the beginning each hut was asked to field a team of only ten men, due to the limited space in the compound. A league was then organised between the teams and the winning team in each line would play each other to determine which line was the victor. All competitions were played under GAA rules. The games were reduced to twenty minutes each half, with three matches played per day. Some of the players had never played football before and most had never played under GAA rules, so a few performances offered great amusement to those watching. Inter-line competitions were held regularly, providing the committee with the opportunity to select the best players from each line.

With football established on a solid basis, the committee focused on other sports to encourage other internees to get involved. In No. 2 compound St Patrick's Day was celebrated with a full programme of sporting events, including running, long jump, handball and wrestling. An order was issued by the camp council that Irish was to be spoken as much as possible on the day and all announcements were made in Irish by the sports committee chairman, Dan Faher, Dungannon, County Tyrone. The games went on until the light began to fade and every winner received a certificate as a trophy.

Sports committees had been formed in both compounds and the committee in No. 2 compound challenged No. 1 compound to an inter-compound sports competition. Nine events were specified, including a football match, and each compound held trials to select the best men to represent them. The respective camp councils made requests to the military authority to allow the competitions to take place, but the British commandant refused.

The No. 2 compound newsletter *The Barbed Wire* carried a section on the GAA activities and praised the efforts of the committee charged with organising teams and competitions. The article was published in the August edition in the section headed 'GAA Notes', which read:

> It was apparent on arrival and experience has proved that athletics in all its branches was essential to camp life. To prevent the stagnation and deterioration of the individual it was necessary to give him a stimulus and an interest to keep him fit both in body and mind. The committee formed to look after the various branches of athletics have done their work well and have been very successful in carrying out efficiently the duties entrusted to them. The GAA Board having now completed various leagues and championships are engaged in the selection of a team to contest a match with a selection from Camp I.[13]

However, the writer was critical of the efforts or at least the discipline of certain skilled and able players:

> Camp II has every reason to be proud of the prowess of its footballers but the erratic performance of some well known players make some of the games disappointing while an occasional lapse from their top form may be excused the good-day bad-day style of some is unfair to selection committees whether for hut or other competitions [*sic*]. It is due to those playing with you to do your best, but don't be selfish. Some players want to do all the playing. It is much better football to give a team-mate a good opportunity

and protect him from attack than to kick wildly and have the ball returned with intent.[14]

The No. 1 compound newsletter *Ná Bac Leis* published an informative article on the GAA competitions held there:

Good football within the wires is not altogether on the decline. The semi-final of the Hut Championship was recently played by teams representing Huts 34 and 35. During the game we were treated to some fine football and with a good breeze in their favour and the popular 'Jimmy' working hard in the forward line the representatives of Hut 35 crossed over with a good margin in their favour. In the second period this lead was increased at the outset but [Hut] 34 soon found their game and taking every advantage of the openings that offered ran out easy winners at the end … The match between Huts 8 and 16 so much looked forward to, proved rather disappointing. The game opened with some fair exchanges and Hut 8 led at the interval there was not much between them on the point of play. But in the second half (Hut) 16's forwards proved rather too weak against their heavier opponents and many openings made by Simon Haugh, Clare, Denny McGrath, Clare and Dick Smith, Cavan, who all played a great game throughout, went for nothing. Play was much brighter towards the end, but when the final whistle blew the Hut 8 representatives had won rather easily. For the winners D. Mackey, Tipperary – J. Tynan, Tipperary – Frank Gregg, Tipperary and William Casey, Tipperary were most prominent in the forward line and centre field. While Thomas Halpin, Tipperary and Mickey White, Tipperary (who sometimes saw red) were always sound in defence. Tom Honan was a capable referee.[15]

This periodical also highlighted the lack of quality football and suggested regular competitions to improve the standard within the compound:

> We have had very little high class football for some time past ... Many of our 'cracks' show signs of Macramé cramp and the sooner they get a chance of working off the rust the better. There is no falling off of good games in No. 2 camp and should our selection cross hands with their best in the near future this idle spell will mean 'RUANE' for our lot.
>
> We would like to see our first fifteen in action again and with the second string ready to be at it HAMAR and TONGS at any time and a few practice games should be arranged. Would not those responsible for our football fare be well advised to start another competition on the Three Hut principle? The late arrivals are anxious to get going and their presence might make a great change in previous form.[16]

The winners of the No. 1 compound Junior Line Championship 1921 were 'A' Company. The team consisted of John Dolan, Roscommon, Patrick O'Grady, Dublin, John McGeraghty, Cavan, Dan Rice, Down, Bob Noonan, Cork, John Kelly, Dublin, Jack Nugent, Dublin, Pat Conway, Tipperary, Christy Rock, Roscommon, Bob Murphy, Dublin, Tom Canavan, Dublin, Jim McCaffrey, Dublin, and William Sherry, Dublin. The reserves or subs in the team were Kevin Halpin, Dublin, Edward O'Connor, Dublin, Edward O'Gorman, Dublin and Patrick Hoban, Mayo. They played six games, won five and lost one with 90 points for and 28 against in total.

'C' Company won the Senior Line Championship 1921. The players were Joe Twomey, Dublin, Patrick Edwards, Dublin and Westmeath, Éamon Bennett, Dublin, T. Cole, Clare, Joe Walsh, Dublin and Meath, Tom Ruane, Mayo, William Rooney, Dublin, Pat Ruane, Mayo, Pat Ryan, Galway, Peter Kirwan, Dublin, Simon Haugh, Clare, Joe Rooney, Dublin, and Peadar Rafferty, Cork. The reserves were John Green, Dublin, Joe Considine, Dublin and Clare, and B. Quigley, Dublin and Longford. They played six games, won five and drew one, scoring 65 points with 32 against.

The final of the No. 1 compound senior championship was held on Saturday 14 May 1921, between 'The Pierce McCans' and 'The Seán Treacys' with the McCans beating the Treacys 14 points to 5 points. The Pierce McCans were Charlie Steinmayer, Dublin, T. Halpin, Tipperary, J. McCormack, Dublin, M. White, Tipperary, J. R. Walsh, Kerry, T. O'Hickey, Tipperary, J. O'Keefe, Tipperary, J. Allen, Tipperary, P. Harty, Louth, M. Ladigan, Tipperary, D. Mackey, Tipperary, W. Casey, Tipperary, and J. Tynan, Tipperary. The referee was Tom Ruane, a member of the Mayo County Board of the GAA.

The junior championship final was held on the same day and 'The Peadar Clancy's' were out-and-out winners of that game. The team were Joe Lynch, Dublin, Christy Seivers, Dublin, Joe Duffy, Armagh, Jim Ormond, Waterford, Tom O'Leary, Dublin, P. L. Kerwin, Dublin, Jim McDonald, Carlow, Dick Smith, Cavan, Martin Clancy, Clare, T. Dolan, Dublin, P. Murphy, Cork, Peter Rock, Dublin, and Alex Kane, Dublin. F. Jones, Dublin, J. J. Whelan, Dublin, and E. Travers, Dublin, were subs.

The referee for the final was Jack Fitzgerald, a member of the Kildare County Board of the GAA.[17]

Handball was also popular and provided an opportunity for the internees who felt they did not possess the skills to play football, to take part in physical exercise. The handball alley had an additional use: to divert attention from an escape tunnel that was being dug in No. 1 compound from the end of Hut 2. Regular games were organised and in early July the men were excavating day and night. A tournament was organised to enable the excess sand and soil to be spread unobtrusively. Pat Ryan, Galway, and Hugh Britton, Donegal, won, having defeated Jim Liddy, Dublin, and Barney Rooney, Monaghan. The prizes were presented by J. J. Green of Dublin.[18]

The growing popularity of handball was also mentioned in the columns of *Ná Bac Leis* and an article appeared in the November edition of the newsletter: 'Hand-ball is all the rage just now.' The internees of No. 1 compound started playing the game in early March at the gable end of Hut 2 and the crack of the rubber ball not only disguised noise coming from the tunnel diggers, but almost drowned out the noise of the rifles on the ranges outside. The game started as a distraction for those with fewer sporting interests: however, it attracted a large number of participants as time went on.

Handball competitions featured in all editions of *Ná Bac Leis*. The November edition carried the following report: 'Bartley's (Patrick Bartley, Meath) figure is familiar on the courts in "E" line while the brothers McGrath (Seán and Michael, London) are also very much in evidence. What a pity that a good alley is not available when we might bring off a series of competitions. However, we must only avail of the facilities to hand in keeping ourselves fit.'[19]

The Quakers were very helpful in providing sports equipment, such as a supply of boxing equipment, including punch balls, sets of boxing gloves, medicine balls and skipping ropes. A committee was established to organise boxing and wrestling tournaments. Many of the participants had never taken part in a boxing bout before and this provided great entertainment.[20]

Just as education served to exercise the brain, so physical activity was an antidote for lethargy. Both disciplines served to counteract the aims of the British in their endeavour to demoralise and crush the resolve of the internees through their internment policy.

National commemorations and drama

The internees organised various events to celebrate the anniversaries of Robert Emmet, Wolfe Tone, the Easter Rising and St Patrick's Day in their endeavour to bring a semblance of normality to their lives. No. 2 compound even had a programme of events to mark Labour Day.

The celebrations to commemorate the birthday of Robert Emmet were held on Friday 4 March, with concerts performed in both camps and Seán Milroy giving the oration in No. 2 compound.[21] However, it was the St Patrick's Day celebrations that gave the first real opportunity for the men to organise a major event within the confines of their cage. No. 1 and No. 2 compounds formed companies at 11.15 a.m. before being reviewed by the commandants of each compound. They then marched around the compounds in columns of four before being dismissed at 12.15. There was a full schedule of events in the recreation fields, followed with concerts in the dining halls in the two compounds until lock-up, which was at 10 p.m. that night. The two compounds timed the parades to take place at the same time and the sight and sound of over 1,600 men marching at the same time certainly caught the attention of the British military.

A unique feature of the St Patrick's Day military parade at Ballykinlar was that the camp was the only place in Ireland where such an event took place that year. The various coercion laws and regulations introduced through the Defence of the Realm Act and the Restoration of Order in Ireland Regulations prohibited such happenings everywhere else in Ireland. Following the St Patrick's Day parade, the British military issued an order forbidding further military parades or drilling in the camp.

The next grand event was the Easter Sunday celebrations, which were restricted to a music and drama presentation held in No. 1 compound. The curtain-raiser was a play called *The Four Provinces*, which was performed by George Nesbitt and Tom Meldon and others from 'D' Company. The second play, *The Pope of Killybuck*, was staged by Louis J. Walsh; this was the second time the play was performed at Ballykinlar, although the first time was when it had been performed for the Ulster Division of the British Army prior to their deployment to the trenches of Europe during the First World War.

The Pope of Killybuck illustrated the amount of humour and humanity that existed between Catholic and Protestant in the north-east corner of Ireland prior to the outbreak of hostilities. It was a revelation to the men from the southern counties, many of whom had believed that unionists and nationalists would not associate or socialise with each other. The cast members of *The Pope of Killybuck* were Frank Doris, Tyrone, P. MacCartan, Tyrone, Tom Larkin, Derry, John Bonner, Donegal, Éamonn Cooney, Belfast and Armagh, Hugh Bradley, Belfast, George Goodman, Belfast, Frank Kearney, Tyrone, and James Lalor, Kilkenny. Henry Dixon was the stage manager for the day.[22]

Labour Day celebrations

In the early part of the twentieth century 'Labour Day' was not the most familiar event in Ireland, having its origins in Canada and America from the 1800s. The celebration marked the achievements of labour movements throughout the world and was only celebrated in Ireland on a few occasions: it was described by Tadhg Barry as being 'as dull as a wet Sunday with the pubs shut'. It did not attract much interest or spur the imagination as did other national commemorations.

The Labour Day celebrations at Ballykinlar No. 2 compound were organised by Tadhg Barry, Cork, who before his arrest had been secretary of the Cork branch of the Irish Transport and General Workers' Union (ITGWU). It was an experimental celebration, as the labour movement in some countries was affiliated to communism and viewed in a bad light within the Catholic Church in Ireland. Although Labour Day would not have been a familiar event to most of the internees in Ballykinlar camp, any opportunity to hold an event was usually welcomed with enthusiasm as it lifted the monotony of camp life. The commemoration was organised for Sunday 2 May 1921, but the British only agreed to its taking place if the organisers could guarantee that no red flags would be flown in the open compound. However, in the morning one internee took advantage of the sunny day and innocently put his red shirt on top of his hut to dry, only realising his error when one of the organisers asked him to remove it. The red-faced internee had to retrieve his shirt to the applause of a few men who had gathered to watch.

The more mischievous internees saw this as an opportunity to have some fun with the military and after mass that morning a red handkerchief was observed flying over one of the huts. A party of soldiers, led by a lieutenant named Sheppard, removed it, but it had happened so quickly most of the internees did not see it. As the news spread throughout the compound, men emerged from the huts to see what the fuss was. Although most had missed the military operation, they did witness four internees carrying a table to the concert hall (a hut specially cleared for the day's events). On top of the table was an internee playing 'The Red Flag' on a concertina. It was not long before other internees realised that this was a way to harass the British and soon red flags appeared on top of many huts. The military moved in quickly to remove the offensive objects and, to add to the fun, the internees began playing a game of cat and mouse with them by hoisting a red flag and then removing it as soon as the soldiers entered the compound. One particular flag was put on such a long pole on top of a hut that a soldier had to be helped onto the roof, and even then could only reach it with a long stick. The internees provoked the military through a chorus of facetious remarks as the hapless man struggled to remove the offending item. One internee shouted 'another great British victory', which enraged the military to the extent that a soldier thrust his bayonet through the flag as he left. As soon as the military were back in the guardroom other flags appeared throughout the compound.

The programme for the day began at 11 a.m. with a lecture in the concert hall. The platform was decorated with the Tricolour and the red flag as a symbol of Gaelic comradeship. Despite the antics of the internees hoisting everything and anything red, the Labour Day programme commenced with the No. 2 compound chaplain and internee, Fr Thomas Burbage, opening the proceedings with prayer. Fr Burbage then introduced Albert Smith, Wexford, who gave the oration on the future of Irish labour. After the lecture, Smith discussed the establishment of a trade's council to end the neglect of organisations on the outside by their comrades in the fighting arena. The lecture concluded with the singing of 'The Red Flag', but the meeting continued up to lunchtime. Leo Henderson entered the hut to inform Tadhg Barry that the British commandant was threatening to withdraw the time extension for a theatrical performance later that evening. The commandant had told Henderson that the normal lock-up hours would apply if the red flags were not removed. Tadhg Barry addressed those gathered in the concert

Men arrested in England and transferred to Ballykinlar internment camp
No. 1 compound. *Courtesy of Kilmainham Gaol Museum Archives*

View of No. 1 compound from the recreation field.
Courtesy of the National Archives of Ireland

Ballykinlar camp orchestra.
Front row (left to right): Frank McKay (kneeling), —, George Goodman,
Tom O'Keefe, —. *Second row:* Frank Hughes, — Walsh, Tommy Dillon,
John Condron, Peter McDonagh; *Third row:* Frank O'Higgins, Ted Neary,
Barney Keogh, Pat O'Loughlin, Thomas O'Rourke, —, Peadar Kearney, Art
O'Donnell, Patrick J. Young, Martin Walton (standing extreme right).
Back row: Patrick O'Hanlon, —, Hubert J. Murphy.
Courtesy of Kilmainham Gaol Museum Archives

Fr John McLister, camp chaplain.
*Courtesy of Kilmainham Gaol Museum
Archives*

Left to right: Dr Richard Hayes, Seán
Nolan, Joseph McGrath. *Courtesy of
Kilmainham Gaol Museum Archives*

The No. 1 compound internee officer staff.
Front row (left to right): Art O'Donnell, Mossie Donegan a.k.a. Thomas
Fitzpatrick, Joseph McGrath, Dr Richard Hayes, Dr T. F. O'Higgins.
Back row: Thomas Meldon, Barney O'Driscoll, Thomas Treacy, D. Hogan.
Courtesy of Kilmainham Gaol Museum Archives

Hut 16. The men in the hut were: Joe Lynch, T. Harmon, James Harmon,
M. Harmon, Dick Smith, Edward Quigley, William Kelly, Denis McGrath,
Simon Haugh, M. Clancy, Michael Kenny, Patrick Fagan, J. Farrell, J.
Murtagh, Art O'Donnell, Edward Travers, J. McArdle, J. Moffat, T. Dolan,
Louis McAvitt, J. McCaffrey, J. Hynes, Phil Foley, Patrick Cavanagh, Joseph
Fanning, John McGrane.
Courtesy of the National Archives of Ireland

Peadar Clancy junior football team.
Back row: Jim McDonald, Christopher Seivers, James Brady, Tom O'Leary, J. Lynch, Joe Duffy, William Kelly.
Middle row: Joseph E. Nolan, M. Clancy, T. Dolan, J. Jones, P. L. Kerwin.
Front row: Alex Kane, John J. Whelan, Éamon Travers, Peter Rock.
Courtesy of Kilmainham Gaol Museum Archives

Men walking around the No. 1 compound.
Courtesy of Kilmainham Gaol Museum Archives

Fr Thomas Burbage, internee and
No. 2 compound chaplain.
*Courtesy of Offaly Historical and
Archaeological Society*

Joseph Tormey, murdered by a
British sentry.
Courtesy of Patrick Tormey

The location where Joseph Tormey and Patrick Sloane were murdered by a
British sentry. *Courtesy of Kilmainham Gaol Museum Archives*

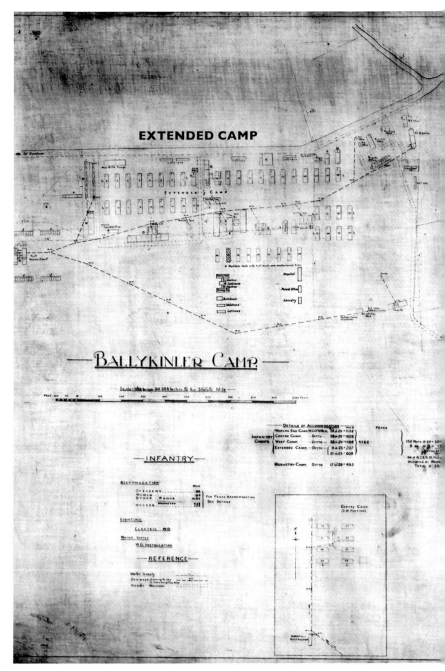

Map of Ballykinlar camp showing the internment compounds in the lower right-hand corner. *Courtesy of the Bureau of Military History*

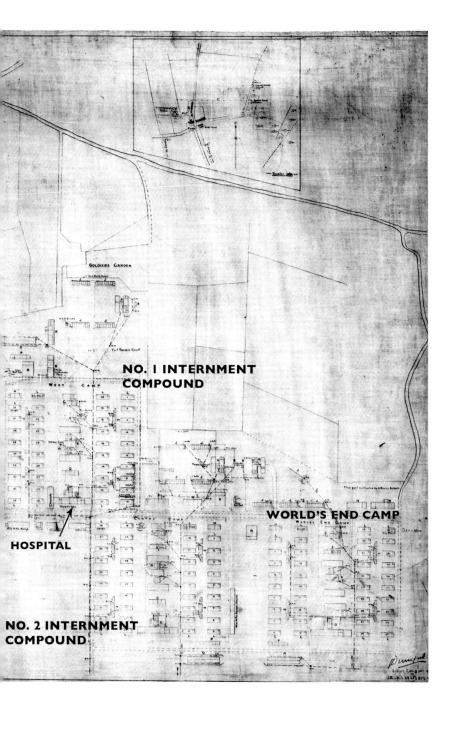

SOLDIERS GARDEN

NO. 1 INTERNMENT
COMPOUND

WEST CAMP

HOSPITAL

WORLD'S END CAMP

NO. 2 INTERNMENT
COMPOUND

The No. 1 compound cooks. The men in the photograph were not named but the cooks from this compound were Thomas Meldon, Declan Horton, John Kane, Jack J. Byrne, Jim Bracken, William Judge, Owen Slowey, Dennis Brennan, Tom Foynes, John Donnelly, Mat Kenney, Pat White and T. Malone.

Courtesy of the National Archives of Ireland

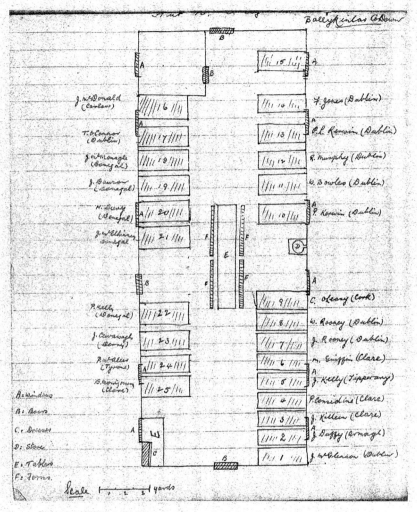

Sketch of Hut 15 by James Dawson, Letterkenny, County Donegal.
Courtesy of Patrick Dawson

Internees on parade in No. 1 compound. *Courtesy of British Pathé*

Hut 28.
Front row (left to right): Joe Behan, Fred Henry, Éamonn Watson, Richard O'Connor, Thomas Brophy, Frank O'Higgins. *Second row:* William Brogan, Jim Roche, Peadar Kearney, Liam Whelan, Andrew Byrne, Frank McNally, William Thorton. *Third row:* Frank Carney, George Traynor, J. Byrne, Liam Ring, Barney Keogh, Patrick Ring, Tom Condon. *Back row:* Gregory Foley, Liam Condon, John Condon, A. O'Reilly.
Courtesy of the Evening Herald

Hut 24. The men in the hut were: Terry Leonard, P. Hegarty-Meehan, Patrick Byrne, James Campbell, James Gibson, P. Swan, Michael Fynes, Tody Fynes, Jim McGeraghty, Michael McGeraghty, F. Donoghue, John Pratt, Thomas McGovern, Thomas Fitzpatrick, Donal Francis Sheridan, Tim Duggan, Thomas Burns, Christy Burns, Patrick Dunne, John Donnelly, M. Cunningham, Denis McGrane, James Cummins, Éamonn O'Kane, Bernard Emmo.

Courtesy of the National Archives of Ireland

Hut 15. *Back row (left to right)*: Joe Kelly, John McElhinney, Jerry Killeen, Patrick Kelly, Seamus Kavanagh.
Second row: Jim McDonald, William Rooney, Dan Montgomery, P. L. Kerwin, Peter Kerwin, Joe Duffy, Eddie Monaghan.
Third row: Dan Monaghan, Seamus McGlennon, Hugh Deery, Jim Dawson, Con O'Leary, James McMonagle, Peter McAleer.
Front row: Jim McClean, Bob Murphy, Liam Bowles, Joe Rooney, Thomas O'Connor, Fred Jones. *Courtesy of Patrick Dawson*

No. 1, VOL. 1.   BALLYKINLAR SEPTR. 1921.   Price.

NABOCLEIS.

When life in Camp seems filled with care
And worries crowd you everywhere,
Be brave-give way not to despair,
        Nabocleis !

When laundry's done and hung to dry,
'Neath sunny morning's azure sky,
It rains in torrents bye and bye,
        Nabocleis !

When in a bout of football play,
You get a knock and bite the clay,
Keep cool-good temper wins the day,
        Nabocleis !

When named each day for Coal fatigue,
Through oversight or Hut intrigue,
You long to join the Looney League,
        Nabocleis !

When comes your turn for hot bath nice,
To banish dirt, disease and---other
        things,
You find the water cold as ice,
        Nabocleis !

When rowdy nights within your hut,
Forbid your weary eyes to shut,
If boot or trestle finds your 'nut',
        Nabocleis !

When things move slowly with the Peace,
Deferring hopes of quick release,
Take heart - your troubles soon shall
        cease,
        Nabocleis.

When racked with family cares
        outside,
Where loving wives and children
        bide,
Trust HIM who ever shall provide,
        Nabocleis !

        J.S. CONSIDINE.

GLEANINGS FROM THE SANDS.

Club-SWINGING is becoming very
popular in the Huts. Heavier material is used in the Hospital.

We understand that the adverse
rate of exchange abroad is responsible for the skittish fit of
the CHIT.

The tortured FLORIN still
shrieks 'twixt and iron. Only at
intervals can one hear the machine guns on the range. Ring off !

GUESTS are being interned daily
AUTOGRAPH HUNTERS are still at
large.

Hand ball in the ── Compound
is having a great vogue. This may
have a bad effect on indoor football ── and cricket. Play the
game !
        (See Page 3).

Front page of the No. 1 compound newsletter *Ná Bac Leis.*
Courtesy of Kilmainham Gaol Museum Archives

Hut 14.
Top row (left to right): John O'Grady, John White, Patrick Hoban, Patrick Ruane, Tom Ruane, Dan Horan, Richard Davis. *Third row:* Maurice Byrne, John Leigh, Michael Nugent, Laurence MacDonnell, Joseph Considine, Henry Dixon BL, John Considine, Patrick Power.
Second row: William Gay, James Maguire, Seamus O'Toole, Hugh Britton.
Front row: Edward McDermott, J. J. Green, Michael Liston, Myles McHugh, Frank McKay. *Courtesy of Jack Britton*

Tadhg Barry – murdered by a British sentry in No. 2 compound. *Courtesy of Tadhg Galvin*

The No. 1 compound teaching staff. *Courtesy of the National Archives of Ireland*

Internees strolling through the mud, mist and rain.
Courtesy of British Pathé

Internees standing behind the barbed-wire fence. *Courtesy of British Pathé*

hall and asked them to decide what to do. The initial reaction was to ignore the military threat, but they decided that the flags should be removed as the hard work of the performers would otherwise have been in vain.

The meeting concluded so the flag issue could be dealt with. Leo Henderson and Tadhg Barry went out into the compound to find every piece of red material being used as flags or as coat badges. The military were visibly riled and some soldiers began threatening vicious reprisals. The internees quickly removed the offending garments when Leo Henderson, the compound commandant, explained the situation. However, as a punishment the military refused access to the recreation field where boxing and wrestling competitions were to be held. The organisers decided not to challenge the decision and simply marked out a ring in the middle of the compound and the competitions were held there. After their evening meal, the internees gathered for a costume competition and parade. The No. 1 compound orchestra set up as close to the wires as permitted and provided the music and soon the No. 2 compound was graced with some strange and amusing figures making their way to the concert hall. The parade began soon after and the various characters walked around the camp to great cheers and laughter from the internees.

An unusual-looking donkey headed the parade led by a jockey in full costume. The internees were even graced with the presence of the 'lord mayor of Ballykinlar', dressed in full robes and chain of office made of barbed wire with a large padlock as a medallion. The lord mayor officially opened proceedings with a speech explaining that he had to do some wire pulling to get the mayoral chain. After his speech, in which he promised special favours to the internees, he introduced the different characters in the fancy dress parade, including a miner complete with a bucket of coal from the pits and an RIC sergeant swinging his baton. Charlie Chaplin even made an appearance as did many other characters of that time and before, with Cú Chulainn also appearing. Labour songs were sung, followed by 'The Red Flag', and the day ended with a rousing version of 'The Soldier's Song'. The only unfortunate incident of the day was the capture of a roll of film with photographs taken of the various events during the day.[23]

The Wolfe Tone commemoration and its aftermath

The annual Wolfe Tone commemoration held at Bodenstown cemetery on the outskirts of Sallins, County Kildare, began in the late 1800s. Theobald Wolfe Tone was buried there in November 1798. In preparation for the centenary of the 1798 rebellion, the 1798 Committee was formed in 1896 by among others Henry Dixon and Frederick Allan, both of whom were internees at Ballykinlar. The first annual pilgrimage was held some time around the latter part of the 1890s. The date of the commemoration was to coincide with the date of Wolfe Tone's birth on 20 June and was marked each year on the Sunday closest to that date.[24]

The commemoration held at Ballykinlar camp on Thursday 23 June 1921 was possibly the only large gathering organised to commemorate the birth of Wolfe Tone anywhere in Ireland that year, and was celebrated with a large outdoor meeting held in the No. 2 compound recreation field. A platform was built from bed boards, boxes and any other useful items. All available chairs were taken to the recreation field. The day's programme consisted of patriotic recitals, national songs, music and dance, with the most anticipated part of the day's programme being a lecture on the life and times of Wolfe Tone.

The British viewed the celebration of a heroic Irish figure with suspicion and, as the lecture was being delivered, the British military listened in from a discreet distance. They viewed the day's events as a propaganda meeting and towards the close of the address a number of officers accompanied by several soldiers entered the No. 2 compound. Given that the military had not anticipated any seditious speeches and had kept their distance from the recreation field that day, they failed to clearly identify the person delivering the lecture and were relying on a general description when they entered the recreation field. After the lecture, a corporal approached Brian O'Kennedy, who had been arrested in London in April 1921 and interned at Ballykinlar on 14 May. The corporal called to a lieutenant and pointed in O'Kennedy's direction. Putting his hand on his revolver the lieutenant ordered O'Kennedy to stand up and said he was being arrested for delivering a seditious speech. O'Kennedy protested his innocence, but he was marched off in the direction of the guardroom. On reaching the gate of the compound the lieutenant obviously had his doubts and returned to the field accompanied by the corporal. By that time most of the men had left or were strolling around, making it too difficult to identify anyone else fitting the description, so the military had to be content with the man they had arrested. O'Kennedy was placed in one of the cells. Later that evening a military police sergeant entered his cell with two soldiers to familiarise himself with O'Kennedy's appearance. The military police sergeant was present the following day when O'Kennedy was taken before Colonel Ennis for a preliminary inquiry.

The corporal who made the arrest addressed the inquiry and said that O'Kennedy had used the following words when giving the speech, 'Here we are inside the wire while our friends are enjoying freedom but soon the day will come when we can strike down the English dogs.' The corporal identified the speaker as having dark hair, being clean-shaven and wearing a light-grey coat and trousers of darker grey. Colonel Ennis asked O'Kennedy if he had anything to say and he said he had not made a speech and that the military witnesses were mistaken. He was then remanded and returned to the cells. That evening a military police sergeant visited O'Kennedy in his cell and asked him to identify the speaker. He said that it would secure his release and that none of the other internees would know. O'Kennedy declined and said he was not prepared to secure his own liberty to the detriment of that of another internee. The sergeant told him that he was facing two years in prison for making the speech, but, realising that nothing was to be gained from threats or bribes, he left.

On Wednesday 29 June a British officer visited O'Kennedy and asked for the names of witnesses for his defence, to which

O'Kennedy said there were several hundred. Brian O'Kennedy asked to speak with the internees' commandant, who by that time was Francis O'Duffy, to draw up a list of witnesses. The officer said that would not be possible and O'Kennedy then referred him to Joseph Boyle, Westmeath, his hut leader, who would supply him with as many names as he wished. The officer said he would not do that either and then left the cell.

On Monday 1 August a commissioner arrived from Belfast to take sworn statements and by then the military had altered the evidence of identification to suit that of O'Kennedy's appearance. The soldiers swore that the speaker wore a sports coat, was clean-shaven and wore a soft trilby hat. All witnesses swore that O'Kennedy had delivered the speech and the sergeant who visited his cell swore that O'Kennedy had told him he had made the speech. Brian O'Kennedy cross-examined a number of internees who had been summoned by the British military, which annoyed the British officers and in particular Sergeant Bryant, who was known for his brutality. When the inquiry concluded, two officers instructed the military police sergeant to keep O'Kennedy in the room until the commissioner had departed. O'Kennedy knew by the look from the two officers that he was in for a beating, having seen the results on other internees who had come into contact with them. They had a reputation for carrying out severe beatings, and on another occasion William Halfpenny, County Down, had been assaulted by Sergeant Bryant, receiving bruising to the face along with other injuries.

When the commissioner had gone through the gate the

sergeant returned with a look of anger on his face and said, 'Bring him in here now', but just at that moment Colonel Ennis walked into the room and asked, 'What is that man kept back for?' With that the sergeant's plan was foiled and he ordered O'Kennedy's return to his cell. The next day O'Kennedy sent a telegram to a London-based solicitor to represent him, in the belief that with the advent of the Truce and the world's attention on the Irish situation an English solicitor would be best placed to protect him against malpractice in Ballykinlar. O'Kennedy hoped he would be in a good position to publicise any under-handed attempts by the military in the camp to convict him or prevent him receiving a fair trial.

On Thursday evening, 4 August, a British officer visited Brian O'Kennedy's cell to inform him that the case against him had been dropped. No explanation was given and O'Kennedy just walked out of the cell without saying a word and returned to the compound to a rousing welcome from his comrades. He had been held for six weeks in solitary confinement, perhaps mostly as a punishment for not revealing the true identity of the man who delivered the speech on the life of Wolfe Tone.[25]

The Ballykinlar Dramatic Society

The Ballykinlar Dramatic Society staged other concerts, and one held on Sunday 16 October was described as the most enjoyable held in the camp. The programme was varied, with a selection of humorous songs sung by the Ballykinlar choir. *Ná Bac Leis* gave the following report on the performances:

The choir were perhaps happiest in the singing of the two rousing martial choruses 'The Soldier's Chorus' (from the 4th Act of Faust opera by George Gounod) and 'The Policeman': the latter of a more melodious and lighter texture. They also gave an effective rendering of a pretty number, 'The Lilies', which was substituted for another item by request. The finished rendering of these items particularly in 'The Policeman' was evidence of meticulous care in rehearsal on the part of their efficient and painstaking conductor, Mr George Nesbitt ... Two 'Come all Yees' entitled 'The Return from the 13th Lock' and 'The Pride of Pimlico' by Tom Cuffe put the audience in merry mood ... The brunt of the work in the 'Rising of the Moon' was borne by G[eorge] Nesbitt, who gave a careful, earnest interpretation of the hunted outlaw in the guise of a ballad singer. As the RIC sergeant, Aodh MacNeill struggled bravely through a part for which he was not quite suited. Some of the dialogue was inaudible owing to indistinct enunciation. Mr E[amon] Morrissey and Mr F[rank] Doris as the constables, made, it is understood, entrances and exits from the stage. 'The Soldier's Song' at the conclusion gave the audience an innings.[26]

Another play was staged in the No. 1 compound dining hall on Sunday 13 November. An adaptation of *The Workhouse Ward* written by Lady Augusta Gregory and Douglas Hyde was performed, with Thomas Cuffe and George Gaynor as the two paupers and Ambrose Byrne as the widow. A report of this play was also published in *Ná Bac Leis*: 'The wrapt attention accorded them throughout was conclusive evidence of their success. As the widow Mr Ambrose Byrne did his best in a role for which he was naturally quite unsuited.'[27]

The No. 2 compound dramatic society also staged many plays during 1921. These included *The Workhouse Ward*, which was staged on St Patrick's night, 1921; *The Building Fund* (28 March); *Hyacinth Halvey* (24 April); *The Eloquent Dempsey* (5 and 6 June); *The Suburban Groove* (24 and 25 July); *The Lord Mayor* (14 and 15 August) and *The Rising of the Moon* (28 and 29 August). A play written by one of the No. 2 compound internees, Henry Murray of Dublin, called *At the Ballykinlar Cross Roads* was staged on 17 and 18 July. Murray got together an excellent company, mostly of men from the north of Ireland, who created the right atmosphere for the play. *Cathleen Ni Houlihan* by W. B. Yeats was performed on 15 and 16 October. *The Duplicity of David* by Bernard McCarthy was staged on the same dates. *The Rising Generation*, a comedy in three acts also written by Bernard McCarthy, was the last performance to be staged in No. 2 compound, on 12 and 13 November 1921.[28]

10

Disputes between the Internees and British Military

The nature of the IRA's campaign against the British establishment in Ireland was centred on confrontation, challenge and disregard for all authority deriving from Britain. The IRA members who found themselves within the prisons and internment camps were merely presented with very different challenges and introduced a new dynamic to the confrontation: challenge and disregard.

The internees at Ballykinlar internment camp were involved in many arguments with the British military during their incarceration, which had the effect of loosening the rigidity of military control and, to some extent, improving the prisoners' morale.[1] The disputes often related to the status of the internees and to internal currency. The British retaliated with searches of the compounds and suspending mail and parcel deliveries, the prisoners with hunger strikes and general disruption tactics.

Disputes over status and treatment of the internees

From the first days at Ballykinlar camp the detainees were adamant that they would not bow to the bullying tactics displayed by many of the British soldiers and officers. The main culprits were the subordinate military officers, most of whom were below the rank of captain and were eager to exert their authority on the defenceless captives. The status of the internees had never been clearly defined and the British government was reluctant to officially recognise them as prisoners of war. The British War Cabinet stated that any members of the IRA arrested and interned were not to be categorised as prisoners of war. One statement by Hamar Greenwood, replying to a written question in the House of Commons, demonstrates the ambiguity of the prisoners' status – they are to be treated in a 'like manner' to prisoners of war:

> Persons interned under Restoration of Order Regulation 14B are allowed to receive visits for special reasons. For example, they may be visited by solicitors to discuss urgent business matters, or by relatives in case of illness. They are allowed to write one letter (not exceeding four sheets) per week, and to receive any number of letters. But all letters, whether incoming or outgoing, are subject to censorship. The regulation provides that persons interned thereunder shall be subject to the like restrictions and may be dealt with in the like manner as prisoners of war, and the restrictions and obligations imposed on them are in fact less onerous than those imposed on prisoners of war in the country during the late war.[2]

Despite the British government's reluctance to recognise the internees publicly as prisoners of war, they were often treated as such by the military in the various internment camps. The internees at Ballykinlar were largely treated as such and received prisoners-of-war rations.

The military demanded that the detainees address the officers as 'Sir' at daily roll call, which was usually carried out by a lieutenant: from the men's point of view these soldiers were usually the most sadistic minions holding the rank of officer. The internees managed to avoid calling them 'Sir' by answering 'Anseo', the Irish for 'Here'. The British may have misinterpreted 'Anseo' as 'In Sir' or accepted the response to avoid unnecessary friction so early in the morning.

Shortly after the camp opened, a lieutenant taking the roll one morning at Hut 26 called out the name of Hubert Wilson from County Longford.

'Here.'

The lieutenant shouted aggressively, 'Here, what?'

'Here, here.'

To the officer's credit, he laughed and carried on with the roll call.

The way in which the subordinate British officers were dealt with was not missed by the ordinary soldiers, who were pleased to see the internees standing up to them. A soldier said to an internee one day, 'These officers have the wind up. If we ask them for anything we get seven days in the clink for cheek, but you people can get anything you want.' According to him, the detainees had better clothes and boots than they did.

There was always friction between the internees and the military, usually involving minor issues, but the relationship between the two became more strained after the deaths of Patrick Sloane and Joseph Tormey. The publication of the internees' Commission of Inquiry in the *Irish Bulletin* incensed the military authorities in the camp. Commandant Patrick Colgan and solicitor P. J. Hogan made regular appeals to the British military authority for a full public investigation.[3]

Trouble began in the days following the shooting of Sloane and Tormey when Dr O'Higgins complained to Colgan about the behaviour of the British medical officer, Major Kyle. Dr O'Higgins was the internees' doctor and worked in the hospital hut with Major Kyle. Prior to the shooting, despite his initial opinion of the British medical officer, O'Higgins had established a good working relationship with Kyle, managing the hospital with great efficiency. Dr O'Higgins had been one of the first at the scene and had assisted in the post mortems, which made him a very important witness at the inquiry into the deaths. After the shootings the British medical officer started making life difficult for Dr O'Higgins by interfering with his work. Patrick Colgan brought the complaint to Colonel Little and was given an assurance that Major Kyle would be spoken to. But Kyle continued to harass Dr O'Higgins and became so aggressive that Colgan ordered O'Higgins to leave the hospital.

Colonel Little ordered another doctor interned in No. 2 compound, Dr Leonard, to report to the hospital hut in No. 1 compound. Colgan met with Leonard and explained the situation, telling him that he would have to resign as he had not been appointed by the camp council. The British military did not have the authority to order an internee who had not been convicted of any offence to take up any position without the agreement of the camp council and the other internees. Dr Leonard refused to obey Colgan's demand and was told that life in the camp could become very unpleasant for him. Dr Leonard asked Colgan if he could relay that to the British medical officer, Major Kyle, and was told that he could tell him whatever he wanted. Patrick Colgan sent a letter to Colonel Little stating that the appointment of Dr Leonard was not acceptable, as the camp council had not appointed him.

On the evening of Monday 24 January 1921, further trouble broke out when Patrick (P. J.) Hogan was arrested and charged with having a coin in his pocket, contrary to camp regulations. Patrick Colgan sent a letter to Colonel Little protesting against the arrest and Hogan was released from the guardroom a short time later. The British military retaliated: at approximately 9 p.m. a party of soldiers entered the No. 1 compound and proceeded to Hut 21, where they arrested Colgan. He was not even allowed to dress and was removed to the guardroom.[4] The British also visited Hut 12 and ordered the men to pack up and be ready to move to No. 2 compound the following morning. The internees learned about the arrest of Commandant Colgan the following morning and a meeting of the camp council was held at which they decided to engage with the British military in their games and prevent the move of the men from Hut 12. The occupants of Hut 12 relocated to other huts and identities were swapped with other internees. Throughout that morning, bed boards and blankets were removed and Hut 12 was 'on the run'. Their disappearance was discovered by the British later that morning, when the line captain carried out the daily inspection of the huts only to find No. 12 empty. As another part of the protest, all other internees refused to answer when the British line captain called the camp roll, to ensure that the military could not identify any of the men to be moved to No. 2 compound. The camp council issued a letter to the British officers outlining the basis of their protest:

> Until our Commandant is returned to us we refuse to allow you to move Hut 12, and our officers will not co-operate with you in running the camp. Furthermore, no prisoner will answer his name for any purpose.

The British were reluctant to allow the dispute to develop and the chief censor, Captain Newton, was directed to enter into negotiations with the camp council.[5] Patrick Colgan was taken before Colonel Little and was charged with:

Threatening a fellow internee (Dr Leonard).

Threatening the same internee with death if he failed to obey illegal orders.

Interfering with the proper running of the camp.

Organising a mutiny amongst the internees.

Publishing false and scandalous stories against British forces (*Irish Bulletin*).

Colonel Little informed Colgan that he was being remanded for general court-martial and when Colgan made a sarcastic comment he was sentenced to seven days' solitary confinement. Colgan made a few more comments and was given a total of twenty-one days in solitary. He was first taken to the punishment cells, where the internees passed food and cigarettes through the windows. Later that night he was moved to the cells in the guardroom. Solitary confinement meant a piece of bread and a mug of water for breakfast, for dinner and for tea.[6] The cell was twelve by eight feet and was only eight feet high, with an opening in the window of twelve inches by nine inches, which was the only means of getting fresh air. There was a small ventilator in the roof, which was stuffed up with dust. The walls and roof of the cell were lined with galvanised iron sheets and the cell was like an oven in summer and very cold in winter. There was no bed, table, chair or stool.[7]

On his first day of solitary confinement, Colgan received a visit from Major Kyle, who informed Colgan that he had been instructed to give him a medical examination. Colgan refused to be examined and Kyle explained to him that he had to report on his fitness to undergo his sentence of punishment, but Colgan again declined. Kyle was accompanied by a British sergeant major, who said that he would force Colgan to take the examination. Colgan jumped up and made a move towards the officer, who ran out of the cell. This impressed the soldiers on duty in the guardroom and one said to Colgan later that he was 'a hell of a fellow for standing up to the swine'. Following this the soldiers on duty in the guardroom were very decent to Patrick Colgan and occasionally gave him tea and food. Despite his twenty-one day sentence, Colgan spent a total of twenty-three days in solitary confinement and on his release was moved to No. 2 compound.[8]

The British upped the ante on Tuesday evening, 25 January, when Captain Newton informed the camp council that all privileges were being withdrawn: this included closing the canteen and refusing to distribute parcels and letters. The British ordered Dr Michael O'Connor, Kerry, interned in No. 2 compound to take up duties in the camp hospital, but he refused. On Wednesday 26 January the British did not unlock the doors of the huts until 10.30 a.m. and also refused to allow the camp chaplain, Fr McLister, to enter No. 1 compound to say mass. They patrolled the compound all day with fixed bayonets and all internees were ordered into their huts at 4.30 p.m. with lights out at 8 p.m. Later that night the military raided the compound and arrested Bernard O'Driscoll in Hut 2 and then went to Hut 21 where they arrested Joseph McGrath and Michael Quish.

In the early hours of Thursday 27 January, the military re-entered the compound and during a raid on Hut 2 smashed up the interior and assaulted some of the men. Bags and boxes were ripped open and smashed, beds were broken and the blankets were soaked with buckets of water. This was repeated in Hut 13. Later that morning the military entered Hut 19 for roll call and, when the men refused to answer, some were verbally abused and some were assaulted. The military pulled down books and smashed up the interior of the hut. This continued each night for the remainder of that week. The internees escalated their protest by removing the locks from the doors of the huts and swapping the hut numbers to confuse the military, who issued a warning that anyone who left his hut during lock-up would be shot. As this was happening the representatives of the two sides were holding meetings to discuss the terms of a settlement.

On Friday 28 January the situation became more perilous as it was military pay-day. That night many were under the influence of alcohol when they entered the compound and were shouting in a threatening manner as they patrolled. The atmosphere was very tense. Joseph McGrath, who was being held in the punishment cells, saw the drunken soldiers preparing to enter the compound and, fearing for the safety of the internees, requested a meeting with a military officer. A conference was quickly arranged and the soldiers were ordered out of the compound. As part of a temporary truce, the arrested men, apart from Patrick Colgan, were released on parole to fulfil the terms of a settlement which had been finalised on Friday afternoon. All privileges were returned with some additional concessions. On his release Joseph McGrath was appointed commandant of No. 1 compound.[9]

The disputes were not confined to No. 1 compound and the internees in No. 2 were also targeted for military aggression. The night patrols ceased for a short time but when they resumed the internees in the No. 2 compound came in for particular attention. The trouble began with the night patrols entering the huts and carrying out vicious verbal and physical attacks on the men as they lay in their beds. The situation became so frustrating that the compound commandant, Leo Henderson, arranged a meeting with the British commandant, Colonel Ennis, on Monday 9 May 1921. Ennis agreed to address the issue of patrols interfering with the men after lock-up hours. However, a week later the guarantees seemed to have been ignored and at approximately 11 p.m. on Sunday 15 May, Lieutenant Sheppard, a sergeant and a private made their way to Hut 35. Sheppard walked directly up to Dr Michael Hayes, who was preparing for bed. Sheppard asked in a very aggressive tone what Hayes was doing with the light. There was no light on in the hut at the time and Hayes replied that he was not doing anything with any light. Sheppard said, 'You had a light in here.' Hayes said he had not been using any light whereupon Lieutenant Sheppard shouted, 'Don't answer me!' and then asked him how he would like to spend a night in a cold guardroom with no blanket. 'I would take you out just as you are' (meaning, in his pyjamas). The officer then shouted, 'The next time I will do it. Now get into bed and be quick about it.'

The lieutenant then walked towards the door as if to leave and an internee who had been woken made some remark to which the sergeant said, 'What's the matter with you – you shut up.' His manner was even more aggressive than the officer's. Some remarks were exchanged between the internee and the sergeant with the latter approaching the bed in which the internee was lying. The sergeant forced him down on the bed by thrusting his rifle butt down on his chest and attempted to strike him in the mouth with a small blunt object. The internee raised his left hand to protect his mouth and received the force of the blow on the hand, which later required treatment by the medical officer.

Lieutenant Sheppard was close to the hut door when the internee was struck. He must have heard the loud angry voice of the sergeant and the blow itself, which was heard by every man in the hut, but proceeded outside. When the internee was struck, Leo Henderson walked towards the door and asked for the officer. The private said he was outside and, going to the door, called him back in. Leo Henderson told him, 'I am the internees' commandant and one of your men has struck one of my men.'

'I don't want to know who you are – thanks!'

'Colonel Ennis had promised me that he had taken measures to prevent unwarranted or undue interference by the night patrols.'

'I am here to keep order among you people and I'll take no back chat from you.'

'You can settle this with Colonel Ennis tomorrow. I shall report it to him.'

The officer made no response, but the sergeant retorted angrily, 'I don't care a damn who you report it to.' Leo Henderson subsequently reported the incident to the colonel, but no action was taken against the lieutenant or the sergeant.[10] The British commandant again assured Leo Henderson that the night patrols would desist from entering the huts and harassing the internees. On other occasions when the internees' commandants raised similar concerns with the British commandant, the night patrols were instructed to cease entering the huts, but this action only lasted a short time. The tactics used by the night patrols were a form of psychological abuse, with the military going to the compounds after 12 a.m. each night and entering the huts, flashing torches in the faces of the internees and shouting in a loud and aggressive manner.[11]

On Wednesday 18 May 1921 an internee from County Kerry, David O'Connor, was asked by a British line officer called Wilson to assist him in closing the door of Hut 24. O'Connor was helping him, but when the officer used unsavoury language he sat down and refused to collaborate. For disobeying an order, David O'Connor received seven days in the punishment cells. In protest against this unfairness, the internees in No. 2 compound refused to stand by their beds for the count that night or answer to their names. They were forced to stand and were subjected to verbal abuse. They continued the protest the following morning. On Thursday evening the internees smashed all doors off the hinges. When, the British military line officer arrived to conduct the night roll call and inspection, he soon left to report the destruction to his superiors. The internees anticipated raids by the military that night and it was agreed that the doors should be put back into position and barricades erected to prevent any surprise raids on the huts that night. At approximately 11 p.m. soldiers entered No. 2 compound fully equipped, wearing tin helmets and with bayonets fixed on their weapons. The military broke down the barricaded doors, entered the huts, smashed up the interiors and assaulted the occupants. This continued down each line, with the contents of the huts being destroyed and thrown out into the compound. The men were beaten with canes and the butts of rifles. Seven, including the vice-commandant Fionán Lynch, were arrested and confined to the punishment cells for one week. On Friday the British delivered a consignment of rotten fish for dinner, but the cooks refused to accept it and it was thrown into the cookhouse by the soldiers and later removed by the internees.

On the morning of Sunday 22 May, the British arranged a peace conference with the officers from both compounds and the discussions went on for most of that day. All issues were raised, some having been in dispute from the first days of the camp, but no agreement was reached that evening. The internees continued with their protest that night and refused to recognise the British line officer's inspection, but there were no military raids. The men arrested were released from the punishment cells on Monday morning and both sides agreed to new conditions. The internees were jubilant as they had been victorious in their battle with the British military. There were other minor disputes between the two sides in No. 1 compound, but the severe actions of the British military were not repeated and any further issues in that compound were resolved through dialogue.[12]

On Sunday 29 May the detainees greatly regretted smashing the doors off the hinges, as there was torrential rain throughout that day and all night. Rain blew in, forcing them to use the broken doors and bed boards to erect barricades to stop the huts from flooding.[13]

Internal currency disputes

The next dispute originated from the British military's claim of discrepancies in the camp currency system. When the camp opened in December 1920 the military retained all hard cash belonging to the internees and issued them with a 'chit' currency system for use within the wires to prevent any attempts to bribe the soldiery – something that had occurred in Frongoch internment camp following the 1916 Rising. The chit system worked satisfactorily, but in late August 1921 the British camp authority accused the internees of some financial irregularities. The prisoners claimed that this was due to mishandling or stupidity on the part of the British camp authorities. The British commandant issued an order on Wednesday 7 September that the internees were to hand in all 'chits' to his office by a given hour and they were then informed that no further currency would be issued. The 'chit' recall also meant the closing of the canteens in both camps. The British commandant gave the internee officers an ultimatum: the canteen would remain closed unless all purchases were made directly from the Naval and Army Canteen Board (NACB).

The internees were reluctant to deal with the NACB because of previous bad experiences and presented a number of alternative schemes to the British commandant, but all were rejected. With the canteen closed, the men had to survive without cigarettes, tobacco or food to supplement their meagre rations. Efforts to resolve the situation continued for approximately three weeks, when the internee camp officers in No. 2 compound decided to initiate retaliatory action.[14]

On Saturday 24 September the men refused to answer to the daily roll call. That night the military entered No. 2 compound in large numbers and on entering Hut 12 one soldier walked around flashing a torch into the faces of the sleeping men. He then shouted to his superiors, 'The fuckers are awake.' They left soon after, but returned at 2.15 a.m. They tried to open the door but although they kicked it a few times, could not get it open. They stood outside, cocking the bolts of their rifles, giving the impression that they were preparing to open fire. This was repeated on Sunday night and continued until 3 a.m. on Monday.

The continuation of the night-time harassment prompted Dr Michael O'Connor to write a letter to the British military commander outlining the effects of the raids:

As a result of this un-soldierly, unchristian and inhuman conduct of what is apparently a prowling squad of marauders … if the said conduct is not prevented the mental equilibrium of many internees who have already suffered much, is sure to be spent and in all probability many will be driven insane. Similar methods were used in the so called dark ages by the Chinese who made a speciality of the art of torture – they placed guards in the cells of prisoners whose duty it was to keep prisoners awake until they were driven insane or committed suicide. We hope that you will immediately take steps to end this intolerable state of affairs.[15]

The internees in No. 1 compound joined in the protest on Monday morning 26 September and all refused to answer to the roll call. The following day the British stopped all incoming and outgoing letters as well as newspapers, which had been allowed into the camp since the Truce in July 1921. The British had the upper hand when any dispute arose, as they knew the internees' simplest pleasures were their letters and parcels from home, so their response was once more to stop all parcels and telegrams into the camp. On Tuesday the internees in No. 1 compound removed the bolts from the hut doors preventing the British military from locking them in at night.

As the dispute escalated three internees were arrested, removed to the guardroom and sentenced to a term of punishment in the cells. The British replaced all bolts to the huts doors and locked the men into their huts each evening from 6.30 p.m. until 7.45 a.m. the following morning. Being locked up for almost fourteen hours a day caused distress and health problems.

An officer from the British military GHQ in Dublin arrived in the camp on Monday 3 October and facilitated a series of meetings between the officers on both sides. After many discussions a truce was arranged on Wednesday 5 October and the GHQ officer promised to recommend the internees' alternative cash scheme to his supervisors. Following this intervention the internees were given permission to arrange their own currency system, that involved the more professionally printed chits.[16]

The compound vice-commandant, Maurice Donegan summed up the attitude of the internees in a letter to *The Freeman's Journal* in mid-October 1921: that British attempts to break the men would always be met with resistance from the internees. 'If it is the hope of the military to break the spirit of the men, then they will have a rude awakening, as we are determined, despite our apparent helplessness to fight to the end against this class of tyranny.'[17]

Searches of the compounds

In late July 1921 a tunnel was discovered under Hut 2, No. 1 compound. As a result, the camp military received strict instructions from their GHQ at Park Gate in Dublin to carry out thorough fortnightly searches of all huts for any signs of disturbance under them or any alterations to the floorboards. The strict search policy involved clearing the huts of all items so that the floors could be thoroughly examined for any trap doors, for example. The new policy was not initiated until the British military engineers had carried out an extensive survey of the tunnel.

The focus of the tunnel searches was initially on No. 1 compound, but later switched to No. 2. The hunt involved raising a couple of floorboards in each hut, but this created an entry for rats, of which Ballykinlar could boast a good supply. The openings also admitted a nauseating smell from rotten refuse which had been dumped there before the camp was opened for Irish internees.[18]

The first actions by the military in No. 2 compound came on Tuesday 25 October when a large number entered and ordered those in lines E and F to remove their beds and other items from the huts. The men refused, so the soldiers began throwing all moveable articles, including bed boards, trestles, mattresses, bolters, blankets and boxes containing private and delicate property out of the huts. Many items were broken and the internees simply left them where they lay. The E Company line captain, Seán O'Donovan from Cork, protested at the aggressive actions and was subjected to a severe beating. He was taken before a court-martial, where, on a charge of insolence, he received fourteen days in the guardhouse on a diet of bread and water.

Later that night the compound OC, Francis O'Duffy, Monaghan, ordered some of the men from E and F lines to relocate to the huts in G and H lines. Although there were no bed boards, they could share mattresses, but that night the military patrol raided after lights out and assaulted the internees who were lying on the floors. One man had his arm badly injured and others suffered cuts and bruises.

On Wednesday night, 26 October, another group moved to the huts in G and H lines and by Saturday night all men had relocated so that there were between forty-five and fifty in each hut, sleeping in very uncomfortable conditions. However, they felt the discomfort was worth it as they were making as much of a protest as they could. The overcrowded conditions in the cold and damp huts resulted in a large number of men becoming ill. On Wednesday 29 October Dr Michael O'Connor and Dr Leo Reynolds examined all those complaining of illness and recommended twelve men report to the hospital. Normally the recommendations by the doctors would be sufficient to get the men into the hospital, but on this occasion when they paraded at the gate they were told to return at 2 p.m. When they had waited in vain for over half an hour for an escort to the hospital, Francis O'Duffy ordered them to return to the huts.

O'Connor and Reynolds resigned as medical officers in protest and two RAMC officers went to them and asked to have the ill internees paraded before them for examination. Dr O'Connor refused and said that he was either medical officer or not, adding that he had recommended the men for hospital because they had chest problems and had lost three nights' sleep due to the cramped conditions. Later that day the internee officers in No. 2 compound resigned en masse, including the commandant, vice-commandant and four line captains. The only officer remaining was the compound quartermaster.[19]

The patients in the camp hospital, although not directly involved in the dispute, did not avoid the attentions of the British military and were barred from receiving letters, parcels etc. The hospital was also the focus of military raids, with the sick men being forced into one ward while the other was thoroughly searched. They were kept out of their beds for over an hour while the search was carried out.[20]

On his return from leave, given the hostile atmosphere, the then British camp commandant, Colonel Browne, made a very unexpected announcement. He summoned ten of the internees to the guardroom and announced that they were to be unconditionally released. The men, all from Dublin, were taken completely by surprise at being instructed to collect their belongings and report to the main gate. One asked Colonel

Browne if the censor officer would subject them to a search and he said no. However, when they later reported to the main gate, the censor officer ordered one of them into an office to present his luggage for inspection. The internee refused, as did the other nine, and the censor did not insist on the search. The men were then taken to Tullmurry Railway Station by the military, accompanied by an officer. At the station they were each issued with a travelling ticket, which classed them as 'ten non-commissioned officers and privates'. They then departed for Dublin and arrived at Amiens Street Station later that day.[21]

Hunger strikes

The most powerful, personal and final form of protest was the hunger strike, which was considered by the prisoners as the most definitive weapon at their disposal to be used against their enemy. A number of such strikes had taken place in Ireland and Britain, with some prisoners fasting to the death. The use of the hunger strike did not bypass Ballykinlar camp, where it was adopted as a protest against the heavy-handed tactics of one particularly unpleasant British military officer, Lieutenant Greenwood. The malevolent Greenwood was in charge of the huts in A Company, No. 1 compound, and was described as 'officious' by the internees. One day the A Company line captain, Michael Nolan, approached Greenwood and made a complaint about the behaviour of the military night patrols. Greenwood immediately ordered soldiers accompanying him to arrest Nolan, who was placed in solitary confinement. The internees of A Company refused to cooperate with Greenwood's orders or any further orders from the British commandant. The camp council demanded the immediate release of Michael Nolan on the grounds that he was only carrying out his duties in raising the concerns of the internees in his line.

Michael Nolan commenced a hunger strike and all other prisoners being held in the cells at the time joined him in solidarity. This was not considered a great sacrifice given that the diet while in solitary confinement was bread and water. However, it was a protest the British loathed, following the deaths of three Cork men in 1920 and subsequent hunger strike protests by internees which had resulted in the release of the men under Prisons Temporary Release for Ill Health Act 1913. Within a few days of Nolan's arrest the camp commandant, Colonel Ennis, escorted by his staff, entered No. 1 compound on a tour of inspection and as he approached Hut 33 he asked if there were any complaints. Gerald (Garry) Byrne, Dublin, replied that the men were not cooperating in protest at Michael Nolan's arrest. He told the commandant that the arrest was unjust and that the internees would refuse to obey orders until Nolan was released. He added that Lieutenant Greenwood was not suited for his position and should be transferred to other duties. The British commandant took issue with Byrne's comments and asked him if he was telling him how to do his job or how to lead his officers. Obviously incensed, Ennis ordered his staff out of the compound without inspecting any other huts. However, all the prisoners being held in the cells were released later that day: perhaps, on reflection, the British commandant did not want the trouble of dealing with men on hunger strike, or it may be that he secretly agreed with the views of the internees.[22]

11

The Irish Products League

One interesting feature of the War of Independence was a campaign of boycotting all products from England and those manufactured or sold by unionist-owned businesses in the north of Ireland. The Irish Products League originated in Cork and was closely associated with University College Cork. All members of the IRA who were responsible for enforcing or promoting the policy strictly adhered to it. The internees at Ballykinlar were conscious that the boycott campaign should be continued despite their incarceration and they were instructed to encourage their families and friends to purchase Irish products when sending parcels of food and other items to the camp.

The initiative for establishing a group to promote the sale and purchase of Irish products from within the barbed-wire confines of Ballykinlar camp originated in mid-April 1921 following a chance encounter in the camp hospital in No. 1 compound. William Sears from Dublin, an internee in No. 2 compound, was sent to the camp hospital for a short period to be treated for a mild medical condition. It was during his stay that he was introduced to Dr Michael O'Connor from No. 2 compound, who happened to be a patient. One day in the hospital William Sears noticed O'Connor carving some letters on the end of a bottle cork with a small penknife. When he had finished, he showed the item to Sears. It read 'Buy Irish Goods', in the form of a circular stamp. O'Connor used this to place the slogan on the top of all letters he sent to family and friends to promote the purchase of Irish products when making up parcels.

The meeting inspired both men to promote the purchase of Irish goods on an organised basis: further discussions followed when they returned to their compound on leaving hospital. They succeeded in persuading a number of men to start the first branch of the Irish Products League in Ballykinlar camp, telling them that it was their duty to support Irish products above any other.

On Sunday 1 May an informal meeting was organised in No. 2 compound consisting of those who had been elected to Dáil Éireann: Seán Milroy, Joseph O'Doherty, Frank Lawless, James Derham, Fionán Lynch, Joseph McGuinness, William Sears, Dr Michael Hayes, P. J. Hogan and Seamus Doyle. Others with an interest in the industrial side of Sinn Féin also attended, including Frederick Allan and Dr Michael O'Connor. William Sears presided over the meeting and a number of pieces of correspondence and leaflets from University College Cork were read out. A discussion followed and those present decided to establish a branch of the Irish Products League. A committee of twelve was selected, with Fr Thomas Burbage elected as president and Frederick Allan and Dr Michael O'Connor elected as honourable treasurer and secretary respectively. The committee selected two men from each line to spread the word and promote the principles of the league. The fee for membership was set at £2 1s, with each member receiving a metal badge. Michael O'Connor was instructed to draw up a circular outlining the aims and objectives of the Irish Products League, a copy of which was to be posted in each hut. Michael O'Riada sketched a design and some illustrations to promote the objectives of the League. Forty copies of the circular were sent over to No. 1 compound with instructions for a branch to be established there. Seán Nolan, a Cork TD, took responsibility for organising the No. 1 compound branch.

The No. 2 compound committee decided to hold a large meeting to encourage all internees to play an active role in the promotion of Irish products. The gathering was organised for Wednesday 11 May and was held in the dining hall of No. 2 compound. William Sears delivered a lecture entitled 'The Knockout Blow'. His opening remarks were about his visit to the camp hospital and meeting with Dr Michael O'Connor. Sears quoted a piece from an English writer who stated that England depended on Ireland for a very large part of her food supply, claiming that in 1919 the USA supplied £242 million-worth of food to England, while Ireland exported £93 million-worth of food, which was more than Canada, India, Australia and New Zealand. Sears announced that although Ireland had exported goods, it had also imported food to the value of £55 million. He described as 'criminality' the fact that Ireland imported goods from England as well as other countries that could and should be produced in Ireland. Sears referred to discussions about the valuable ship-building industry of the Belfast shipyards that only produced £10 million per annum, whereas the value of eggs produced in Ireland each year was estimated to be £15 million and there was much less talk about the poor hens that laid all the eggs. He said that the hen kicked up less of a row than the Belfast nut- and bolt-throwers the internees had met en route to the camp.

The committee had ordered two rubber stamps with the logo designed by Michael O'Connor, but having been sent from Dublin these were not received by the committee. The internees used stamps carved by Dr O'Connor, but the British military censor made a point of erasing the print from the letters and flaps of the envelopes. However, some stamped letters managed to slip through the net.[1]

The committee ordered 100 badges from the Irish Products League headquarters in Cork at a cost of £5. A total of 335 members enrolled and by the end of June this had nearly doubled with the paid-up members numbering 630. By mid-July the membership had increased to 780. The establishment of the 'League' was also mentioned in the No. 2 compound newsletter *The Barbed Wire*, which emphasised the importance of the League and the benefit to the nation:

> A branch of the above league [Irish Products League] was started in No. 2 Cage early in May at an informal meeting consisting of the members of An Dáil and a few others interested. As a result

of the activities of its founders this branch has now over 760 members and it is confidently hoped that each member will act as a Pioneer when he gets home and so carry on outside the good work, which is so essential for our National Welfare if we are to keep our young people at home.[2]

The branches of the Irish Products League in Ballykinlar camp were certainly proactive and many lectures were delivered with instructions as to the best methods of promoting the sale of Irish-made goods both inside and outside the camp. The committee hoped that some of the lectures delivered under the education programme, including the future of Irish agriculture, milk for cities and towns, rural labour problems, cottage industries, Irish coal mines, commercial Ireland and the fishing industry, would instil the importance of their objectives in the internees so that on their release they would return to their villages, towns and cities to continue the work.[3]

12

Escape Attempts

One of the first thoughts in an internee's mind from the moment he entered Ballykinlar camp was how he would get out again. Escape was a popular topic of conversation in the early days of the camp and various ideas were presented to the compound commandants. The internees at Ballykinlar and similar camps enjoyed one type of luxury compared to men confined to cells in the various jails around the country: they could converse with fellow internees on a daily basis. Given that the huts held up to twenty-five men, and there were up to several hundred men in the compounds, many were probably saved from the desperate isolation normally attributed to the jail system. However, the freedom to mingle with fellow internees on a daily basis did not alleviate the stress of being confined. The loss of liberty merely increased their desire for freedom and thoughts of escape were never far from their minds. Imprisonment as a result of conviction for a specific crime carried a sentence or a defined period of detention, but for those given an indefinite period as a result of mere suspicion or simply based on the malicious motives of certain individuals, the strain was all the more unbearable. Despite the fact that the internees were uncharged and untried, as IRA Volunteers they considered it their duty to escape or at least attempt to escape.

Escape plots were varied, and carried out concurrently, so events that affected one sometimes impacted on others. Events both inside and outside the camp also affected the plans.

The swill-cart idea

One of the early escape ideas was to make use of a 'swill-cart', which was filled each day with waste from the cookhouse and removed from the camp by a local farmer. The idea was to put a man at the bottom of the cart and cover him with old coats, which would then be covered with the food waste. In preparation for this a despatch was sent to the local IRA division for background on the farmer and whether or not he could be relied upon to remain silent should the plan be executed. The local farmer could be trusted, but the internees later discovered that the 'swill-cart' was emptied by the military at the outside gate and refilled each time before leaving the camp. This put an end to the 'swill-cart' escape plan.[1]

Tunnels

Another idea put forward was to tunnel under the lines of barbed wire into the open countryside. However, the location of Ballykinlar camp on a coastal strand presented a challenge to the IRA engineers. The ground was composed of sand and earth, was saturated most of the time due to the inclement weather, and was only four to five feet above water level in most parts. The internees tested the ground shortly after their arrival and on discovering the water level ruled out tunnelling until the weather improved in late spring.[2] The British military engineers were also convinced that tunnels could not be constructed due to the water level. However, the IRA engineers in No. 1 compound discovered that tunnels could be dug at certain locations without reaching water level.[3]

The direction of the tunnel they planned would lead past the guardroom and surface outside the camp. Hut 2 was selected for the location of the tunnel entrance as it was situated just inside the barbed wire barricades and almost directly under a sentry box – the internees may have thought that the sentry would be looking out across the camp rather than down below the box.[4] A trap door was cleverly cut out of the floor of the washroom, which was partitioned from the remainder of the hut. The floorboards were lifted in one complete section so that they could be replaced in a matter of seconds. A few men were selected to construct the tunnel, most of whom had experience in engineering and mining. There was a gap between the bottom of the huts and the surface of the ground, and this was initially used as an area for hiding the excavated earth. The internees feared that the military would notice the difference in the ground level, but the problem was solved when the handball alley was developed adjacent to Hut 2. The excavated sand and soil were removed and spread over the alley. The earth was removed from the tunnel using bath pans, which were supplied for the collection of garbage. The roof of the tunnel was propped up using bed boards, which were commandeered from nearly every hut on the orders of Joseph McGrath, the compound commandant at the time. When the British line captains found out about the missing bed boards the men maintained they were either broken or had been used as firewood.[5] When the officers asked to see evidence of broken boards, they were shown planks that were always kept for that purpose. This seemed to satisfy them, as the boards were always replaced. The bed boards were propped up using broom handles.[6]

The work was monotonous and at times dangerous, as there was always the threat of the tunnel collapsing on the diggers. Scouts were placed at different points near Hut 2 and a signal system was established should any military enter the camp or be seen observing the activities around the hut. As the tunnel progressed, the men placed on the base wooden rails made from broom handles which were split in half, and a small wooden truck or bogey was made and attached to a rope so it could be pulled back and forth. There was a bell at the entrance and one at the tunnel end to signal to the man in the hut to pull the truck out, and to the tunnel digger to pull it back in again once emptied. The excavators would pull the wooden truck filled with earth and sand to the entrance, from where it would be taken outside so that its contents could be scattered on the ground, or, depending on the weather, dispersed under the huts.

The tunnel was lit by candles, and pipes from the heating system in the huts provided ventilation. The pipes were pushed through the roof just breaking the surface. Before long the tunnel digging was being carried out day and night. The diggers were instructed to push up markers at regular intervals to ensure the shaft was progressing in the right direction. After a couple of months it was over 100 yards long. The surface of the road was only one and a half feet above the roof.[7]

Although the Truce was announced on Monday 11 July 1921, the internees continued with the tunnel, as there was no guarantee that the Truce would last. Joseph McGrath was released on Sunday 24 July and Thomas Fitzpatrick (Maurice Donegan) from County Cork was appointed as No. 1 compound commandant in his place.[8] About the end of July the tunnel had reached a sufficient distance to plan a major escape of up to 100 men. However, with the on-going Truce and negotiations between the Irish and British leaders, the internees were reluctant to mount a mass escape without the authorisation of IRA GHQ.[9] Maurice Donegan sought the advice of Patrick Colgan, who was then in No. 2 compound. He feigned illness and was sent to the camp hospital where Donegan visited him and they discussed the possibility of escape, but both agreed that authorisation from the outside would have to be sought first. They had to get a despatch to IRA GHQ to arrange transport, etc. Patrick Colgan had his doubts about their despatch carrier Sergeant Farrell and spoke to Maurice Donegan about the matter. Donegan told Colgan that he had also had his suspicions in the past, but that there was no proof. Colgan asked Donegan for permission to send a message out with Farrell and spoke with the camp chaplain about Farrell.

Fr McLister agreed that he was possibly untrustworthy, as he had requested payment for the job as courier. Colgan asked Fr McLister to carry a message to Fr Fullerton of St Paul's in Belfast, to be passed on to the IRA adjutant general, Gearóid O'Sullivan. The message sent with Fr McLister stated that Farrell would be carrying a despatch concerning the tunnel and the escape plan.

The communication given to Farrell explained that the tunnel was complete, that approximately 100 men would escape on a particular night in the first week of August and that transport would be required.[10] On Wednesday 27 July, the British began digging a trench around the camp, at about 2 p.m., much to the amusement of the internees. A soldier had been digging at a certain point outside the barbed wire when he shouted to an officer, 'I can't dig any further, sir, there's a lot of wood here.' The officer immediately lifted an axe and smashed through the wood, exposing the tunnel.[11] There had been just enough time to recall the men who were at work in the tunnel.[12] At the time it was not known if Farrell had communicated the information in the despatch to his superiors or if the tunnel was discovered by coincidence, since there had been an underground escape from the Curragh camp a short time earlier.

British military engineers were called into the camp and there was great amazement as to how the tunnel had been constructed. They made a detailed inspection and eventually traced it back to Hut 2. The military mounted a raid on Hut 2 and all occupants were arrested and taken to the punishment cells. The tunnel was said to be about three and a half feet by four feet, extending from Hut 2 near the roadway, under the sentry's observation post, within a yard or two of a guardroom. It ran under the camp road to an adjoining field, under the hedge and rows of barbed wire to within a few yards of a potato field, which would have given the internees perfect cover. The military engineers believed the tunnel would only have needed another twelve hours' work to complete.[13]

The No. 1 compound commandant, Maurice Donegan, was summoned by the British commandants to answer questions about the tunnel. He was cross-examined by an array of officers, but said that he could not possibly know everything that went on in the compound and eventually the matter was dropped. The British engineers carried out a thorough inspection of the tunnel and detailed every part of it. They then dug a trench through the camp inserting metal spikes at regular intervals to prevent further attempts at tunnelling. They also introduced large searchlights that shone throughout the night and were so bright that the internees were unsure if it was night or day.[14]

The discovery of the tunnel was raised at a meeting of the British cabinet the following day, in a way which suggested that Farrell did in fact pass on the information to the camp military. An extract from the cabinet meeting memorandum stated:

On the 27th July in consequence of information received, a search was made at Ballykinlar Internment Camp and revealed the existence of a cleverly constructed tunnel some 215 feet long leading under both the obstacles surrounding the camp. This tunnel has been under construction for probably five to six weeks, and there is evidence to show that an escape of at least 20 of the most important internees was planned …

The memorandum also suggested that the release of Joseph McGrath some days earlier at the behest of republican leaders was to make arrangements for the escape:

> Evidence exists that Joseph McGrath, who was conveniently released at the insistence of the government on 24 July, has, since his release been in consultation with Michael Collins regarding the selection for escape by this tunnel, of those internees who would be most valuable to the IRA in the event of hostilities being recommenced.[15]

Despite the British military engineers' attempts to thwart further tunnelling, the internees in compound No. 1 discovered another secure route and started work almost immediately after the first was discovered. However, another tunnel was discovered under Hut 36 in No. 2 compound on Tuesday 27 September. The following day a large trench was dug at the rear of the chapel and adjoining huts. The military carried out extensive searches of all huts, throwing beds and bed boards out. The internees carried their beds back in, but the soldiers threw them out again. When ordered to carry the beds and bed boards back in again, the internees refused. The military shouted at the internees and some men were struck, which created tension. The following day the military returned to the huts and ripped up floorboards in G Line. They withheld all letters and parcels from the internees, and continued to do so until Thursday 3 November.[16]

The second tunnel was progressing well until Tuesday 15 November, when a military lorry, loaded with internees who had been granted parole that day, made its way out of the camp. It drove over the tunnel, collapsing its roof. Luckily no one was in the tunnel, but that was the final attempt at tunnelling out of No. 1 compound.

The incident came shortly after a shocking and high-profile incident in which Tadhg Barry was shot dead by a sentry.[17] Perhaps this subdued the British military's response, because they did not react as they had done over the discovery of the first two tunnels; in fact there was very little reaction at all. They discreetly repaired the road by filling the hole, while engineers were observed quietly tracing the direction of the tunnel.[18]

Despite the trench dug around the camp perimeter, the men of No. 2 compound discovered that it would be possible to construct a tunnel that would go under the British officers' mess, which was about twenty-five feet from the compound and on an elevation. They had been working on the project for a few weeks and were making great progress by the beginning of December 1921. No. 2 compound had an expert tunnel engineer, Michael Sheehy from County Offaly, who happened to be working in the shaft on Wednesday 7 December 1921 when he was handed a copy of the *Irish Independent* newspaper which carried details of the Treaty agreement between the Irish delegation and the British government. Sheehy read the terms of the Treaty and thought that it was no longer necessary to continue digging, as the internees would soon be released. A few days later the internees were informed that all the men were to be released as part of a Treaty amnesty and the tunnel was subsequently abandoned.[19]

According to one member of the British military, they had been on the lookout for signs of tunnels for many months prior to the discovery of the first tunnel in late July. When the camp was eventually evacuated in December 1921, the British carried out a thorough search of the huts and discovered that there were seven tunnels either in progress or abandoned.[20]

Cutting through the wires

In early October 1921 a group of internees in No. 2 compound decided to cut their way out through the wires. The plan was sanctioned by the No. 2 compound camp council, although some thought it not only dangerous, but foolish, as it relied on accurate timing, with the men having to cut their way out of the recreation or football field and make their way into the military quarters. The plan originated with Seán O'Riordan, County Waterford, and the others involved were Colm Lawless, Dublin, and Seamus Brennan, Jimmy Mahon and Michael Sheehy, all from County Offaly.[21] During Brennan's time at Ballykinlar he had been repeatedly summoned on jury service, but as he was a resident of the camp he was unable to attend and received a fine each time he failed to appear before the court. By October 1921 he had amassed fines amounting to £50 and the RIC had called at his residence to collect them. His family merely told the police to refer the matter to Ballykinlar camp for payment.[22]

On the day of the planned escape, Friday 7 October, a special football match was organised to facilitate it and the signal for the men to put their plan into action was the call for their evening meal. At that moment Seán O'Riordan dropped to the ground and snipped the wire. The men were shielded from the sentry posts by the other internees watching the game, who were told to ignore those cutting through the wire. By the time the five men got out of the field and into the lavatory connected to the military church, the other internees were ordered to leave and not to look in the direction of the escapees. This was at 5 p.m. and as they waited in the lavatory they could hear someone playing a harmonium and organ in the church. The men had planned to get into the church when it was safe and at night mingle with the British soldiers leaving the nearby cinema, and so pass by a sentry post. They timed this for 10 p.m., but as they crept along the ground a sergeant out walking his terrier came along. The dog started sniffing around where the men were lying motionless on the ground, but the sergeant, thinking his dog had discovered a rat, moved it away. Suddenly a group of soldiers walked past, but the men could not be seen in the shadows. O'Riordan and Sheehy decided not to follow the original plan, but instead cut their way into the compound at an old trench since they could crawl diagonally across and sever the wires at the other end.

O'Riordan had cut his way out and was on the outside lying face down on the ground when a British officer, Colonel Ennis, came along smoking a cigar. The men could smell the smoke of the cigar before they noticed the officer as he walked along and passed them. Sheehy cut the wire and passed through with O'Riordan now some distance ahead of him. The officer must have noticed or heard something, as he called out the guard just as Colm Lawless, who had followed O'Riordan and Sheehy, was cutting through the wire. One of the soldiers spotted Lawless and pushed his bayonet to his head but was reluctant to pull the trigger. Another soldier was standing on Michael Sheehy's sleeve and Sheehy said in a low voice, 'Don't shoot', which gave the soldier such a fright that he almost collapsed on top of him. Colonel Ennis told the escapees to get back into the camp: 'Go back into camp whatever men are behind the wire.'

'You might as well shoot them as order them to go back into camp,' said Michael Sheehy.

A soldier then asked, 'How many of you are there?'

'Five of us.'

The men were rounded up and taken to the intelligence officers' quarters where they were stripped naked and all personal possessions were confiscated. They had managed to dispose of all notes and their instructions before being rounded up, with some having eaten the paper. After an hour their clothes were returned and they were placed in the cells. The charge preferred against the five did not relate to the actual escape but with 'damaging his majesty's property' (cutting the wires). They got twenty-one days each in solitary confinement on a diet of bread and water.

While there Michael Sheehy was visited by a soldier attached to the King's African Rifles, who commended him: 'That was a great attempt to get out.' Sheehy, recognising the London accent, asked the man where he was from and was told north London. Sheehy was familiar with the area as he had spent some time studying there. The soldier then became friendly and said, 'I'll get you lads out of here. You made a damn good attempt to escape and we all have admiration for you because of it. I'll get you out.' He went on to say that if Sheehy watched on a certain night he would see him help two other men get out of the camp, and that he would get the five of them out the same way. Michael Sheehy told the others, who were delighted to hear the news.[23]

Walking out of the gate

The most daring escape attempt took place in mid-October 1921, the idea originating with the north London soldier who had spoken to Sheehy. He had previously suggested the plan to Patrick Colgan, who had been given two British military uniforms while he was staying in the camp hospital. One day when Maurice Donegan was visiting the hospital, Colgan asked him if the would be willing to escape dressed as a British soldier and explained how it would be done. Donegan considered it very dangerous, but when Colgan produced the uniforms he knew he was serious. There were no unit badges on the caps or markings on the uniforms and there were very few buttons on the tunics.

The day before the planned escape Maurice Donegan feigned

illness and was admitted to the camp hospital for treatment. On Sunday evening, 16 October, Colgan and Donegan made up dummies and put them in their hospital beds. They went to the isolation hut and donned the shabby uniforms over their own clothes. When darkness fell they left the hospital hut and followed an officer and soldier out of the compound. They waited at the gates until they were let out; the inner gate was carefully locked by the guard before the second gate was opened for them. The few minutes felt like hours as they waited to be let through each gate, but the guard asked no questions and they found themselves walking down the road outside the compound. Maurice Donegan walked along towards the perimeter of the camp with Patrick Colgan following a few yards behind.

When Donegan rounded a corner a sentry challenged him but just at that moment an officer came along and Donegan saluted him and the two men said goodnight. This satisfied the curious sentry and Donegan walked on, but he was nervous as he did not know if Colgan, who was some distance behind him, would think of saluting the officer. He glanced back and to his relief Colgan saluted the officer as he passed.

When Donegan was a safe distance from the camp he waited for Colgan and they joined up with a number of soldiers going on local leave. They crossed to the village of Dundrum on a ferry and walked down the village street. To their surprise they met Sergeant Farrell, who was standing on the edge of a footpath. Farrell was fairly intoxicated, but recognised the two men. 'How did you get out?'

'We crawled under the wire,' said Maurice Donegan as he did not want to disclose the real method of escape.

They asked Farrell where they could get a car and he led them to Savages' garage where they were able to hire a car and driver. They made off in the direction of Dublin and discarded the uniforms along the road. They travelled through the night until they arrived at a point near Drogheda in County Louth where a military checkpoint had been set up. The military called on the car to halt and it was surrounded by a mixed party of military and RIC. Patrick Colgan was pulled out of the vehicle but Maurice Donegan tried to bluff by saying that he was a cattle dealer on his way to Holyhead for the morning boat.

One of the RIC said, 'Sure, you might as well give that up. We know who you are, all right.'

The two men were taken to a military barracks at Drogheda and were left on an open lorry overnight with a guard of four soldiers watching them. An officer came over to the lorry and said, 'Hard luck, Fitzpatrick you made a good try for it anyway.' The officer, Captain Mathiesson, a Scotsman who had been an intelligence officer at Ballykinlar, was a decent sort. He took the men and sentries over to the canteen and treated them to a drink. The next day Captain Mathiesson shook hands with them and said he hoped they would meet some time under happier circumstances. The pair were returned to camp the next day and put into solitary confinement for about six weeks. They were later taken to Belfast and tried by court-martial, being sentenced to six months' hard labour. They believed that they had been apprehended when Sergeant Farrell informed his superiors about the escape, a suspicion that was supported when an RIC constable at Belfast jail said, 'You were mad to think you could do it. You weren't gone an hour when the authorities knew all about it.'[24] At 9.15 p.m. on the night of the escape the military at the camp had searched the hospital looking for them and had also entered Hut 2 where Maurice Donegan had been staying.[25]

As it turned out, the suspicions about Farrell were well founded and confirmed during the Irish Civil War when the anti-Treaty IRA occupied the Four Courts in Dublin. In 1926 Leo Henderson told Patrick Colgan that they had found correspondence there from Farrell to the British demanding back pay for intelligence work while based at Ballykinlar camp.[26]

Following Maurice Donegan's escape and subsequent re-arrest, the role of No. 1 compound OC passed to his vice-commandant, Thomas Treacy from Kilkenny. One of his first actions as commandant was to write a letter that was smuggled out to *The Freeman's Journal*: 'On behalf of this camp I must thank you for the wide publicity you have given through the medium of your journal to the grievances of the prisoners. At the same time I must ask you for further space in order to bring under the notice of your readers some further facts and further actions of the English military, which have so far escaped public attention ... .' Here Treacy referred to the escape of Maurice Donegan and Patrick Colgan calling their re-arrest a 'breach of the Truce':

We looked on this arrest as a breach of the Truce, and endeavoured by wire and registered post to communicate with the Liaison officer for this area and also with the chief Liaison officer in Ireland. These communications were held up by the intelligence officer here. Consequently we are anxious to publish the facts in order, firstly, to see if it were possible to obtain the release of these men and secondly to see if a junior officer of the British Army is entitled to seize correspondence addressed to the chief Liaison officer while the Truce is in being. Of course, the only reason why we mention this arrest is because it took place away from this area.

Treacy also highlighted that since the Truce the British military in the camp had become more aggressive in their endeavours to break the men in the camp:

Here we have had three months bitter experience of the fact that a truce does not improve things in prison camp as it releases more soldiers and consequently enables them to practice brutalities and keep their 'hands in' on unarmed prisoners. The point has about been reached when even unarmed prisoners must put up what fight they are capable of in order to rid themselves of intolerable conditions, as contracts between prisoners and their jailers are daily being dishonoured by the latter.[27]

Escape by 'bluff'

The British established an appeals process through an advisory committee in January 1921 to review the applications of persons who considered their internment as mistaken or unwarranted. Many who had no association with the IRA appealed to the advisory committee to have their internment orders overturned. Although initially all Volunteers were barred from applying to the committee, a decision was later taken to allow certain men to do so. These were usually those who held important roles in their areas, so their release was necessary to bolster the local war effort.

An application to the advisory committee for release, made by a member of the IRA, was considered a form of escape by 'bluff'. The individuals concerned were advised to have a watertight story and present what would be perceived as a genuine reason when making the initial application. The first step was to seek permission from the compound commandant and then fill out the necessary form.

Patrick O'Daly from Inchicore, Dublin, had been arrested in late November 1920 while staying at a house in Cecil Avenue, Clontarf. A member of the Squad, he had been involved in many operations and was responsible for killing many British personnel. He was not directly involved in the operations of Sunday 21 November, but was arrested afterwards. From the time of his arrest he denied any association with the IRA or Sinn Féin. His wife had died while he was a prisoner at Mountjoy in 1919 and he had four children, one of whom was staying at the house in Clontarf. A local RIC man, Dick McCarthy, who was one of Michael Collins' agents, vouched for O'Daly on another occasion shortly before his arrest.

O'Daly had been only a short time at Ballykinlar when he suggested to Frank Lawless that he was considering applying to the advisory committee to secure his release. Lawless advised against the idea as he thought that the military would make enquiries and that O'Daly would draw unnecessary attention to himself and could possibly be identified by someone. O'Daly was adamant that if enquires were only made in the Clontarf area he would be safe. He approached the compound OC, Leo Henderson, requesting permission to apply to the advisory committee to have his internment order reviewed. He experienced some difficulty in persuading Henderson and others, but told them that Michael Collins approved of the plan. While the compound staff were considering his request he applied to the advisory committee. A short time later, he was called before the committee, which consisted of Judge J. Doyle and two military officers. O'Daly told them of his personal tragedy and that he had four young children to look after. He was questioned about various aspects of his life, his employment, etc. and was then asked if he knew Michael Collins. He told the committee that he had never met him and said that he did not think Collins actually existed, that he was something akin to a banshee or a bogey man. Judge Doyle laughed and asked him why he said that. O'Daly said he never met anyone who could say he had met Collins. He even used the line that the British intelligence service was the best in the world and that if Collins did exist they would have easily captured him.

The advisory committee seemed convinced by O'Daly's story and on Sunday 20 February 1921 he was informed that he was to be released. He and six other men were set free. Two of O'Daly's friends, Dan Brophy and Paddy Sheehan, arranged to have a group inside the wire to jeer and shout abuse at him as he left the camp to give the impression that he was a traitor.

When O'Daly arrived back in Dublin two days later he met Michael Collins and related what he had told the advisory committee, whereupon Collins laughed heartily and told him that Judge Doyle was not a bad sort and he had been lucky to have him on the panel.[28]

As more and more men arrived in the camp the internees were updated on how the war was proceeding in the various counties. In late April 1921 word was received that the Volunteers in the Ballybofey area, County Donegal, had become almost inactive due to the large British presence and they were moving freely around that area at the time. A meeting of the Donegal internees and compound officers was convened to consider the appropriate candidate to apply for release to address the problem in Donegal. James McCarron, who was an officer in that brigade area, was selected as he had served with the British military in the 1914–18 war and received a pension. He had suffered a leg wound during that war and was the best candidate to persuade the advisory committee that he was of no use to the IRA or any threat to the British. McCarron made the request for release and easily convinced the committee.[29] He was granted release on condition that he report to the local RIC head constable and the local barracks every twenty-four hours. However, he did not report to the RIC in Ballybofey and instead returned to duty with the IRA. He formed a flying column in his area and set about increasing the war effort against the British there and in the surrounding areas.[30] McCarron was subsequently killed during an ambush on a British fishing party at Trusk Lough on the outskirts of Ballybofey in early June 1921.[31]

13

The Ballykinlar News-letters and Photography

Newsletters

The internees came from various professional backgrounds and many applied their knowledge and trades as best they could. Among them were a number of journalists. One such group in No. 1 compound started putting together a monthly newsletter, *Ná Bac Leis* ('Don't worry about it'), which was first produced by hand and circulated to the compound. Due to the time-consuming efforts of creating a handmade newsletter, only a small number were produced and had to be shared between the huts. Some time later they succeeded in getting a despatch out of the camp requesting the necessary items to produce a more professional publication. Art O'Donnell made contact with a friend in Dublin requesting a portable Corona Typewriter, a Roneo duplicator, a supply of stencils and duplicating paper. The requested items were acquired and sent to the camp in a large tea chest, but unfortunately arrived during one of the many disputes with the military when delivery of all letters and parcels was suspended. On this occasion, the post was held up at Tullmurry Station for almost two weeks, but this worked to the internees' advantage as the military censors had the job of sifting through over two weeks' worth of parcels and the sorting office was filled to capacity.

The internees working in the sorting office were informed about the special delivery containing the printing equipment and the importance of getting it delivered into the compound. The tea chest caught the attention of the censor, Captain Farrer, who ordered it to be opened and was very much intrigued by a bottle labelled 'lubricating oil'. He removed the bottle, deciding to open and smell the contents. The bottle smelled of whiskey and he ordered the box to be set aside for confiscation. He then continued to examine the parcels, occasionally glancing at the chest. When one of the internees saw that the captain was distracted, he removed the tea chest and smuggled it into the compound. Farrer only noticed the box was missing when the censoring process had been completed. He ordered a thorough search of the compound, but the contents had been concealed in a safe place by that time. Captain Farrer was obviously only concerned about the bottle of whiskey and, on the last night of the camp in December 1921, asked Art O'Donnell what became of it. O'Donnell told him that the men had drunk it.[1]

Ná Bac Leis was produced monthly and featured many articles, caricatures, story series, poetry, gardening notes, editorials and the results of football matches and other sports. Hugo McNeill was the artist and caricaturist, with Joseph Considine as editor.

Contributions were submitted by many of the internees, with various articles focusing on the events that occurred in the camp. Editions produced following the Truce in July 1921 contained extracts from the daily newspapers and there were many references to events around the country.

A copy of the newsletter was purchased by each hut for eight shillings and provided much-needed entertainment for the men. A similar newsletter, *The Barbed Wire*, was published in No. 2 compound, but due to the lack of equipment had to be painstakingly produced by hand each week. The newsletters carried a number of advertisements and other humorous and interesting anecdotes mostly concerned with camp life and activities. One advertisement carried in the August edition sought suitable persons for a pantomime. The advertisement read, 'Wanted – Principal boy and other well shaped ladies for panto. Send waist measurements to this office. Bring own tights unless prepared to wear macramé mantle border as substitute. – Apply to Box 1921.'

Other pieces were published to express the internees' appreciation of friends on the outside. The No. 2 compound library had been established in mid-January 1921 and an article was published to recognise the contributions made by various individuals and organisations in helping to set up that resource:

In the second week of January a library was opened in No. 2 camp with a 'Capital' of about 100 books presented by internees. Under the care of Dr. Michael Hayes, TD, the library grew up so well that there are now about 2,000 books on its shelves. To the Christian Brothers (Synge St., Dublin), University College Cork, The Society of Friends (Quakers), The Talbot Press Ltd, and individuals inside and outside the barbed wire the thanks of the reading-loving internees is [*sic*] due.[2]

The newsletters gave the intellectual and creative internees an outlet to pen articles, poetry, songs and gossip on life in Bally-kinlar. Joseph Considine, the editor of *Ná Bac Leis*, was also a regular contributor and his sonnets described many aspects of camp life. One sonnet was entitled 'Nabocleis' and went as follows:

When life in Camp seems filled with care,
And worries crowd you everywhere,
Be brave – give way not to despair, Nabocleis!

When laundry's done and hung to dry,
'Neath sunny morning's azure sky,
It rains in torrents bye and bye, Nabocleis!

When in a bout of football play,
You get a knock and bite the clay,
Keep cool – good temper wins the day, Nabocleis!

When named each day for Coal fatigue,
Through oversight or Hut intrigue,
You long to join the Looney League, Nabocleis!

When comes your turn for hot bath nice,
To banish dirt, disease and … other things,
You find the water cold as ice, Nabocleis!

When rowdy nights within your hut,
Forbid your weary eyes to shut,
If boot or trestle finds your 'nut', Nabocleis!

When things move slowly with the Peace,
Deferring hopes of quick release,
Take heart – your troubles soon shall cease, Nabocleis!

When racked with family cares outside,
Where loving wives and children bide,
Trust HIM who ever shall provide, Nabocleis![3]

There was much emphasis on presenting articles with a humorous slant to temporarily lift the spirits of the internees and the editorial of the first edition in September was written in a comical tone. The editorial predicted that the Ballykinlar newsletters would be received with great fanfare and the world press would sit up and take notice. The editorial read:

Dear Reader – Within the next few days there will be unparalleled excitement in the editorial sanctums of the world's press on the appearance of a new and brilliant luminary in the literary firmament – *Ná Bac Leis*.

The mission of our modest organ will be to provide light, wholesome reading for our little commonwealth. Our outlook will be broad and sympathetic. If at times individual idiosyncrasies are touched on in our columns the barbs of our shafts will have been sterilised in the front of our magnanimity and softened in the thurificating [*sic*] flame of our benevolence.

To ensure the correct atmosphere we have dispersed with printers' devils and all such demonical accessories of modern yellow journalism, and installed the Angel of Charity as the presiding genius of our enterprise. If our language in the editorial sanctum is sometimes of the crimson variety the kindly Angel blushingly turns his back knowing that stress of work and the permeating lethargy of camp life is enough to make even his less stern brethren weep. Well *Ná Bac Leis*.

Owing to the circumscribed nature of our surroundings, this, our first issue, will be necessarily limited and we have arranged for first aid parties to cope with accidents in the rush to procure copies. We seek no bloated profits and only wish that the expenditure of our humble energies will be repaid with 'Compound' interest. Do not smile, gentle reader, there is no occasion for levity and if we have trespassed beyond the bounds of PUN-ctilious editorial propriety, *Ná Bac Leis*. Our organ has come to brighten your lives and blight our own. – The Editor.[4]

The 'Chit-Chat' section of the inaugural issue of *Ná Bac Leis* was written by Joseph Considine, Dublin, and Seán O'Reilly, Armagh, and made a comical, yet serious, reference to the tunnel that had a short time earlier been discovered in No. 1 compound. It praised the efforts of the tunnellers and might even have been a cipher broadcasting a warning to the internees:

The tunnel revealed plenty of SAND in our Engineer Officers. Some of the enemy 'SANDYS' are only 'stick-in the muds'. Do we also possess a 'Judas'? Hard lines on the trolley-workers! It was a big under-taking. Even a 'miner' *issue* would have been a 'dig' at the foundations of British Rule.[5]

The aftermath of the tunnel discovery remained a comical topic in the columns of 'Chit-Chat'. The October edition of the newsletter carried the following observation on the British manoeuvres following the discovery of the tunnel:

Any men interested in the subject of Applied Intelligence and Detective Engineering should attend on 'A' line every forenoon, there will also be a matinee on odd days with full Company Reports of the performance are [*sic*] subject to the censors.

Come and see the human moles and ferrets in their Tunnel DIS-locating Act. The Strike continues. Nightly raids on the huts are expected ... In the course of military Operations in D line during the Strike the full enemy 'intelligence' and engineering staffs concentrated their attention on the floors in No. 1 Hut in search of the missing Tunnel. Some wag among the spectators outside gently closed the door and wedging it, 'bagged' the lot. It was a weighty capture physically and numerically, but mentally there was nothing in it.

The plight of the imprisoned ones was pitiful. There was no means of egress though we are informed that one of the ferrets escaped through the stove-pipe and alarmed the guard outside the wires who came in with fixed bayonets at the double and released the captives.

The silly appearance of the officers in their blundering situation was highly amusing and they made for the exit of the cage thoroughly dejected amid the bantering cheers of their late captors and the sly grimaces of their own armed guard. Absent minded Beggars after all.

The impending peace negotiations between the Irish and British delegations were ever present in the minds of the internees and also appeared in the 'Chit-Chat' columns. 'On turning up the Editorial Calendar for October 11th the date fixed for the conference, we find the apt Shakespearian quotation: "As the sun breaks through the darkest clouds, so honour peereth in the meanest habit".'[6]

By November the negotiations were causing great anticipation among the internees about the future of the camp and that month's edition of *Ná Bac Leis* carried a number of articles relating to the release of the internees. The front page carried the following: 'Since the Conference began the anxious waiting for news of its deliberations has produced a new disease in the camp. Though the trouble is mental rather than physical it has been paradoxically diagnosed as BALLYKINLAR HALT, and the symptoms will entirely disappear with the opening of the Gates and the first rush for the STATION.'[7]

Among the internees were a number of men who would come to prominence in later years in various walks of Irish life, including Peadar Kearney, famed for penning the words of 'The Soldier's Song'. During his time at Ballykinlar, Kearney composed many songs with one, 'O Loydy George' about life in the camp, being published in *Ná Bac Leis*:

O Loydy George

My name is John Fitzwilliam Smith,
I come from Inchicore,
I was always brave and bold,
When down the Circular Road I strolled,
But now alas! My rambling days are o'er,
For the bull dogs came one wintry night,
And dragged me off in a terrible fright
And landed me here an awful sight,
On Ballykinlar shore.

Chorus:
I'm one of the curfew birds, I'm an Internee,
O! Loydy, Loydy George,
See what you've done for me.
You started out to buy a dog,
And only got a pup,
O! Loydy Loydy George,
See what you've rounded up.

You should see me cutting it fine,
Along the Esplanade,
Whenever I had a bob to spare,
If you were in Bray you'd find me there,
But now alas! I'm very much afraid,
I'll spend the rest of my life instead
Gobbling spuds that feel like lead,
And spreading the Margo on my bread,
Disguised with marmalade. (*Chorus*)

The Susans and the Mary Janes,
May fade away and die,
They'll be all old maids I see,
If they sit on the bench to wait for me,
For now alas! They'll never see me more,
I'll be here to the end of my days I know,
Carrying buckets to and fro,
And I'll go where martyrs go,
On Ballykinlar shore. (*Chorus*)

Some articles were about the history of the country and the on-going war, some about fallen comrades, but an article by an internee arrested in London and transported to Ballykinlar gave an interesting depiction of the camp life and the surrounding landscape. Entitled 'The Mountains of Mourne', it was written by Emmet Fox:

Those of us who are in Ballykinlar have at least one advantage over our comrades at the Curragh and elsewhere – The Mountains of Mourne Sweep Down to the Sea. To the men behind the barbed wire the greatest of all hardships is the simple sheer monotony. To the Irish mind in particular, so much more alert and active perhaps than any other in the White Race, pure monotony can become more painful than any mere physical suffering. But as long as there is a range of mountains within view, it is always easy to escape, for a few seconds at least, from wind, sand and corrugated iron.

The Mourne range are never the same for half an hour at a time. Under the endless play of light and shade the aspect of

Slieve Donard changes like the expression on a human face. Thus it becomes possible to conceive how primitive peoples are led to personify and worship natural objects, and we ourselves come to have a natural sympathy for, and even a vague understanding of, some of the lost secrets of the old mythologies that remain mere childish nonsense to the city dweller.

It is easy, of course, to say that the prisoners should overcome the monotony by concentrating their minds on study, but one cannot study all day long and every single factor in the life of an internment camp is hostile to any study at all. Privacy and quiet are both essential for many people if any mental work is to be done and both are out of the question in the 'cage', perhaps fortunately. Above all, the uncertainty of tenure that hangs over the head of an internee, kidnapped without charge and imprisoned without trial, liable to be released at any moment on the throw of the dice at Westminster, makes any fixed programme impossible for all but the most Spartan. If a man knew that he was to be in for six months or two years or any other definite period he could lay his plans accordingly and settle down. As it is the thing is hardly to be done. Needless to say those who devote their whole time to the service of the rest of us are the happiest men in the camp.

Nevertheless, it takes a good deal to depress an Irishman and we do pretty well all things considered. We know that the ocean is there, although we see it only as a faint blue streak and we sometimes hear the roar of the waves at night (when neighbouring huts are behaving themselves). When we are tired of carving frames or knotting 'crammey' inside or tramping round and round the compound, we can look up at the mountains again.

Fifteen hundred years ago Saint Donnaght used to say Mass on the summit. With a good glass he could have made out the site of our own altar without any trouble: and at a date so remote that it would make the Saint appear modern to us, our ancestors had a Druidical temple there and worshipped the Dawn and the Elements. We can still see the remains of the Trigonometrical Station erected by the foreign occupation in the early nineteenth century, but it is now obsolete and fallen into ruin – not a bad symbol of the British authority itself.[8]

Joseph Considine gave his last editorial in the November edition of the No. 1 compound newsletter, which was published shortly after the death of Tadhg Barry and described the feelings of the men in the camp:

Dear Readers,

We have great pleasure in noting the growing appreciation among our numerous readers of our modest efforts to furnish in our columns themes of varied interest to all. The demand for our last issue far exceeded the supply though we used up all available paper in the endeavour to meet it. Hence the delay in issuing the present number.

Since our last going to Press there have been many changes in camp. Our commandant and ex-commandant are now in close captivity as a consequence of their plucky effort to regain their liberty.

The gloom of the recent tragedy in our midst still lowers over the two camps. We had already gone to press when the appalling crime was committed and have but very limited space to refer to it.

The flitting of such a heroic spirit as poor Tadhg Barry is a severe blow to the Nation and we heartily condole with his relatives in their heart-rending anguish. Our unbounded sympathy also goes out to his immediate friends and to his gallant comrades in camp 2.

We note in the columns of a Daily Contemporary that *Ná Bac Leis* had been paid a high tribute by the Enemy – it has been proscribed as 'Seditious'. We are grateful for the high honour and needless to say our future numbers will live up to the glorious commendation. – The Editor.[9]

The editorial team of *Ná Bac Leis* received much correspondence from the internees and many topics and queries were addressed in the portion 'Answers to Correspondence'. For example, 'Anxious' wrote: 'Can you please let me know when the camp will close?' The reply read: 'Your query is unique. The chief anxiety seems to be when it will open. As to when we shall get out I have only inside information but shall endeavour to get some outside and will give you the full "inns" and "outs" of the case in our January issue. Meanwhile keep your feet warm and your head cool – if you can in the present miserable weather.'

An irate internee took issue with the choice of wording used by the Ballykinlar drama committee in a concert held in mid-October. Using the initials 'J. D.' he wrote, 'What was the idea in calling Sunday night's entertainment the "First" Farewell Concert. I always associated the word "Last" with farewells. Also was it a coincidence that "The Rising of the Moon" was performed a few hours before the Eclipse of that

Luminary?' The typical witty response read, 'We shall consult our astronomical expert as to whether the one phenomenon produced the other or vice versa.'

There was other correspondence from internees' reminiscing about life before their incarceration. 'Nature Lover' wrote, 'There were some glorious sunsets during the past summer but they pale into insignificance before one I beheld in 1913 when Guinness was three pence a bottle.' The response was, 'You are indeed cruel in your reminders. Yet I am told that equally beautiful sky tints are to be observed in camp when camouflaged Bovril arrived.'[10]

The 'Gardening and other notes' section was written by Daniel Hogan, Dublin and Tipperary, and offered some peculiar advice for those interested in gardening. This section was very much a tongue-in-cheek column and was obviously written to lighten the mood for the men. The following is a selection of the column contents: 'The man who talks about what his forefathers did is like a potato – The best of it is underground.' 'Although the soil in Ballykinlar is poor, yet a good crop of time is put in.' 'Why is the potato like an oculist? Because its very existence is made up of eyes.' 'Emulate the cucumber – keep cool.' 'If you want cowslips in winter – drive cattle on ice.' 'Never sow seeds of dissension.'[11]

The November edition of *Ná Bac Leis* was to be the last, as the camp closed a few weeks later. The internees who were released unconditionally or on parole before the general release usually took copies of the newsletters as souvenirs with them. However, the British military classed the periodical as seditious material and confiscated them if found.

Photography

The focus for many internees was the collection of souvenirs of their time at the camp. Many men acquired autograph books and had their fellow hut members and friends inscribe them with personal messages, poetry and artwork. One internee thought that the ultimate souvenir would be a photograph of each hut group. However, the strict military rules prohibited certain items, including cameras, from being sent into the camp. Frank McKay from Dublin gave considerable thought as to how a camera could be sent in and, just as important, how he could get a letter past the censor requesting it. A cryptic message was eventually sent to a friend in Dublin and before long a large home-made cake arrived in the camp. The small, fold-up camera was cleverly placed inside and escaped the censor's knife when he cut the confectionery into slices to determine if there were any forbidden ingredients inside. It was delivered to McKay in Hut 14. The films arrived soon after hidden in parcels of tea and sugar. The chemicals required for developing the films were to be found and sometimes manufactured in the chemist's laboratory attached to the hospital. As many of the huts were without lights the darkroom was easily created and the films were usually developed at night.

Photographs were taken of the members of the various huts, the No. 1 compound chaplain, Fr McLister, and different groups including the violin orchestra, camp staff and the football teams. As the compound was often patrolled, the group photos required a cordon of men to give cover for the photographer and were usually taken in a corner out of view of the sentry boxes. A number of scouts were usually posted near the photo shoots to give warning should the military enter the compound. On a number of occasions, a military officer would enter the compound unnoticed and the large gathering of internees would heighten his curiosity. The sudden appearance of the officer would lead to someone giving an impromptu lecture on history or the Irish language, allowing the photographer an opportunity to escape.

The negatives were hidden, and due to the constant searches for contraband, some had to be destroyed in the hut stove, but many were smuggled out.[12]

The internees in the No. 2 compound also managed to have a camera smuggled in, but it was discovered as the remains of John O'Sullivan were being removed from the camp in early May 1921. Unfortunately, the only photographs that survived were of the No. 1 compound and its inhabitants.[13]

14

Ballykinlar and the 1921 Elections

The 1921 general election in Ireland was the first time that the people exercised their franchise in favour of candidates in two separate jurisdictions. This election was the prelude to the establishment of two separate parliaments in Ireland – one in Dublin and the other in Belfast, or one nationalist and one unionist respectively, under the Government of Ireland Act 1920.

Despite the on-going hostilities in the country, the Government of Ireland Act came into being on 23 December 1920 and divided Ireland into two separate political entities. It provided for 'a Parliament to be called the Parliament of Southern Ireland ... and there shall be established in Ulster (hereinafter referred to as Northern Ireland) a Parliament to be called the Parliament of Northern Ireland ... ' Section 2 of the Act contained the naïve aspiration that the two parliaments and governments would work in harmony relating to matters affecting the whole of Ireland.[1] Whether this was the true belief of the

British government or merely an appeasement to those taking an interest in Irish affairs, it was wishful thinking.

In his speech for the Prorogation of Parliament in December 1920, the British King, George V, announced:

> I have given my assent to a Bill for the better government of Ireland. This Act, by setting up two Parliaments and a Council of Ireland gives self-government in Irish affairs to the whole of Ireland, and provides the means whereby the people of Ireland can of their own accord achieve unity ...[2]

The Government of Ireland Act was in its most blatant outward appearance a pacifier to the unionists of the six north-eastern counties who vowed to oppose the introduction of Home Rule by the use of violence, setting up the Ulster Volunteer Force in 1913 for this purpose. This led to the widespread introduction of the gun into Irish political affairs in April 1914.

The elections were scheduled for Tuesday 24 May and the deadline for nominations was Friday 13 May 1921.[3] Ballykinlar internment camp housed sixteen Sinn Féin candidates, six of whom (John Walsh, Derry; Seán Dolan, Queen's University, Belfast; Seán Milroy, Tyrone and Fermanagh; Pat Lavery, Down; Denis McCullough, West Belfast and Louis J. Walsh, Antrim) represented some of the constituencies under the new north-eastern counties jurisdiction.[4]

In the early election preparations, close scrutiny was focused on County Antrim, where it was considered that there was the possibility of returning at least one anti-partitionist or Sinn

Féin candidate. The candidate, Louis J. Walsh, gave his address as Hut 19, No. 1 compound, Ballykinlar camp. Walsh was a native of Ballycastle, County Antrim, and had been living in Maghera, County Derry, at the time of his arrest in December 1920. He had previously been elected to the Antrim County Council for the Ballymoney electoral area in 1920. In early May, Walsh's election agent posted the necessary election forms to Ballykinlar for him to sign and return. A few days later, on Monday 10 May 1921, a military sergeant walked into Hut 19 and shouted, 'Pack up, Walsh and be at the entrance gate in ten minutes!' Louis Walsh was not sure if he was being released on parole or unconditionally. All election candidates then in Ballykinlar camp had made formal requests for parole. When Walsh reported to the front gate he was brought before Colonel Ennis who informed him that he was being unconditionally released and that he was the only candidate in the impending elections to be released.[5] The majority of the Sinn Féin election agents were 'on the run' and many of the candidates were either in internment camps, prisons or also 'on the run'. There were very few Sinn Féin candidates addressing the electorate from platforms anywhere in the country.

Another issue of the 1921 general election was the eligibility of the internees to exercise their franchise, particularly those from the constituencies of the six north-eastern counties, given that they were being held at Ballykinlar. There were over 100 internees from these counties and public opinion was that these men should be given the opportunity to vote, considering the efforts made during the 1918 election and several subsequent by-elections, to allow British soldiers to exercise their right to vote even though they were serving abroad.[6] However, the opportunity for any of the internees to exercise their franchise did not materialise. The polling for the election was held on Tuesday 24 May, but as none of the nominations in the twenty-six counties was contested by any other than 128 Sinn Féin and the four Trinity College candidates, all were returned unopposed.

The results of the election for the new parliament in Belfast set the scene for future hostilities, establishing a unionist-dominated political system with six nationalist and forty-four unionist candidates returned to constituencies in the six north-eastern constituencies. Seán Milroy was elected to two constituencies: Tyrone/Fermanagh and Cavan. None of the Sinn Féin TDs recognised the partitionist parliament in Belfast, and opted to represent their constituencies through the second Dáil. The four Independent Unionists elected under the Trinity College or Dublin University constituency sat in the new parliament in Belfast.[7]

The elections for the second Dáil resulted in the return of fifteen internees: Seán Nolan, Cork; Joseph O'Doherty, Donegal; Joseph McGrath, James Derham and Frank Lawless, Dublin; Seán Milroy, Tyrone/Fermanagh and Cavan; P. J. Hogan, Galway; Fionán Lynch, Kerry; Joseph P. Lynch, Laois and Offaly; Dr Richard Hayes, Limerick City and East Limerick; Joseph McGuinness, Longford and Westmeath; William Sears, South Mayo and Roscommon; Seamus Doyle, Wexford; Dr Michael Hayes, National University of Ireland, and Éamonn O'Dea, Waterford and Tipperary.[8]

The new 'Northern Ireland' parliament was officially opened by George V at Belfast City Hall. During his speech at the opening on Wednesday 22 June 1921, the King appealed for peace:

> I speak from a full heart when I pray that my coming to Ireland today may prove to be the first step towards the end of strife among her people, whatever their race or creed. In that hope I appeal to all Irishmen to pause, to stretch out the hand of forbearance and conciliation, to forgive and forget, and to join in making for the land they love a new era of peace, contentment and goodwill ...[9]

For its first decade the new northern parliament met at the Presbyterian College close to City Hall as the new parliamentary building was being constructed at Stormont in east Belfast.

15

The IRA and British Truce – July 1921

The Truce was announced on Monday 11 July 1921 and the internees believed that they would be released soon after: however, that hope faded as the weeks and months passed. By late July public feeling was reflecting manifest uneasiness over the delay in releasing those who were held without charge or trial.

Despite the Truce, the British secretary of state for war, Winston Churchill, pressed ahead with arrangements to house additional numbers of internees. In a memorandum to the British cabinet on 20 July 1921 he stated that a number of empty prisons in Britain, including Derby, Wakefield, Warwick, Reading, Devizes, Chelmsford and Lewes, had been identified as possible accommodation for up to 2,600 additional internees from Ireland. Under these circumstances, the military would have been charged with maintenance, guarding and provision of equipment. Churchill also suggested that the British Admiralty should be tasked with sharing responsibility for the accommodation, administration and custody of internees, and said that the Admiralty would take charge of 2,000 internees at Scapa in northern Scotland. Osea Island in eastern England was also suggested as a possible location for an estimated 600 internees.[1]

Stories of ill-treatment in the different camps were beginning to have an undesirable effect on the general feeling of goodwill following the Truce announcement. There had been trouble in all internment camps: Rath Camp at the Curragh, Bere Island, Spike Island in Cork and Ballykinlar, which was manifested in passive resistance, demands to be treated as prisoners of war and hunger strikes. The lack of public inspections added to the frustrations both inside and outside the camps. Only one press inspection had been permitted with one journalist from England and one from America being given access to Ballykinlar camp in the earlier part of the year. However, the correspondents were compelled to submit their reports to the military before publication to prevent the true conditions of the camp becoming known to the general public in Ireland and abroad.[2]

Following the Truce the first requests for early release received by the advisory committee were from the fourteen members of Dáil Éireann who were being held at Ballykinlar. The first TD to be released on parole, Sunday 24 July, was Joseph McGrath, TD for the St James's constituency in Dublin.[3] The first internee to be unconditionally released post-Truce was Denis Costello from County Tipperary. In August Patrick Brett, a county councillor in Westmeath, was released after a nine-month internment. At a homecoming celebration in Mullingar he stated that the severest trial the country had ever had to endure had passed, and that the heel of the oppressor would soon be lifted once and for all from the neck of the Irish nation.[4]

The British sanctioned the release of all TDs in early August to enable them to attend a meeting of Dáil Éireann on 16 August 1921 and all but one of the TDs in Ballykinlar were released.[5] The British cabinet memorandum for the week ending 8 August 1921 stated that the goodwill generated by release of all TDs was overshadowed by their refusal to release Seán MacEoin, TD for Longford-Westmeath. MacEoin had been sentenced to death for killing an RIC Inspector. The British cabinet memorandum stated:

The good effect upon public opinion of the decision to release all members of Dáil Éireann in crown custody (in order that they might be free to attend the meeting of Dáil Éireann summoned for the 16th August) was almost completely eclipsed by an amazing public outcry against the part of the decision, which precluded the release of one member, John McKeon [sic], who had been convicted of murder. McKeon, by reason of a striking personality, by certain acts of consideration towards members of British forces who, after fighting, had fallen into his power, and by a dramatic speech from the dock when he was sentenced – all of which matters have been fully advertised by Sinn Féin propaganda – had attained a remarkable place in Sinn Féin esteem ...[6]

Due to pressure, the British military began granting parole requests and, in some cases, early release, on a phased basis. Up to 20 August 1921, seventy-two internees, excluding the members of Dáil Éireann, were released.[7]

Henry Dixon was released on Monday 19 September after almost twelve months in Ballykinlar camp. He had been one of the most prominent supporters of Charles Stewart Parnell in Dublin at the time of the split in the rank of the Irish Parliamentary Party in 1890. He was also one of the principal organisers in establishing the annual pilgrimage to the tomb of Theobald Wolfe Tone at Bodenstown. Seán O'Dea, Waterford, was released on parole on the same day so that he could attend an examination at the National University's medical faculty.[8]

The Truce period releases provided the general population with an insight into the conditions of the internment camps. Louis Walsh had been arrested in December 1920, arriving at Ballykinlar in early January 1921. He was released in May 1921 and began writing a book mostly based on his experiences in Ballykinlar. In September *On My Keeping and in Theirs: A record of experiences 'on the run', in Derry Gaol, and in Ballykinlar Internment Camp* was published. When the internees received copies of the book, they were not impressed by the disclosures and believed that it was giving inside information to the British military. Those in the No. 2 compound showed their resentment by holding a ceremony in the centre of the compound and burning their copy.[9]

Many of the men who were released or paroled gave interviews to the press, while men who were still interned had letters smuggled out, many of which were passed on to *The Freeman's Journal* and subsequently published. A letter by Hugh Bradley, Belfast, described the mental torture meted out by the British military and how it affected the internees:

> At night we can't get sleeping. The military have 'dug-outs' below each hut and these are filled with soldiers who keep quiet and spy on us until we are about to sleep and then they begin bawling. We are subjected to all kinds of insults and our patience is being tried sorely. The cells, like the hospital are filled up. The least thing is an offence and penalties ranging from three days to fourteen days bread and water are being inflicted unscrupulously.[10]

The release of internees on parole in the months following the Truce took many men by surprise as they themselves had not requested it. A military sergeant would enter the compound and call out the name or names of internees and order them to the guardroom. There they would be informed of their unconditional release and ordered to collect their belongings. When they returned, they were subjected to a thorough search that included their boots and socks. Their clothes were also rummaged through despite their protests. Some were treated very roughly and one man had his clothes violently removed when he refused to be searched. He was taking the newsletter *Ná Bac Leis* home as a souvenir, but it was confiscated by the military as a seditious document. The letters published in the press may have been the reason for the intrusive and thorough searches of all men thereafter.[11]

The parole process was callous: when men were gravely ill or when the close relative of an internee was seriously ill or had died, parole could still be refused. Denis McCullough, Belfast, was thirty-eight years old and had been very ill for several months. When in late September 1921 his condition deteriorated he applied for parole, but the request was refused. His condition was considered so serious by the internees' doctors and commandant, that a telegram was sent to his wife, but when she arrived at the camp she was refused admittance.[12]

The following month Michael Bradley from Dunmanway, Cork, received word that his mother was seriously ill, and applied for parole to visit her, enclosing a medical certificate about her health. The application was refused and his mother subsequently died on Wednesday 5 October. He applied for release on parole and on Friday 7 October he was informed that as his mother had been buried that day his release could not be recommended.[13]

On the afternoon of Monday 17 October, Liam Sheridan, a County Meath internee, was informed that he was being unconditionally released. He had not made any formal request for parole and was surprised. He had been interned at Ballykinlar for almost ten months following his arrest on Sunday 7 December 1920. His journey home was long, as, having walked the three miles to Tullmurry Station, he discovered that the last train had already left. He was then forced to make his way to Newry by car and then on to Dundalk where he caught a train to Dublin. On arrival at his home in Drumlerry, Oldcastle, County Meath, a reporter from the *Meath Chronicle* interviewed him. Sheridan said his health was good, but on describing the camp said the food was insufficient and that sand and dust were mixed with all meals and men had often had to tie handkerchiefs over their eyes to save them from the sand. He also said that they were subjected to very cruel treatment from time to time.[14]

Another example of the callousness of the parole system was exemplified by the case of two internees whose eyesight had deteriorated to the extent that they faced blindness. Joseph Clarke, Dublin, and J. Tully, Cavan, both suffered eye infections from the effects of the sandstorms at Ballykinlar. Their condition could not be properly treated in the poorly equipped camp hospital. Their plight was reported by the camp doctors to the military medical officers and the men made formal requests for parole to travel to Dublin where they would receive the appropriate treatment, but their requests were refused.[15]

Some of the internees gave detailed interviews to journalists from national newspapers. In an interview for *The Freeman's Journal*, two men released in mid-November described conditions in the camp as being calculated to depress the internees: 'One of them expressed the view that no other nation could produce a body of men capable of enduring the hardships to which the internees in Ballykinlar are subjected.' The article also referred to the detrimental effects of the unpredictable weather: 'During the past fortnight sandstorms in the camp had been frequent, while one could almost row a boat in parts of the compound. The sand told upon the eyesight of the internees and many were wearing glasses.' Despite the change in atmosphere on the outside following the Truce, the military in the camp showed little sign of recognising the peace: 'The attitude of their guards is still one of the principal causes of complaint on the part of the men. Rev. Father Burbage, who is interned and acts as chaplain was threatened last week, and other incidents of a similar character were mentioned by the men interviewed.'[16]

The military night patrols became more aggressive, engaging in a campaign of looting internees' property. The looting began on Thursday 6 October, when the canteen and boot stores were raided and a number of items were stolen including razors, shorts, socks, tobacco, cigarettes and small personal belongings. This incident was reported to the British commandant the following morning, but it is not known what, if any, action was taken. On the night of Friday 7 October the canteen was again raided and more items were stolen including toothbrushes. Again this was reported to the British commandant the following morning. On Saturday 8 October the night patrol turned its attention to the huts and everything near the open windows was stolen. The British commandant's response to the thefts was that he would not be responsible for any article which was not under lock and key at night. This implied that the thieves would not be punished and that their actions were somehow legitimised.[17] The *Irish Bulletin* of Thursday 13 October published a series of extracts from statements smuggled out of the camp. In one, Jack Fitzgerald, Kildare, complained of the disappearance of parcels, postal orders, clothing hanging out in the compound, foodstuffs, razors and many other items.[18]

In October 1921 the Truce had been in place for over three

months and the continued incarceration began to unsettle the peace. An Irish delegation travelled to London in early October to begin treaty negotiations with the British government, and there was great anticipation in Ireland that, as part of the early negotiations, the Irish delegation would request the immediate release of all untried and unconvicted men from the internment camps and other centres of detention. The Irish expressed the opinion that the release of the internees would be an immense help in easing the tensions between the two sides, but the British believed that their release at that time would be prejudicial in the event of the negotiations failing to reach a permanent and successful conclusion. In other words, if the talks failed the British did not wish to have to deal with the possibility of several thousand additional men rejoining the ranks of the IRA.

The issue of ill-treatment in jails and internment camps arose at the early sessions of the negotiations and it was agreed that a joint Irish and British body be established to enquire into the complaints. The Irish representative on the Prisons and Camps Inspection Committee was Commandant Michael Staines. The news was announced in an official communiqué issued in Dublin on Saturday 15 October: 'The Irish and British representatives have agreed to the constitution of a joint visiting body for all camps and prisons. As this body will investigate the conditions it is considered advisable that further action in the prisons should be deferred for the moment.'[19]

Throughout October 1921 resolutions were passed by county councils, urban councils, boards of guardians and many other public bodies, all calling for the immediate release of internees. Carlow County Council raised the plight of the internees at their October meeting. Councillor Michael Governey said that no matter how much Lloyd George had been the political trickster in the past, it was unthinkable that he would go down in posterity with another betrayal to his credit. A resolution on the motion of Councillor Brophy demanding the immediate release of the internees was unanimously passed.

At Westmeath County Council, on a motion by Councillor O'Reilly seconded by Councillor O'Brien, the members protested 'against the continued detention in jails and internment camps of thousands of Irishmen and women'. The council called on the Irish delegation to cease negotiations with the British until all internees were released. Longford Urban Council also passed a resolution, on the motion of John Murray, demanding the liberation of all internees and prisoners.[20]

The following institutions passed similar resolutions:

- Borough Councils: Cork, Limerick, Clonmel and Kilkenny.

- County Councils: Galway, Waterford, Roscommon, Wexford, Westmeath and Carlow.

- District Councils: Rathdrum, Killarney, Mullingar, Roscrea, Croom (Limerick), Carrick-on-Shannon and Youghal (No. 2).

- Board of Guardians: Pembroke (Dublin), Killarney, Thurles, New Ross, Longford, Carrick-on-Shannon, Listowel, Baileboro and Youghal.

Other bodies that demanded the release of internees and prisoners were the Irish Dominion League, Cork County and City Land and Harbour Health Assurance Society, Ennis Trades Council, Cork Tied Vintners Association, Offaly County Homes and Hospital Committee, the Committee of Management of Leix Mental Hospital, Cavan County Home Committee and Cork Insurance officials.[21]

At a special meeting of Louth County Council held in Dundalk, a resolution was adopted demanding the release of the political prisoners detained in internment camps and jails. The motion, moved by P. Butterly, focused on the claim by the British government of their desire for peace. Introducing the motion Butterly said, 'Their acts are not in keeping with their professed sentiments, and an atmosphere of peace cannot be created while thousands of internees are suffering unjustly.' Louth County Council called on Dáil Éireann to withdraw the delegation to the Peace Conference in London until unconditional freedom was given to all prisoners. Councillor Patrick McGee suggested that it was not admissible to request the withdrawal of the Peace delegates, but the resolution was passed.[22]

In late November a journalist from the *Irish Independent* met a group of new parolees at a hotel in Newcastle, County Down, and reported that some of them showed signs of a hurried grooming while the others were dressed as they had been while in the camp, with rough, ill-fitting clothes. The journalist noticed that the released men were not entirely at ease with even the basic items of everyday life. One man sitting at the table let a cup slip so it rattled the saucer. He said, 'It is easy to see that I haven't had a cup in my hand for some time. At the camp I drink my tea out of a jam pot and eat my dinner off the lid of an "N.K.M. Toffee Box"'. (N.K.M. was a Kerry-based company manufacturing confectionery items.) The journalist accompanied the men to Dublin and listened to their stories of camp life. One tale concerned the Dublin internee bestowed with the honour of 'mayor of Ballykinlar', who had presented the Mons Star to the man awarded the medal while being held. The journalist recognised the irony of the award – when the internee received the decoration he was still suffering for 'the rights of small nations' in Ballykinlar camp. The men also reported that on his release the 'mayor' wore his mayoral robes and chain of office: the reddish military blanket and his mayoral chain, made of barbed wire.

There was a touching scene when the train arrived at Drogheda and the internees were bidding farewell to their comrades travelling on to Dublin. As one of the released men stood at the carriage door a young girl approached him enquiring if he knew a particular individual in No. 2 compound. 'I do and well he's looking, as you will see if you turn round.' The girl turned around, gasped, looked at the young man for a brief moment and sobbed before embracing him. One of the other men whispered into his ear and the man said in a loud voice, 'No. She's not. She's my sister,' and the other men smiled. The train then carried on to Amiens Street Station in Dublin where the journalist and the released men parted company.[23]

16

The Murder
of Tadhg Barry

On the morning of Tuesday 15 November, the internees received news from the British camp commandant, Colonel Browne, that he had been given permission to release thirty internees on parole: fifteen from each compound. There was great excitement as the names were called out and the men were informed that they would be taken by lorry to the Tullmurry Railway Station later that day.[1] However, unknown to the internees the goodwill gesture was to coincide with a visit from the Prisons and Camps Inspection Committee. The joint Irish-English commission was established as part of the negotiations in London and was charged with the investigation of complaints of maltreatment in jails and internment camps.[2] Commandant Michael Staines was the IRA representative and chief liaison officer on the committee, which arrived at Ballykinlar that morning at approximately 11 a.m. and was given a selective and limited tour of the camp, ensuring very little contact with the internees. At the conclusion of the inspection the committee was taken to the British commandant's office for refreshments and further discussions about the camp. This was at approximately 2.30 p.m., and at the same time two lorries arrived in the camp to transfer the paroled internees to Tullmurry Railway Station.[3]

Commandant Michael Staines was standing in the British commandant's office looking out the window when he saw one of the lorries drive into what looked like a large hole in the road. He heard one of the British officers remark, 'Another tunnel.' They went out to inspect the scene.

In the No. 2 compound a group of men had gathered near the gate approximately two yards from the wire to wave goodbye to their comrades. They included Seán D. MacLochlainn, Donegal, Con O'Halloran, Clare, and Tadhg Barry, Cork. Staines was talking to a number of internees as he passed the compound and Barry gestured that he wanted to speak to him.[4] He was standing on top of an upturned bucket to see over the galvanised iron fence which lay between him and the lorries. Barry was giving a parting salute when an eighteen-year-old soldier called Barrett, manning a sentry box some twelve yards away, shouted at the group to get back from the wire. The men did not think they were too close and refused to move. Barry said, 'If one of us got shot while the liaison officer is in the spot it may be the means of putting an end to the camp.'[5] One of the other internees repeated what the sentry had shouted and Barry said, 'I am coming down.'[6] He had barely uttered the words when the sentry raised his rifle and took aim, first at MacLochlainn and then, moving his aim, at Barry. He fired and hit Barry in the chest, killing him instantly.

At the same time Maurice Horgan was waving to the parolees from the roof of the washhouse in No. 1 and could see the internees gathered at the gate to No. 2. He heard the shot and saw Tadhg Barry clutch his chest and fall to the ground.[7] Barry had been hit in the heart, the bullet passing through his body and ricocheting off the ground and lodging in the hut used to censor the mail.[8] The sentry then aimed his rifle at the other internees around Tadhg Barry as Con O'Halloran dragged his body back from the gate, and an angry crowd gathered around their fallen comrade, some of them shouting at and denouncing the sentry. The young guard continued aiming his rifle at the angry internees.

The volatile situation was calmed by the quick thinking of Seán O'Sullivan, Tipperary, who called on the internees to kneel down and say the rosary. In an instant the men were on their knees. Fr Burbage arrived and administered the last rites to Barry and the doctors pronounced him dead at the scene.[9] Some internees dipped their handkerchiefs into Barry's blood, held them up and called on the guards to shoot them also.[10]

In the meantime a British officer had entered the sentry box and the soldier who had killed Barry was replaced.[11] The parolees were standing on the back of the second lorry, and when the British officers saw what had happened they shouted to the drivers to move off.[12]

The British medical officer, Captain Harlow, was impressed with the internees' discipline in light of the tragedy and complimented Francis O'Duffy, the No. 2 compound commandant, the following day. The shock and sorrow was clearly visible on the faces of everyone in the compounds that day and cast a dark cloud over the camp. For several months they had been in high spirits at the prospect of being released, but this tragedy brought the men back to the reality of their situation. Although the internees had been more relaxed since the Truce, the British military had proved that it was business as usual at Ballykinlar camp. However, some British officers expressed regret about Tadhg Barry's death and even consulted the internee officers regarding funeral arrangements. They offered the use of a building outside the camp to accommodate the remains and also consented to a group of twenty-four internees standing guard until the body left the camp, on condition that they agree not to use the opportunity to escape.

Later that day the remains were removed from the hospital for transfer to the building outside the camp. A British sergeant stepped out and attempted to remove the Tricolour from the coffin, but was chastised and prevented from doing so by another officer, Lieutenant Joselyn.[13]

On reaching Dublin, one of the paroled internees gave an interview to a reporter from *The Freeman's Journal*. When asked about the shooting he related:

We were getting into the lorries outside the guardroom when we heard a shot. Then we heard loud shouts from our comrades when we were leaving. They were shouting angrily, 'Now you've done it! Now you've done it!' We got up as high as possible in the lorries – some of us on tip-toes and some kneeling on the side – to get a view of what had happened. We saw lying on the ground a man whom we afterwards found to be Tadhg Barry. The blood was spurting from his side, and covering the ground around him. Then we saw a sergeant approaching the sentry-box. But that was all, for when the officers realised what had happened they shouted peremptorily to the drivers of the lorries to drive away. The order was obeyed and we were compelled to leave without knowing whether our comrade was alive or dead. We could think of nothing else the whole way down in the train.[14]

Barry had been a member of the republican movement from very early on and for many years was an earnest worker. In his early days as a journalist he was a member of staff for the *Cork Free Press* as a sports reporter. He was also a member of the Cork County Board of the GAA. After the 1916 Rising he was arrested for a speech he delivered in favour of the republican movement and was sentenced to two years' imprisonment. He spent some time on hunger strike while in Cork jail in 1918. In March 1920 he was an active figure in the national stoppage of work organised by Irish labour organisations as a protest against the incarceration of prisoners.[15]

At the time of his arrest in 1921, Barry was a prominent member of the labour movement in Cork city and was branch secretary of the Transport Workers' Union. He was arrested on Monday 31 January 1921 at the courthouse in Cork city as he was attending a meeting of Cork Corporation to elect a lord mayor for the city. At approximately 1 p.m. a party of military and Black and Tans entered the meeting, arresting all members of the corporation. As they were being led away a crowd gathered and the military fired shots into the air to frighten them off. Barry and the other members of the corporation were held in Cork Barracks until the following morning when they were taken to Cork jail. They were not given any food for the first day at the jail and all parcels sent in were withheld. They were held there until Saturday 19 February when they were taken to Spike Island and put into huts that had previously been used to treat soldiers with venereal disease. On Wednesday 23 February they were taken to a vessel and started the journey to Belfast en route to Ballykinlar camp. The sailing lasted for approximately twenty-two hours and Barry suffered from the rough weather. On arrival at Belfast they were marched off the vessel in single file and completed the remainder of the journey to Ballykinlar by train. As they were about to set off a British military officer warned them that anyone found looking out the window would be shot.[16] Barry and the new arrivals were sent to the No. 2 compound and his first job on arriving at the camp was to clean latrines filled with urine and excrement.

During his time at Ballykinlar camp Barry was very popular, involving himself in all camp activities. He volunteered to act as hut leader in the 'old men's hut', which was specially fitted to accommodate twenty-five of the oldest men in the compound. He delivered many lectures and in the week before his death gave a talk on 'Slavery, Ancient and Modern', which was well attended and well received.[17]

The British issued an official statement from Dublin Castle

the day after the shooting: 'In accordance with the normal procedure of law, a coroner's inquest by jury will be held to inquire into the circumstances attending the death yesterday of Alderman Tadhg Barry, interned at Ballykinlar.'[18]

The following day, Thursday 17 November, a deputation including TDs, councillors and prominent members of the GAA and union officials travelled to Ballykinlar camp: chief liaison officer, Commandant Michael Staines, TD; Liam de Róiste, TD; Donal O'Callaghan, lord mayor of Cork; J. J. Walsh, TD; J. J. Kane, president of the GAA; L. O'Toole, secretary of the GAA; L. McAlinden, Newcastle, County Down; J. King, solicitor, Newcastle, County Down; Fr McLister, camp chaplain; Councillors R. Daly and Joseph Forrest, representing the Transport Workers' Union; and Commandant Joseph McKelvey.[19] They spent some of their time speaking with the internees in No. 1 compound through the wires. Some of the Cork internees spoke with members of the delegation and an internee from Kildare shouted to Liam O'Toole, 'Is the stand finished yet?' referring to Croke Park.

'It is indeed,' replied O'Toole, 'and we gave Kildare a fine whacking there a few Sundays ago!'

The other internees laughed heartily at that remark.

Some of the Cork internees recognised Patrick Barry, brother of Tadhg, and shouted to him, 'Bear up, Paddy boy: we'll win yet.'

After some further exchanges, the group of visitors was informed that they could view the body which lay in a brown habit in a coffin in the centre of one of the rooms. On each side a guard of honour stood to attention as the guests walked in. It was a touching moment when Barry's heartbroken brother, friends and colleagues stood sadly looking over his remains. They all knelt for a few moments and prayed in silence for the repose of his soul before quietly rising and leaving. Afterwards some of the visiting group held a meeting with the Cork internees and asked the British commandant for special parole for a number of men to accompany the funeral cortège to Cork.[20]

The inquest into the death of Barry was opened at Ballykinlar camp on the morning of Friday 18 November by the coroner, Dr Wallace. At first members of the press were refused admission and a military officer stated that it was by the direction of the British military's general headquarters. The internees' solicitor, Mr King, pointed out that the press and public were entitled to be present and the coroner agreed, so the inquest was opened to all and an undertaking was given that facilities would be available for the investigation of the tragedy. The only witness at the opening of the inquest was Patrick Barry, brother of the deceased and sole remaining member of the family, who gave formal evidence of identification. He testified that his brother was secretary of the Irish Transport Workers' Union in Cork and also a journalist. He stated that his brother was thirty-nine years old and that the last time he saw him alive was at his arrest. The family's solicitor, Mr J. King, then made an application for an adjournment until 29 November and this was granted.

The remains of Tadhg Barry were then removed from Bally-kinlar camp. Commandant Seamus Wood, Belfast, representing the Northern Divisions of the IRA, took charge of the funeral procession and made all arrangements. Shortly after 11.30 a.m. the funeral cortège began the journey from Ballykinlar, headed by Patrick Barry, and was joined by the Cork internees who had been released on special parole: James Dunne, Cork city; Thomas Lynch, Kinsale; Robert Lynch, Bantry; Thomas Murphy, Clonakilty; and Michael Bradley, Dunmanway. The funeral cortège was afforded little respect from the soldiers who were present, only two of whom gave the customary military salute. The others directed insulting remarks at the mourners and shouted, 'rip their bastard tyres' with several mimicking cutting the tyres of the vehicles. In contrast the funeral procession was accorded the greatest respect and sympathy for the remainder of the journey to Dublin.[21]

The cortège travelled through Castlewellan, Newry, Dundalk and Drogheda, arriving at Whitehall, Drumcondra, at 7.30 p.m. It was accompanied from Drogheda by Laurence O'Neill, lord mayor of Dublin, Austin Stack, Cathal Brugha, W. T. Cosgrave, Kevin O'Higgins and many TDs. An estimated 200,000 people gathered along the route from Drumcondra to St Mary's Pro-Cathedral in Dublin, where the coffin remained overnight.[22] The remains left Dublin the following morning and the funeral was held in Cork city on Sunday 20 November. Michael Collins had been engaged in the negotiations in London, which were at a crucial stage, but when he heard of Tadhg Barry's death he immediately returned to Ireland and attended the funeral in Cork.[23]

Cork city came to a standstill for the ceremony. At the

head of the procession marched twenty Volunteers bearing floral offerings and several thousand Volunteers marched three deep, with eight bands. Over eighty clergy attended as well as representatives from Cork Corporation, the Harbour Board, the Board of Guardians, the Rural District Council and the County Council, and people from all over Ireland. As well as Michael Collins, Austin Stack, TD, representing Éamon de Valera, was in attendance. The funeral was one of the largest ever to take place in Cork city, with the procession stretching for over two miles. At the graveside Seán O'Hegarty delivered an oration following which three volleys were fired and the 'Last Post' was sounded.[24]

The Barry family solicitors maintained that at the start of the inquest the coroner had directed that facilities be made available to them to interview internees who had witnessed the shooting. However, the British military stated that no such request had been made, contending it had to be in writing. On Thursday 24 November the family's solicitors wrote to Dr Samuel Wallace, coroner for County Down, reminding him that they had applied for facilities for interviewing witnesses. Despite the fact that the military representatives had undertaken to provide every assistance to the lawyers in the preparation of the case, when Mr King visited the camp he was not given an opportunity to take statements. The solicitors subsequently informed Patrick Barry that they would be writing to the officer in command at Ballykinlar to apply for a further adjournment. They also wrote to the commander of the British forces in Ireland, General Nevil Macready:

The order of the coroner has not been complied with and the undertaking given has not been kept. Accordingly we shall not be ready when the inquest resumes on Tuesday next, and intend to ask for a further adjournment.

We think it right to acquaint you with the facts and to send you copies of these letters, feeling sure that you will give direction at once that the members of our firm and their assistants be facilitated in interviewing and taking statements of evidence in the camp.

Since coming to Dublin we have received a telegram from our Downpatrick office that the local military authorities require us to lodge a written application for permission. In view of our letter and undertaking given in the Coroner's court, this is a strange request. We can only assume that it has been made by some officer not personally aware of the facts.[25]

The British military's reply stated that the solicitors had failed to comply with directions and that no official written request was received seeking interviews with witnesses:

The instructions this officer gave to you were confirmed, as being correct, from these headquarters on 19 November. It is therefore not understood how you can pretend that the request to do so is in any way 'strange' … So far you have not informed any military authority with whom you desire an interview, except that on 23 November you asked, by telephone, to see the internee supervisor of No. 2 Cage, but as it is understood the supervisor was not present when the internee was shot, the reason for your request is not understood.

I am commanded to say that if you are not ready when the inquest is resumed that it is not due to any difficulties the military authorities have made, for you must know that the camps are within a prohibited area and permission to enter the area must be obtained; so if you wish any of your assistants to interview internees will you please let me know the name of such assistant.

Despite all this, the inquest reopened on Tuesday 29 November, but was again adjourned – until 13 December – and after that, once more until mid-January. By the time the inquest resumed all the internees had been released and the feelings aroused among the public by the tragedy had lessened somewhat. The inquest had clearly been delayed for that reason and was a blatant attempt by the British to cover up the circumstances of the shooting. In addition, the two principal witnesses, the sentry who fired the shot and the officer of the guard, failed to attend. The only witnesses produced by the British were Colonel Browne and an officer from the engineer corps. The colonel gave evidence regarding the orders forbidding internees to approach the barbed wire and for them to obey sentries. The officer testified that the prisoners had made tunnels to try to escape, which had no relevance to the circumstances of the killing. The officer of the guard on the day of the killing was Lieutenant Sheppard and he gave the sentries specific orders 'to stand no nonsense'. However, he was not called as a witness.[26]

The barristers for Patrick Barry were Albert E. Woods, James Geoghegan and Paddy Lynch. Mr Babington and others appeared for the British military. Albert E. Woods tried to make the case that Barry was deliberately shot because he was Tadhg Barry – but he could not support this idea. It had also been alleged that someone entered the sentry box shortly before the shot was fired, but there was no evidence to support that either, though an officer did enter the sentry box after the shot was fired.[27]

Albert E. Woods told the jury that the military, through their advisers, had dodged the issue and that there was something sinister behind the fact they did not produce the sentry who fired the shot, the sergeant nor the officer of the guard. Paddy Lynch asserted, 'We are being deliberately insulted in the grossest way by counsel for the military authorities and if you, Mr Coroner, do not restrain this sort of thing we will walk out.'

'Certainly you are entitled to some courtesy,' was the reply.

One internee who gave evidence was John Walsh, Dublin, who said he was standing at the water tower watching the parolees get into the lorry. Tadhg Barry joined him and then moved to the front of the tower. John Walsh said the soldier in the sentry box shouted, 'Get back.' 'I looked at the sentry and saw him bring the rifle over the box and level it at us. I turned the corner and then heard a shot. I turned and saw the deceased stagger on his heels and say, "I am shot." The whole affair lasted about three seconds.' Walsh also said he had stood there on previous occasions and had not been challenged.

Two other internee witnesses, Patrick Landers and Daniel Minogue, gave similar evidence and said that Barry had a perfect right to be at the water tower. Another witness, Leo McKenna, stated that he had frequently stood at the location where Barry had been shot and had never been challenged.

Edward Watson, Dublin, testified that he was standing on a bucket in No. 1 compound and had a good view of the sentry box. He was waving to the lorry when the gate to No. 1 compound was opened and a military policeman admitted a soldier on fatigue duty. At that moment he heard the sentry shout to someone in the adjoining compound and then heard one of the officers at the gate say, 'Put one into them.' Immediately a shot rang out and he saw the sentry withdraw the rifle after firing it. Another witness, John Byrne, corroborated Watson's evidence.[28]

Francis O'Duffy, internee commandant in No. 2 compound, gave evidence that he had a conversation with one of the British officers, Colonel Andrews, who told him that in all probability the sentry would be charged with manslaughter. O'Duffy also stated that he was present when Colonel Andrews asked the camp commandant, Colonel Browne, if he knew of any reason why Tadhg Barry had been shot. He replied that he knew of absolutely none. O'Duffy explained that he found a fresh bullet mark in the galvanised iron sheeting on the post office and a grooved mark in the hard roadway, which he concluded was caused by the lethal bullet.[29]

Mr King stated that despite the undertaking given by the military authorities, the report of the officer of the guard at the time of the shooting had not been supplied to him and the officer was not present at any of the inquest sittings. He went on to accuse the British of placing difficulties of every kind in their way, while they had produced every man on their side connected with the case. There was no proof that Tadhg Barry had interfered with the fence and there was no case made that he attempted to rush the gate or was touching the wires. Mr Babington for the British said that it did not matter whether Barry had touched the wires or not, he had disobeyed orders.

The jury retired to consider their verdict and after two hours the foreman announced that they could not agree on a verdict. The coroner asked whether they could come to a decision if he gave them more time or assistance. The foreman stated that there was no possibility of an agreement.

The coroner then asked if twelve out of the eighteen could agree on a verdict, to which the foreman replied no, but added that the jury had agreed that the deceased died from a gunshot fired by a sentry at No. 6 post. They could not agree whether it was done feloniously or not. After further consultation with the coroner, the jury unanimously agreed to the verdict of 'death from shock and haemorrhage caused by gunshot wound inflicted by a sentry in the execution of his duty'.[30]

17

The Treaty and Release

The Treaty negotiations concluded in the early hours of Tuesday 6 December 1921, with the signing of the Articles of Agreement by the Irish and British delegations. The British government recognised the significance of the immediate release of the internees as a means of assisting the Irish delegation in securing the acceptance by Dáil Éireann of the Articles of Agreement. The British were conscious that a release of prisoners would help to bolster the pro-Treaty side against the more hard-line elements within Dáil Éireann.

The commander-in-chief of British forces in Ireland, General Nevil Macready, was present at the British cabinet meeting held at 10 Downing Street, London, on Wednesday morning, 7 December. He said there would be no objection from the military point of view to the immediate release of the internees. It was pointed out at the meeting that it would be more difficult for Dáil Éireann to reject the Articles of Agreement if the men were released as an act of clemency before the Irish political leaders debated the terms of the agreement. The British cabinet unanimously agreed that the British prime minister, Lloyd

George, should convene an urgent meeting with King George V, suggesting that instructions be given for the immediate release of all internees.[1] The meeting took place later that day, following which the British cabinet reconvened at 10 Downing Street at 4.15 p.m. and the secretary of state for war, Laming Worthington-Evans, was directed to take the necessary steps to release persons interned under Regulation 14(b) of the Restoration of Order in Ireland Regulations. The following statement was then issued to the press:

> In view of the Agreement signed yesterday between the representatives of the British Government and the Irish Delegation of Plenipotentaries, HM has approved of the release forthwith of all persons now interned under Regulation 14 (b) of the Restoration of Order in Ireland Regulation. Instructions have been given accordingly.[2]

The number of men interned or awaiting internment in the various camps and jails around the country at that time was 3,627. A total of 4,368 internment orders had been issued up to the Truce of July 1921. The issue of convicted prisoners was also discussed and arrangements were made to review each sentence through a special judicial tribunal, with particular consideration given to those under sentence of death.[3] Meanwhile Ballykinlar was buzzing with rumours of a peace settlement and counter rumours of a breakdown in negotiations. On the morning of Wednesday 7 December the news of the Treaty signing swept through the camp.[4]

The terms of the agreement were published in the national newspapers. The internees in No. 2 compound were well advanced with their tunnel and someone informed Michael Sheehy of the development, handing him a copy of that day's *Irish Independent*. He remained in the tunnel and read the full details of the Treaty agreement.[5]

The internees received official confirmation of their release at 4 p.m. on Thursday 8 December when a general parade was called in the two compounds. Colonel Browne addressed the men and said he had been instructed to read a statement signed by George V, which meant they would be released forthwith. The statement was received by the internees in silence, but a short time later the gates between No. 1 and No. 2 compounds were thrown open and there was much jubilation.[6] Later there was complete freedom in the camp and men walked freely between the two cages, meeting friends for the first time in twelve months. The camp was humming with excitement with men exchanging addresses, signing autograph books and gathering their belongings to go home.[7]

That evening the British officers summoned the internees' commandants or their representatives to their offices to discuss the issue of compensation claims for the destruction of camp property by the internees. Francis O'Duffy, was the officer commanding the No. 2 compound, and the representative from No. 1 compound was Adjutant Art O'Donnell. The two men were asked to remain behind so they could accompany the military officers on a tour of inspection.[8]

The internees attended mass for the last time in Ballykinlar

camp, celebrated at 5 a.m. on Friday 9 December in both compounds. Then at dawn the British began making preparations
for the men's release and the gates to the camp were opened
shortly after 8 a.m. The men began making their way in batches
along the three miles of muddy road to the railway station at
Tullmurry. They sang songs and were whistling and laughing
as they walked, and carried bundles or items, bags of clothes,
camp souvenirs and some musical instruments. The British
military assisted by transporting luggage in military lorries.

The people living in the vicinity gathered outside their
homes to wave and cheer as the first train departed from
Tullmurry Station at approximately 9.45 a.m. Even the British
were said to be very pleasant to the men as they left the camp.[9]
Three special trains were organised, with the first carrying
413 men, the second carrying 646 and the last with 450 who
were mainly from Dublin city and suburbs. The train followed
a route through various County Down towns before joining
up with the main Dublin line. All internees had to travel to
Dublin before making their own way to their home counties.[10]

As the first train arrived at the Newcastle goods' yard a large
number of locals, including members of Cumann na mBan,
were waiting.[11] The local population had arranged a reception,
supplying the men with tea and other refreshments, which was
appreciated, as many had not eaten since the previous day. The
trains departed from Newcastle amid rousing cheers, while the
Tricolour fluttered from the open windows of the carriages,
and workers in the fields, women and children waved.[12]

As the last commandant of No. 1 compound, Thomas

Treacy remained in the camp until the last batch was ready to leave. By the time they had boarded their train, there were rumours that one of the earlier trains had been attacked. The last train travelled through Newcastle where it received a warm welcome and then passed Castlewellan without incident, but it was attacked between Ballyward and Katesbridge. A party of unionist gunmen were lined up on one side of the track and opened fire as the train passed.[13] Over the next few miles shots were fired from the left-hand side of the track and then from the right. One bullet passed through the window of a packed carriage, smashing the glass and sending splinters over Patrick Mulcahy, Waterford, John Fitzgerald, Cork, and Patrick Cahill, Cavan. Cahill's face and head were severely lacerated. Patrick Mulcahy was sitting by the window when a bullet passed in front of his face and out of the open window on the other side of the carriage. As the bullets whizzed over and through the train Thomas Treacy shouted to the men in the other carriages to stuff parcels and belongings across the windows as a shield.

The train was attacked several times, but continued travelling at speed. Then it suddenly slowed as if preparing to stop, and shouts could be heard from another carriage that one of the men was seriously wounded. Stephen Treacy, Dublin, had been shot in the foot and someone had pulled the communication cord, which automatically clamped the breaks. Dr O'Higgins and Dr Reynolds were on board the train and administered first aid. Dr Reynolds examined Stephen Treacy and his wound was found to be slight. The train continued at approximately eight miles per hour as gunfire was directed at the carriages from different locations along the line between Ballyward and Katesbridge. It eventually pulled into the railway station at Katesbridge and the men, in the belief that the driver had colluded with the gunmen, approached the engine. They were angry and were shouting at the driver and fireman in a threatening manner.

Thomas Treacy quickly got out of the carriage to prevent anything happening to the driver and fireman and stood between the driver and the group of men, telling them to stand back. Treacy questioned the driver, who pointed out that someone had pulled the communication cord, causing the train to slow down. The driver and fireman had kept the train moving despite the breaks and at times had been forced to lie on the footplate as the bullets whizzed around them. Treacy then asked if there was any possibility that the train would be attacked again. The man replied that he had heard a rumour that a much larger ambush was planned for their arrival at Banbridge where the train was scheduled to stop for fifteen minutes.

Treacy instructed the driver to ring Banbridge Station to arrange for the train to pass straight through. This was not possible, but after considerable difficulty the driver had the stopover period reduced to two or three minutes. The train travelled at full speed arriving at Banbridge some minutes early and as it pulled into the station men with rifles could be seen at points around the station. An angry crowd of several hundred stormed onto the platform, but the men on the train were at the doors to prevent any of them getting on. The unionist mob started attacking the train with stones and bricks, smashing every window on the platform side. A vicious hand-to-hand fight developed at each carriage door with the unionist mob attempting to gain entry and the former internees desperately trying to keep them at bay. A sudden rush of the crowd prevented those at the train doors gaining entry, as they became squashed in the surge, and also barred the gunmen from shooting as they were caught up in the crush. As the train began to pull out some of the crowd tried to gain entry on the other side of the train from the tracks, but it was easy for the men on the train to repel them. The throng then began to throw stones at the train, but it managed to pull away from the station safely.[14]

While the trains passed through the mixed scenes of celebration and raw sectarian hatred in the north-eastern counties, large crowds of men, women and children eagerly awaited their return at various railway stations along the route to Dublin. There were five Drogheda men on the train and approximately forty Meath men who were warmly welcomed when they arrived at Drogheda.

At Clones thirty-four men arrived from Ballykinlar, with some proceeding to Cavan and others to the midlands, and they were honoured by a procession through the streets with members of the IRA in uniform, Cumann na mBan, Na Fianna boy scouts and members of public bodies. The released internees from Tyrone also disembarked at Clones before continuing their journey home. Dungannon greeted the liberated men with a large procession through the town and a reception at St Patrick's Hall. There were similar scenes when Armagh's former internees arrived at Lurgan Railway Station.

The homecoming of the Dundalk men was eagerly awaited:

a large number of people had assembled at the railway station from early that morning. When the train appeared there was much cheering and waving of flags. The streets were filled with people and the men were loudly cheered as they drove past. From the windows of several houses in the town republican flags were waved, and several bonfires were lit in the streets. The employees at the railway locomotive works stopped work at noon to attend the celebrations. Among the released men were two elected representatives, Seamus (James) Magill, county councillor, and Joseph McGinley, urban district councillor.

The former internees from Wicklow were greeted by large numbers of Volunteers, Cumann na mBan, Na Fianna and townspeople headed by the Irish National Foresters' Brass Band assembled at Wicklow Railway Station.

When the first train arrived at Amiens Street Station in Dublin at approximately 1 p.m., some fifty men from the west of Ireland were given a rousing reception before continuing their journey home. The next train arrived shortly after 2 p.m., carrying men mostly from the southern counties, so they did not alight, but travelled on to Kingsbridge Station from where they continued their journey. Friends and relatives were waiting for the return of the men on the last train, which had received most of the vicious loyalist attacks. There was great excitement and anticipation in the air, but this suddenly turned to fear and anxiety when the news of the attacks reached the city. Rumours began circulating that at least two men had been killed and many others injured. The presence of three ambulances fuelled the anxiety.

When the train arrived at about 5 p.m. the crowds were overjoyed at the sight of the freed men hanging out of the windows waving the Tricolour. The St James' Brass and Reed Band played 'The Soldier's Song' as the train pulled into the station. Companies of Volunteers endeavoured to keep a clear thoroughfare, but they were brushed aside by delighted relatives eager to greet their loved ones. Many people wept with joy. There were several Tricolours waving as the men made their way from the station. Horse-drawn carriages, hackney cars, cabs, motor cars and lorries were requisitioned to convey the men to their homes.

Stephen Treacy was taken to the Mater Hospital in a Fire Brigade ambulance. He had to undergo surgery to have the bullet removed and later made a full recovery. The other men injured in the attacks were also taken to the Mater Hospital.

A large number of released men lined up in military formation and headed by the St James' Band marched proudly through the city. Many had a strange look, which gave some indication of the psychological strain of enduring the terrible conditions of the internment camp. The Irishtown road was ablaze with bonfires and there were similar scenes throughout Dublin, with large numbers of people gathering in the different areas to welcome the men home.

At Athlone an explosion of fog signals marked the arrival of the released internees. Volunteers were on duty on the platform, where a large crowd had gathered. Deafening cheers were heard as the men walked to waiting motor cars and other modes of transport. A torchlight procession accompanied the men from the west of the country who had to walk to the midland station to catch a train home.

Bonfires blazed in Waterford and the surrounding areas when the released men arrived on Thursday night. Escorted by a torchlight procession they marched from the station through cheering crowds. Waterford Corporation adjourned their monthly meeting so that members could take part in the celebrations. Before doing so, however, they expressed sympathy with the relatives of the late Tadhg Barry and the citizens of Cork.

The former internees from County Offaly arrived at Tullamore on Friday evening. The local railway station was filled with relatives, friends and comrades. All businesses were closed to enable workers to join in the celebration. Flags were displayed from the houses and a large crowd accompanied by bands awaited the arrival of the train. Over thirty men stepped from the train to an enthusiastic welcome.

Tragedy befell the released internees at the Thurles Railway Station as the train conveying them from various parts of County Tipperary, from Cork and from Kerry arrived on Friday 9 December at approximately 7 p.m. As the train passed under the parapet of a bridge at the entrance to the station, a group of RIC and Black and Tans, under the cover of smoke created by setting off fog signals, threw a bomb at the first carriage. The scenes of jubilation among the large crowd that had gathered quickly turned to panic and confusion as the device blew splinters everywhere, broke windows and injured both passengers and people standing on the platform. One of the former internees, Declan Horton, Ardmore, County Waterford, was seriously injured. Two other men were also hurt, with James Coleman, Cork, receiving a nasty cut to the head. The stationmaster, Mr Moore, his wife, sister-in-law and his little daughter were all wounded, as was a young boy called George Gorman, the son of a railway porter. The injured were transferred to Thurles Hospital where doctors Barry and Callan attended them. Unfortunately the medics were unable to save Declan Horton, who died of his injuries later that night. A bomb was also thrown at a train carrying former internees as it arrived at Glanmire terminus in Cork, but missed its target and no one was hurt.[15]

The British cabinet memorandum 'Weekly Survey of the State of Ireland' referred to the Thurles tragedy and suggested as ludicrous the claims that any elements of the British forces were involved. The attack on the train was suspected of being a reprisal for an assault on the RIC at Thurles earlier that day:

> The train outrage at Thurles Station on the night of 9th instant is one of the few serious breaches of the Truce that have been charged against the crown forces. Although the facts as originally reported appeared to constitute a very strong *prima facie* case against the police, the latter investigations made on the spot by the chief of police in conjunction with the local Sinn Féin Liaison Officer have not resulted in the production of any substantial evidence ... It appears to be clear that only one bomb was thrown, but no witnesses to the act of throwing have yet come forward and the only ground for the allegations brought against the police

is the natural assumption that no members of the IRA would be likely to throw bombs at a train containing internees among its passengers ... In view of the inconclusive nature of the joint preliminary investigation the chief of police proposed to the Sinn Féin Liaison Officer that the matter should be referred to a military Court of Inquiry, and there is a possibility of this suggestion being adopted.[16]

While the internees were making their way home on the special trains, Art O'Donnell and Francis O'Duffy were still waiting at the camp to conduct the tour of inspection, but after several hours the British commandant informed them that they would not tour the camp on that day and asked them to return the next morning (Saturday 10 December). O'Duffy and O'Donnell agreed and told the British commandant to have a car at Tullmurry Station at 10 a.m. to drive them to the camp. As they set off to walk to the railway station, Fr McLister arrived with a car and gave them a lift to Downpatrick. They had tea at the presbytery and later that evening took the train to Newcastle where they stayed at the Donard Hotel. The following morning they returned to Tullmurry and had to wait for some time before a British officer arrived to pick them up.[17] They conducted a tour of the camp and inspected all huts, but did not find any damage that could not be attributed to wear and tear. The British estimated a total cost of £1,935 16s 9½d resulting from both damage to property and general wear and tear. However, Art O'Donnell and Francis O'Duffy refused to accept any responsibility for the estimated damage. The British requested that they attend a meeting at Victoria Barracks, Belfast, the following week to discuss arrangements for compensation, but neither man attended.[18]

Saturday 10 December was also the day when the released internees from Derry and Donegal made their way home from Dublin. Tar barrels blazed and bands played when they reached Strabane late on Saturday evening. Cars were waiting to transport the fourteen Derry men to their homes, and they were accorded a rapturous welcome in the city.

Some seventy Donegal men took the train to Letterkenny where a large crowd was waiting. The men from other areas of the county then set off on their journeys home and in each town and village there were great celebrations. A number of prominent figures addressed the gathering in Letterkenny, including Peadar O'Donnell. Having extended a hearty welcome to the returned men, he addressed the subject of the Treaty and challenged whether it was a good or bad deal. He said he did not wish to say anything that would strike a wrong note, but it would be well to be frank since the terms came and would come in for comment, especially as many of those present were IRA men.[19]

The men who had been arrested in London and transferred to Ballykinlar were also afforded a welcome celebration on their return. The reception was held at the premises of the Roger Casement Club, Blackfriars Road, London, on Monday 12 December. There was a large attendance and the freed men were given an enthusiastic welcome.[20]

The release of all internees and the events that marred the otherwise joyous occasion were referred to at the British cabinet meeting of Monday 12 December 1921. Although not entirely accurate, the memorandum of the meeting confirmed that the release of the internees was designed to aid the Irish negotiating team in selling the terms of the Treaty to Dáil Éireann and the general public:

> In accordance with a cabinet decision of the 7th instant, all persons detained in internment camps in Ireland have now been released. This step has undoubtedly had a good effect in conciliating public opinion in Ireland and in strengthening the hands of the leaders of the peace party in Sinn Féin. The return of the internees provoked scenes of great enthusiasm in many places, but was marked by two very regrettable incidents in addition to that at Thurles ... Two of the special trains conveying internees from Ballykinlar to Dublin being attacked while passing through County Down by gangs of Orangemen, who assembled at various places along the line and fired revolvers and threw stones at the passengers, three of whom received minor injuries.[21]

The final task for the former internees of the Ballykinlar internment camp was the disposal of camp property, which included mostly books and the camp piano and harmonium. All the items were transferred to the store room at Tullmurry Station on the day the camp closed and were later transported to Dublin. The camp currency was in the most part retained as souvenirs and some money was not redeemed. This and the profits from the canteens in both compounds amounted to £165. It was decided that this would be donated to two of the neediest causes to be identified at a later date. The first of these were the dependants of the Belfast prisoners, who received £75 in 1922. The balance was finally donated to the Irish Red Cross in June 1941.

The books from the libraries in the two compounds were boxed up and it was decided to send them to University College Cork. The boxes were sent first to the Gaelic League offices at Parnell Square, Dublin, but when a group of former internees arrived at those offices to transport them to Cork they discovered that the boxes had been broken open and all the books stolen.

The camp piano and harmonium were transported to Denis McCullough's shop in Belfast for much-needed repairs. McCullough's shop was later destroyed by unionist mobs and both items perished in the fire. The sports equipment disappeared shortly after the news was received of the impending release in early December.[22]

Postscript

An indication of the true scale of the internment policy of the British government could be seen in late May 1921 when General Nevil Macready, commanding officer of British troops in Ireland, made 'urgent representations' to Winston Churchill, secretary of state for war, requesting further accommodation for the growing number of internees. Macready stated that he required accommodation for up to 2,000 internees, as all other camps were full to capacity, and estimated that it would take six to twelve months to erect another internment camp in Ireland at an approximate cost of £300,000.

The British cabinet met on Thursday 2 June to discuss the problems facing the military posed by the growing number of internees. A decision was taken at that cabinet meeting that 'as a matter of policy, the Irish internees should continue to be interned in Ireland' and this was communicated to General Macready. At that time, the four internment camps at Spike Island, Bere Island, Ballykinlar and the Curragh were already full to overflowing, but despite this large numbers of arrests continued on a daily basis.

The British had been considering extending martial law to all twenty-six counties, a move that would have increased the number of internees to between 8,000 and 10,000 (these figures were given by General Nevil Macready in a memorandum to the

British cabinet in June 1921).[1] In preparation for such a move, the military had been arranging additional accommodation for detainees with a third compound at Ballykinlar and a tented camp at the Curragh, to accommodate up to 5,000 more internees. General Macready had suggested that the British Admiralty should be involved in the internment policy and provide out-of-date battleships for the purpose. He recommended that two ships be anchored off Dublin and one in Belfast Lough, with others located in areas to cater for the west and south. Another proposal was to transfer prisoners to northern Scotland for internment at Scapa, on the Orkney mainland, where hutted accommodation for several hundred was available.[2]

A new concern soon arose regarding internment in Britain that made the issue of internees even more problematical – the expiration of the Defence of the Realm Regulations, the only mechanism under which Irish internees could be detained in Britain. The British attorney general stated that from 31 August 1921, Regulation 14(b) of the Restoration of Order in Ireland Act would be *ultra vires* (invalid) concerning internees held in Britain. In the absence of fresh legislation before that date, the internees would have to be either released or returned to Ireland. If there was no suitable accommodation in Ireland the internees would have to be released on their return.[3] It was only with the implementation of the Truce that these issues were finally resolved.

***

Those who survived their incarceration would never forget the time they spent in the custody of the British. Ballykinlar internment camp stood on a bleak, sandy and marshy landscape on the edge of Dundrum Bay, County Down. Its location exposed its inhabitants to extreme weather conditions: the most striking characteristics of the internment cages being rain, mud and barbed wire. These features, coupled with the harsh treatment meted out by the British military in their endeavour to smash the spirit and aspirations of the internees, only served to strengthen their resolve. The year between December 1920 and December 1921 was difficult and challenging for both sides, and witnessed great hardship and injustice. Despite this, the spirit of comradeship and sheer determination amongst the internees to make the very best of a lamentable situation was overriding. Not only did they exercise minds and bodies, they also provided opportunities that would otherwise not have been experienced or enjoyed by most internees on the outside. The Education Committees enjoyed a silent victory in their educational pursuits and possibly saved the sanity of many men. Many former internees secured employment after their release by presenting certificates in various disciplines from their time at Ballykinlar.

Escape plans also kept the men focused, and, ironically, the skill employed may have inspired the British to use the same methods when they later found themselves behind the barbed-wire confines of prisoner-of-war camps in Germany.

Some of the men who endured the Ballykinlar cages later served as politicians, judges and senior military officers. Some

were successful in business and other areas such as the Garda
Síochána (the Irish police force). They also included a future
Taoiseach. However, the close-knit friendships established
inside the barbed wire under the shadow of the Mourne
Mountains were shattered within seven months of their
release when the horrors of Civil War broke out. Many former
internees took opposing sides in the eleven-month war that
ripped through the country, and the memory of the animosity
from this period would taint these men and the country for
decades to come.

Appendix 1

List of internees in Ballykinlar No. 1 Compound*

Antrim:
A. P. Carey
Alastair McCabe, Cloghmills
Hugh McShane, Whitehall,
    Aghagallon

Armagh:
E. Cooney (Belfast and Armagh)
Patrick Kelly, Mullaghbrack
James Mallon, Keenaghan, Moy
John J. McCabe, Annarea,
    Middletown
Brian (Barney) McCann,
    Foraghmore, West Lurgan
Manus McMenamy, Blundell's
    Grange, Loughall
Seán O'Reilly
P. Toner

Belfast:
Joe Allan, 25 Stranmillis Gardens

Seán Allan, 25 Stranmillis
    Gardens
Hugh Bradley, Ardoyne
T. Cleary
T. Corr
S. Dolan, MA
P. Dempsey, 40 Locan Street
Robert Foley, 41 Locan Street
Joe Goodman, 15 Quadrant
    Street
George Goodman
D. Harron
Éamon Hayes
Éamonn Hughes, 2 Mount
    Delphi, Antrim Road
Liam P. Mac Giolla Mhuire
    (Liam P. Gilmore), 345
    Crumlin Road
Hugh Magill, 37A Hamilton
    Street
Donal McDevitt, 455 Falls Road

---

* The lists of internees in the two appendices were compiled from a number of different sources. While the lists are as accurate as possible, some names may be missing due to their omission from the sources, as men were released from the camp before the lists were compiled. For example, a number of names found on photos of the internees and reproduced in this book were not in the sources and could not be assigned a county or compound. They could not, therefore, be included in these appendices. There may also be some misspelling of names.

Éamon Quinn, 55 Old Lodge Road
J. Totter
V. Watters (Belfast and Cavan)

Carlow:

Denis Brennan, Borris
Seamus Byrne, Graiguecullen
Seán Donnelly, Rathvilly
John Dooish, Leighlinbridge
Eoin Kinsella, 4 Barrack Street, Carlow town
John Kinsella, 4 Barrack Street, Carlow town
P. Maher, Royal Oak, Carlow
James McDermott, Raheen, Killedmond, Borris
Patrick McDermott, Tullow Street, Carlow town
Seamus McDonald, Raheen
David Murphy, Leighlinbridge
Éamonn Nolan, Tig Cnoc
Seamus Nolan, Tig Cnoc
Patrick O'Mescalf, Bagenalstown
Patrick O'Toole
Seán Smith, Bagenalstown

Cavan:

P. J. Bartley, Prospect House, Mountnugent
E. Boyle
James Brady, Carriga, Stradone
Peter Connity
J. Corry
Bernard Emmo
Thomas Fitzpatrick
J. Fitzsimmons
Michael Fynes, Butler's Bridge
Michael Kenny

Terry Leonard, 89 Main Street, Cavan town
Tom Leonard
Roland Lynch
Joseph McCaffney, Aughill, Ballinagh
Ernest McDonald, Virginia
Jim McGeraghty, Ennismore, Butler's Bridge
Michael McGeraghty, Ennismore, Butler's Bridge
Thomas McGovern
James McPhilips
P. McShane
Bert O'Donoghue
Henry O'Reilly, Swanlake, Gowna
H. O'Reilly
James Plunkett, Cornacross, Kilcogy
John Pratt, Derrygoss, Butler's Bridge
Charles Robinson, Crossdoney
Mat Smith
Richard Smith, Bridge Street, Cavan town
T. K. Walsh

Clare:

M. Clancy
Joe Conroy, Tulla
Pat Considine, Craggaknock
William Cooper
Martin Griffin, Kildysart
Simon Haugh
Jerry Killeen, Dunsallagh PO, Miltown Malbay
J. Lanigan
Thomas McAteer
Denis McGrath, Cooraclare

Dan Montgomery, Dunogan,
Mullagh, Miltown Malbay
Michael Nugent,
Bearnafuinshin, Barefield,
Ennis
John O'Dea
Art O'Donnell, Tullycrine
John O'Grady, Cappamore,
Crusheen
Denis Shannon, Coolmeen
Daniel P. Sheehy, Corraclare,
Ennis
John White
T. Wright

Cork:

Liam Bernard
Eoin Buckley, Cobh
John Buckley
Andrew Callanan, Mallow
Maurice Collins, Coolraheen,
Rosscarbery
Tadhg Cotter, Rathcormac
Denis Cremin, Glaundine,
Dromahane, Mallow
Thomas Cremin, Mogeely
Denis Cronin, Mogeely
Seamus Cronin, Skibbereen
Cornelius Crowley, Kilbrittain
Maurice Cullen
Thomas Delamer, Mitchelstown
Maurice (Mossie) Donegan
(Thomas Fitzpatrick),
Passage West
Michael Dowling, Fermoy
Cornelius Doyle, Youghal
James Dunne, Cork city
Seán Egan, Mogeely
Cathal Finn, Cobh
Seán Fitzgerald, Kilbrittain

Seamus Hayes, South Main
Street, Bandon
Peter Hession, Coachford
Denis Hickey, Glenfesk
Patrick Holmes, Mogeely
Patrick Hughes, Bere Island
J. Keating, Kanturk
Seamus Kelleher, Rathcormac
Thomas Kilpatrick, Kanturk
Denis Lenehan, Quartertown,
Mallow
Denis Linehan, Mogeely
Liam Lydon, Clonakilty
Robert Lynch, Bantry
Tadhg Lynch, Kinsale
Dermott Lucy, Fermoy
Philip Magner, Youghal
Michael Murphy, Mogeely
Nicholas Murphy, Mogeely
Tadhg Murphy, Clonakilty
Seamus Murnane
Dan McCarthy, Millstreet
Michael McGuinness, Midleton
Michael Nolan, Knocknagree
Seán Nolan
Bob Noonan, Mitchelstown
Andrew O'Callaghan, Mallow
Tadhg O'Connell, Cobh
Barney O'Driscoll
Micheál Ó Gura, Ballydorgan
Cornelius O'Leary, Clonakilty
Matthew O'Leary, Cobh
Michael O'Neill, Timoleague
Seán O'Neill, Castletown
Cornelius O'Sullivan, Bantry
Donal Pyne, Rathcormac
Maurice Quinn
Peadar Rafferty, Cobh
Seán Ryan, Fermoy
Patrick Sullivan, Cobh

Seamus Sherman, Mallow
Patrick Thornton, Glantane
Seán Trainor, Youghal

Derry:

Seán Breathnach, Maghera
Seamus Dempsey, Aghadowey
Willie Doherty, Shiels Yard,
    Derry city
Seamus Kavanagh, 17 Alexandra
    Place, Derry city
Tom Larkin, Magherafelt
Éamon McDermott, 35 William
    Street, Derry city
Tomás Ó Lorcáin, Ballyronan
Seán Walsh, Maghera

Donegal:

A. Anderson, Frosses
Seán Bonner, Summerhill
James Boyle, Letterfad,
    Letterbarrow
Hugh Britton, Donegal town
Donal C. Byrne, Bunglass, Teelin
Donal C. Byrne, Doonin, Kilcar
Michael Byrne, Carrick
Seán Callan, Castlefin
James Campbell, Castlefin
James (Jim) Dawson, Southwell
    Terrace, Letterkenny
Hugh Deery, Ballyboe,
    Letterkenny
Hugh Doherty, Seaview,
    Dungloe
Eoin Gallagher, Ardfarn,
    Bundoran
John Gorman, Dungloe
Jim Hannigan, Ballybofey
Michael Hannigan, Brockagh
Pat Hannigan, Killygordan

Charles Haughey, Loughmuilt,
    Dunkineely
P. Hegarty-Meehan
Matthew P. Higgins, Carrick
    (Arrested in England)
John J. Hirrell, Carndonagh
John Kane, Ballyshannon
John James Kelly, Drumdoit,
    Castlefin
Patrick Kelly, Killygordon
Seán Mailey, Carrigans
Frank Marley, Mounthall,
    Killygordon
James McCarron, Ballybofey
P. McCarton, Main Street,
    Dungloe
John McElhinney, The
    Diamond, Raphoe
Thomas McGlynn, Liscooley,
    Castlefin
James McMonagle, Castle
    Street, Letterkenny
Conal McShane, Teelin,
    Carrick
Joe Meehan, Menacully
G. Meehan, Castle Street,
    Donegal town
John Melley, Farrigans,
    Lettermacaward
Edward Melley, Farrigans,
    Lettermacaward
Seán Molloy, Dunkineely
Frank Murray, Kilcar
John E. O'Boyle, Dungloe

Down:

Seán Byrne, Crossgar
Donal Corr, Magheralin
Éamonn Cunningham,
    Carrigenagh, Kilkeel

Thomas E. Cunningham,
Harbour Road, Kilkeel
Éamonn Doran, Kilkeel
Tom Farren, Gilbert's Hill,
Killowen
Donal Francis Sheridan, Newry
Seamus Gill, Loughinisland
Hugh Gribbon, Burran,
Warrenpoint
Liam Halpin, Loughinisland
Frank Kearney, Newry
Patrick Kearney, Crossgar
Patrick Moore, Downpatrick
Donal McCreesh, Magheralin
Seamus McDermott, Grange,
Kilkeel
Patrick McNamara,
Loughinisland
Brian Mullen, Annacloy
Philip Rodgers, Kilcoo

Dublin:

P. Allan
Bernard Anderson
Seoirse Arthon, 22 Manor Place
Liam Arthon
Thomas Atkins, 10 South
Spencer Street
M. Barrett
(?) Barry
Art Behan, 17 Carling Road
Éamonn Behan, 17A, Carling
Road
H. Behan, Drumcondra
Joe Behan, 257 Richmond Street
Patrick Behan, Drumcondra
Richard Birmingham, 42
Lombard Street
Art Bolger
G. Bould

Peter Bowes
Liam Bowles, 5 Carmac
Cottages, Dolphin's Barn
Seamus (Jim) Bracken, Briar
Road
M. Brady
Fintan Breen
P. J. Breen, 39 Church Avenue,
Drumcondra
A. Brennan, Dolphin's House,
Dolphin's Barn
William Brogan, 7 Frankfort
Cottages
Thomas Brophy, Feltram
Cottage, Malahide
Fintan Brown, 61A Richmond
Road
Seán Brúansáin, 27 Wellington
Street
J. Brunswick
Thomas Bryson, Merrion Road
Richard Buckley
Richard Butler, 28 Harold's
Cross Cottages
Christy Burns
Maurice Burns, 433 Harold's
Cross
Michael Burns, 115 Harold's
Cross
Patrick Burns, 33 St Ultan Road
Seán Burns, 62 Lower Gardiner
Street
Seán Burns, Maine Way
Thomas Burns
Ambrose Byrne
Andrew Byrne
C. Byrne, 33 St Alban's Terrace,
South Circular Road
Chris Byrne, 33 Ultan Road,
Crumlin Road West

E. Byrne

Gerard Byrne, Donore Avenue, South Circular Road

J. Byrne

J. J. Byrne

Jack J. Byrne

James Byrne, Bath Street, Irishtown

Joe Byrne, 3 Harcourt Street

John Byrne, 56 Mary Street

Maurice Byrne

Patrick Byrne, 33 St Alban's Terrace, South Circular Road

R. J. Byrne, St Joseph's, Ranelagh

Thomas Byrne, Blackpitts

William Byrne

(?) Byrne Snr

J. Caffrey

W. K. Cahill

Tom Canavan

Michael Caney, Clanbrassil Street

Joseph Canny, 128 Capel Street

M. Carey

Thomas Carey, 27 Lower Mount Pleasant Avenue, Rathmines

B. L. Carroll, 5 Mallon Terrace, Grove Road, Harold's Cross

William Carroll

P. Carroll

J. Carpenter

J. Cassells

Thomas Cassidy, 22 Bolton Street

Patrick Cavanagh

S. Cavanagh

Chris Chambers, Mount Merrion

John Clarke, 34 Hamilton Street

Seán Cleary

John Condon

Tom Condon

Frank Condron, 19 Stella Gardens, Irishtown

Liam Condron, 19 Stella Gardens, Irishtown

Thomas Condron, Irishtown

F. Conroy

John Conroy, 59 Capel Street

Joseph Conroy, 8A, Lower Mercer Street

Joseph Considine

Chris Coppinger, 76A, Gloucester Street

John Corrigan

Jack Costelloe, 59 King's Avenue, Ballybough

John Crimin, 14 Mulgrave Terrace, Dún Laoghaire, Co. Dublin

Tom Croke, Drumcondra

T. Cummins

Seán Curran, 49 St George Street

Joe E. Curran, South Great George's Street

D. Curtin

Tom S. Cuffe, 4 Pleasant Street

James Cummins, 50 Daniel Street

M. Cunningham

L. Daly, 38A Mary's Lane

(?) Dalton

J. Darmon

Richard Davis

Henry Dixon, 19 Cabra Road

T. Dolan

John Donnelly, 34 Hardwick Street

Seamus Donnelly, 34 Arboe Street
William Doran, Langrishe Place
John Dorman, 7 Meath Place
J. Dowling
Joe Downey, 3 New Inniskeen Road
Henry Doyle
J. Doyle
Patrick Doyle, Ring Street
Martin Duffy, 34 Great Western Square, North Circular Road
Patrick J. Duffy, 34 Great Western Square, North Circular Road
Matt Dunleavy, 8A Richmond Hill
James Dunne, 4 Upper Erne Street
Patrick Dunne, Washington Street
P. Edwards
Hubert Earls
Patrick Fagan, 200A Phibsboro Road
Stephen Fagan, 7 Stafford Street
M. Fannam
Joseph Fanning, 12 Usher's Quay
J. Farrell
Richard Farrell, 3 Rossa Road
Seán Farrell, Goatstown
Turlough Farrell
Peter Fearon, 30 Viking Road
Maurice C. Fitzsimmons, 8 Blessington Place
Cormac Flanaghan
F. Flanaghan
M. F. Flanaghan
John Flood

John Flynn, 5 Henrietta Street
Liam Flynn, 412 North Circular Road
P. Flynn
Gregory Foley, 42 Bath Street, Irishtown
Louis Foley, Irishtown
Tom Foynes
Patrick Franklin, 30 Gardiner Place
Tody Fynes, 1 Donmore Avenue, South Circular Road
Paddy Garland
William Gay, 11 Sandford Avenue
Arthur Gaynor, 9 Aughrim Villas
James Gibson, 7 Lower Gardiner Street
J. Gilfoyle, Synge Street
James Gilligan, 18 Sandwith Place
Philip Glynn, 62 North Arran Street
John P. Goodman, Capel Street
Edward Gordan, 3 Henrietta Street
Fred Gordan, Henrietta Street
Joe Gordan, 3 Henrietta Street
Ned Gordon
Stephen Gordan, Henrietta Street
P. Gorman
John Grace
Patrick Grace
Eoin Green, 38 Martin Street
John Green
John J. Green, 26 Mount Eden Road, Donnybrook

William Greene
John Halpin
K. Halpin
Tom Hanan (Dublin and Clare)
Donal Hannon, New Row
P. J. Hardiman
James Harmon
M. Harmon
T. Harmon
Val Harris snr
Pat Harrison, 2 Waterford Street
Dr Richard Hayes, TD (Dublin
    and Limerick)
Patrick Healy
Brian Henderson, 19A Brigid
    Street
Michael Henderson
Thomas Henderson
Jim Hennessy
Fred Henry, 116 Ring Street
Michael Henry, 14 St Kevin's
    Road
Michael Heverin, 33 Queen
    Street
D. Hogan (Dublin and
    Tipperary)
Donal C. Hogan, 149 Phibsboro
    Road
Liam Hogan, Killarney Street
Patrick Hogan, 12 Green Way,
    Harold's Cross
Dan Horan
Daniel Horan, 85 Cork Street
W. Horris
P. Hosey
J. Hubbart
Frank Hughes, 28 Redmond's
    Hill
Myles Hughes, John Street
Patrick Hughes or McHugh,

115A, James Street
Richard Hughes, Thomond
    House, Rialto
J. Hynes
Fred Jones, 7 Margaret Place,
    Bath Avenue, Sandymount
William Judge, 10 Blackhall
    Parade
Alex Kane
P. Kane
Patrick Kavanagh, 36A, South
    King Street
Peter Kavanagh, 4 Ross Road
Sam Kavanagh, 4 Ross Road
Seamus Kavanagh, Henrietta
    Street
Frank Kearney
Peadar Kearney
Laurence P. Keegan, 8 & 9
    Moore Street
M. Keegan
Frank Kelly, 74 Marlboro Street
Isaac Kelly, 23 Longwood Avenue
Jack Kelly
James Kelly, 9 Aungier Street
John Kelly, 9th Lough,
    Clondalkin, Co. Dublin
Patrick Kelly, Drumcondra
William Kelly, 15 Usher's Quay
Seán Kennedy, 22 Parnell Street
Mat Kenney
Patrick Kenny, 19 Kings Avenue,
    Ballybough
D. Keogh
Denis Keogh, 12 Synnott Place
Patrick Keogh
Peter Kerwin, 18 Dodder View,
    Ballsbridge
Patrick Leo Kerwin, 18 Dodder
    View, Ballsbridge

F. Kieran
Thomas King, 6A Richmond
Place West
Robert Kirk
Patrick Landers, 151 North
King Street
John (Jack) Leigh
Seán Lemass
Tom Leonard
Brian Levy, Sherrard Way/Street
John Liddy
Seamus Liddy, 24 O'Sullivan
Street
Michael Liston, Goatstown
Paddy Lochlan
Anthony Lynch, Aughrim
Street, North Circular Road
John Lynch
Joseph Lynch, 28 Usher's Quay
Stephen Lynch, Henrietta
Street
James Maguire
J. Maher
Ross Mahon, Drumcondra
J. Malone
T. Malone
C. Malphy
Harry Mangan
Christy Manweller
Gerry Markey, Ranelagh
Éamon Martin, 6 Kings Way
P. Masterson
Martin McAdams, 67 Francis
Street
Seamus (James) McArdle
Louis McAvitt
Seamus McBride, 7 Middle
Gardiner Street
John McCaffrey, 49 Mountjoy
Street

M. McCarthy
Brian McCaughey or Kehoe, 2
Richmond Way
J. McConnell
Edward McConville, 29 John
Dillon Street
Christopher McCormac, 76
Lower Gloucester Street
J. McCormack
Peter McDonagh
Jim McDonald, 23 North
Strand
John McDonnell, 23
Marrowbone Lane
D. McDonnell
Larry McDonnell
Louis McEvett, 31 Usher's
Quay
Seamus McGilligan
Chris McGlynn
C. McGowan, 45 Dolphin's
Barn Street
Chris McGrane, 32 Middle
Gardiner Street
Denis McGrane, 32 Middle
Gardiner Street
Joseph McGrath, TD
Michael McGuinness, 83
Ballybough
H. McHill
Myles McHugh
Patrick McHugh, 115 James
Street
Frank McKay
Séamas Mac Lidhir, Mount
Merrion
Frank McNally, 1 O'Sullivan's
Avenue, Ballybough
P. McNally, 10 O'Sullivan's
Avenue, Ballybough

Hugh McNeill, 109 Seville Place

Patrick Meade

Peter Meehan, 39 Hardwick Street

Thomas J. Meldon, 45 Lower Gardiner Street

Joseph Moffat

Joseph Moffat, 14 Primrose Street

John Monaghan, 12 Belvedere Avenue

Éamon Morrissey

Donal Morrisey

D. Morrisy

Thomas Muldowney, 45 Lower Gardiner Street

Christopher Mullan, 3 Spencer Terrace, Ringsend Road

C. Mulligan

Thomas Mulligan, 32 Monck Place, Phibsborough

Cathal Mulready, 89 Ballybough Road

Patrick Mulvey

Bob Murphy

Hubert J. Murphy, 31 Usher's Quay

Peter Murphy, 65 Pearse Place

Robert Murphy, 31 Usher's Quay

John Murray, 93 Lower Gardiner Street

Michael Murray, 99 Lower Gardiner Street

William Murray

J. Murtagh

Edward Neary, 30 Little Mary Street

George J. Nesbitt, 'Bessboro', Kimmage, Terenure

Éamon Nolan, 1A Baggot Court

Joseph E. Nolan, 16 Sandford Avenue, South Circular Road

Jack Nugent

John Nugent, 74 Marrowbone Lane

Art O'Brien, 6 Sitric Road

Michael O'Brien, 6 Sitric Road

Richard O'Brien

T. O'Brien

James O'Connell, 15 Upper Mercer Street

E. O'Connor

John O'Connor, 67 Wellington Street

Ned O'Connor, 67 Lower Wellington Street

Peter O'Connor, 125 Harold's Cross Road

Richard O'Connor, Blackrock

Thomas O'Connor, 158 North Strand Road

Micheal O'Donnell

Eoin Ó Durmon

Terence O'Farrell, 32 Mountjoy Street

C. O'Glynn

P. John O'Grady

C. O'Hanlon

J. O'Hanlon

Éamonn O'Kane, 27A Redmond Street

Thomas O'Keefe, Rathmines

Tom O'Leary

Seán Ó Moinséal

Éamon Ó Muirgeara, Drumcondra

M. O'Neill

Seán O'Neill, Back Road, Rathgar
Thomas O'Neill
T. O'Neill
A. O'Reilly, 24 High Street
C. O'Reilly
Con O'Reilly, 11 Lower Gardiner Street
Donal O'Reilly, 43 Francis Street
Martin O'Reilly, 12 Kings Avenue, Ballybough
Richard O'Reilly, 90 Aughrim Street
William O'Reilly, Grosvenor Gardens, Harold's Cross
Christy O'Rourke, 5 Summer Row (Off North Summer Street)
J. T. O'Rourke
Thomas O'Rourke, 13 Ultan Road, Crumlin Road West
D. O'Toole
Liam O'Toole, 4 Ardan Lorne
Seamus O'Toole
Brian Parker, 44A, Aughrim Street
T. Pentory
Alfred Piggot, 20 Lower Sherrard Street, South Circular Road
H. Porter
Edward Quigley
Christopher Quinn
Joseph Redmond, 22 Stamer Street, South Circular Road
Chris Reilly, 12 Kings Way
Donal Reilly, 43 Francis Street
Liam Reilly, 27 Hamond Street
Peter Reilly, 90 Aughrim Street

Richard Reilly, 27 Hammond Street
Liam Ring, 4 Sackville Gardens
Michael Ring, 11 Ormond Market, Off Ormond Quay
Patrick Ring, 6 Sackville Gardens
Jim Roche
Tadhg Roche, 8 Coburg Place
L. Rocheford
Laurence Rochford, 180 James Street
Peter Rock
Joe Rock
Patrick K. Roe, 142 Francis Street
Joseph Rooney, 64 Buckingham Street
William Rooney, 64 Buckingham Street
John Ryan, 7 Parkgate Street
Christopher Seivers, Lusk, Co. Dublin
Donal Sands, Inchicore
Patrick Sands, Inchicore
J. Sexton, 2 Mountjoy Place
Liam Sheridan, Mayfield Road
Billy Sherry
James Shiels
Seamus Shiels, 33 Berboro Way
Joe Spain
T. Stanton
Charlie Steinmayer
Anthony Swann
P. Swan
T. Tallon
William Thornton, 7 Lower Dominick Street
Jack Timmons
Joe Timmons, 23 Lower Clanbrassil Street

William J. Toomey, 32
    Mountjoy Square
George Trainor/Traynor
Joe Trainor, 1 Leitrim Place
Éamon Travers, 134 Parnell
    Square
Edward Travers
Richard Travers, 134 Parnell
    Square
Stephen Treacy, 44 Upper
    Wellington Street
Joseph Twomey
J. Walsh, Sitric Road
Joe Walsh
Leo Walsh, 4 North James
    Street
Seamus Walsh, 4 North James
    Street
Thomas Walsh, 4 North James
    Street
Martin Walton
Patrick Ward, Glenmlaure
    House, Rialto Bridge, South
    Circular Road
Peadar Ward
Richard (Dick) Ward
Éamonn Watson, 13 Sinnons
    Place (Off Summer Hill)
J. Welshe
Leo Welshe
John J. Whelan, Mount Merrion
Joe Whelan, 92 Lower Gardiner
    Street
Liam Whelan, Townsend Street
Michael Whelan, Kilmainham
James White
Pat White
Patrick Williams
P. J. Young, 37 Hamilton Street,
    South Circular Road

Fermanagh:

Frank Carney
T. McEntaggart
Dan Monaghan, Kesh
Eddie Monaghan, Kesh

Galway:

John Egan
P. Lacey
? Moloney
Pat Ryan
Pat Tully

Kerry:

Phil Foley
Maurice Horgan
M. O'Connor
P. O'Connor
P. Sullivan
J. R. Walsh

Kildare:

Michael Corry, Naas
Frank Doran, Rathangan
John Fitzgerald, Newbridge
Joe Havlon, Monasterevin
Seán Kavanagh, Mill Street,
    Maynooth

Kilkenny:

James Lalor
J. Tierney, London and Kilkenny
Thomas Treacy

Laois:

P. Corcoran
Thomas Cribbin
T. Fox
John Lacey
G. Lawlor

Joseph P. Lynch, TD
Dr T. F. O'Higgins

Leitrim:

Seán Farrell, Dromod
Thomas Gilligan,
    Manorhamilton
Peadar Harris, Carrigallen
Turlough Lineham, Manor-
    hamilton
Patrick McAvenny, Ballinamore
Andrew Mooney, Drumshambo
Turlough Mulrooney, Manor-
    hamilton
Samuel Nulty, Carrick-on-
    Shannon

Limerick:

Richard Hayes, TD, East
    Limerick
Donal Moran

Longford:

Tom Bannon
John Comisky
M. Connolly
Jim Fullam
Luke Higgins
(?) Keenan
P.J. McCrann
Patrick McKeown
J.P. O'Neill
John Reynolds
M. Ryan
Jim Savage
John Sullivan
B. Williams
Hubert Wilson

Louth:

Matthew Agnew, Dundalk

Patrick Agnew, Cú Chulainn
    Terrace, Dundalk
William Atkinson, Dundalk
F. Coffey
Tadhg Coffey, St Mary's Road,
    Dundalk
P. J. Cosgrove
Tom Diver, Greenore
Joe Duffy, 5 Castletown Road,
    Dundalk
Michael Ferguson, Carlingford
Joe Fitzsimmons, Dundalk
Seán Garvey, Hill Street,
    Dundalk
Philip Hearty, Dublin Street,
    Dundalk
Sam Holt
Frank Kerley, Burr Street,
    Dundalk
Seamus Lean, Dunleer
Seamus Magill, The Square,
    Dundalk
Joe McGinley, UDC, Dundalk
Seamus (Jim) McGlennon, 12
    St Mary's Road, Dundalk
Patrick McKevitt, Dundalk
Owen Slowey
J. White

*All men listed below were
arrested in County Louth and
arrived at Ballykinlar camp
on 7 September 1921 and were
housed in tents.*

Gerald Coburn
Joe Cotter
James Cunningham
A. Curran
J. Dooly
P. Donnelly

Prisoners of War

John Fearon
Owen Fearon
P. Flynn
A. Green
Pat Lennon
J. Mandeville
J. Markey
L. McCooey
Mat McGeown
Owen McGough
F. McLaughlin
M. McLaughlin
P. Melia
T. Murphy
James O'Neill

Mayo:

(?) Connolly
F. Donoghue
(?) Fanning
Martin Gill
M. Griffin
Patrick Hoban
Peter Hynes
J.J. Molarchy
Felix Murray
Terence Rooney
F. Ruane
Patrick Ruane
Tom Ruane
(?) Tarpey
(?) Toban
(?) Toole

Meath:

Patrick Bartley
Frank O'Higgins

Monaghan:

Seamus Boland, Scotstown

Owen Boland, Scotstown
John Brennan, Scotstown
Tom Brennan, Scotstown
Peadar Connolly
Tadhg Daly, Ballybay
Henry Duffy, Castleblaney
Seán Finn, Castleblaney
Thomas Hughes, Ballybay
Thomas Lineham
Seamus Maguire, Kilmore,
    Scotstown
John McCabe
Joe McKenna
Patrick McKenna, Scotstown
Seamus McKenna, Scotstown
Joe McMahon, Ballybay
Brian Mulrooney
Feargal O'Connor,
    Carrickmacross
Joe Salley, Castleblaney
Michael Sherlock, Tydavnet
Owen Smith
Lorcan Reilly

Offaly:

W. Mooney

Roscommon:

Patrick Armitage, Castlerea
Seán Cassidy, Castlerea
Michael Doherty, Church
    Street, Roscommon
Seán Dolan, Castlerea
Ian Durnin, Castlerea
Patrick Finneran, Castlerea
Michael Flanagan, Castlerea
Raymond Kelly, Athleague
Seán Synnott, Roscommon
Liam Ward, Ballydangan

Sligo:
(?) Keegan
M. Leonard

Tyrone:
Frank Carney, Fintona
Charles Cavanagh, Dungannon
Dan Cavanagh, Dungannon
Joe Cavanagh, Dungannon
T. Devlin
Frank Doris, Clogher
Peter McAleer, Brook Street,
Omagh
J. McCaffry
P. McCartan, Carrickmore
Jim McGuigan, Dungannon
B. Molloy, Newtownstewart
Vincent Quinn
J. Scott

Tipperary:
Liam Clarke, Cahir
Liam Clarke, Gladstone Street,
Clonmel
Liam Condon, Cloghan
Seán Cooney, Clonmel
John Crean, Cahir
Seamus Finglas, 77 O'Connell
Street, Clonmel
Tom Gorman, Cahir
Thomas Halpin, Clonmel
Domnick Hughes, Gladstone
Street, Clonmel
Joe Kelly, The Cresent,
Templemore
Seamus Kennedy, 17 Irishtown,
Clonmel
Seán McCallan, Albert Street,
Clonmel
Seán McDonald, Nenagh

D. McGrath, Ballyporeen
Patrick McGurren, Ballina,
Killaloe
Patrick McNamee, Toomevara
Dermott Molloy, Ballyporeen
Patrick Morcell, O'Brien Street,
Tipperary town
Patrick O'Brien, Aherlow
Sorley O'Brien, Aherlow
Éamonn O'Hanrahan,
Ballyporeen
Patrick O'Kane, Ballina
Denis Ó Rubaigh, Clogheen
Patrick Power
Michael Ryan, Clonmel
Liam Sisk, Cahir
Maurice Walsh, Clogheen

Waterford:
M. Cotter
T. Hancock
(?) Hassett
Declan Horton
T. McCarthy
Éamonn O'Dea, TD
P. C. O'Mahony
M. O'Neill
J. Ormond
E. O'Shea
M. Ryan
W. Walsh

Wicklow:
A. Anderson
Alfie Henderson, Gleann na
n-Iolar
J. Keogh
Pádraig Ó hAirt, (P. Harte)
Baltinglass
J. Rodgers

Seán Roe, Baltinglass

Westmeath:
John Blayney, Athlone
Joe Brick, Mullingar
Seamus Conlon, Moate
Arthur Costello, Moate
Michael Dillon, Athlone
Patrick Dowd, Emmet Street,
    Mullingar
Cornelius Duffy, Moate
Éamonn Duffy, Moate
Seamus Gill, Moate
Joe Henry, Athlone
Larry Kelly, Castletown
    Geoghegan
Michael Kelly, Moate
Thomas Maguire, Moate
Patrick Manahan
Patrick McBride, Mullingar
Thomas McCarthy, Athlone
Michael Murphy, Moate
Thomas Noonan, Mullingar
Seán O'Farrell, Wolfe Tone
    Place, Athlone
Patrick Sloane, Legan, Moate
Joseph Tormey, Hall, Moate
Éamonn Whelan, Patrick Street,
    Mullingar

Wexford:
Patrick Donaghy, New Ross
Thomas O'Neill, Ballybeg, Ferns

England:
Charles Barrett, 109 Gladstone
    Road, Liverpool
Michael Byrne, 192 High Park
    Street, Liverpool

Denis Carr, 58 Nichlos Square,
    Hoxton
John Joseph Carr, 58 Nichlos
    Square, Hoxton
Philip Coyne, 2 Chapel Terrace,
    Liverpool
Alfred Doyle, 11 Bank Road,
    Bootle, Liverpool
Robert Duggan
Charles B. Dutton, 4 Fairbourne
    Road, Tottenham
Thomas Faughnan, 44 Mayfield
    Road, Manchester
Joseph Emmet Fox, 10 Chester
    Street, Kensington
Matthew P. Higgins, 64 Blythe
    Road, West Kensington
John Lynchehan, 18 Dutton
    Street, Liverpool
J. J. Fintan Murphy, 16 Effra
    Road, Brixton
James Maclean, 230 Victoria
    Square, Liverpool
Michael McGrath
Seán McGrath, 182 Shaftesbury
    Avenue, London
Daniel O'Brien, 182 Shaftesbury
    Avenue, London
Edward O'Connor, 72 Underley
    Street, Liverpool
Brian O'Kennedy, 63 Queen's
    Road, London, NW8
Thomas Reidy, 304 Great
    Howard Street, Liverpool
Peter J. Rowland, 304 Great
    Howard Street, Liverpool
Thomas Tighe, 52 Great
    Crosshall Street, Liverpool

Appendix 2

List of internees in Ballykinlar No. 2 Compound

Antrim:
Dan McAllister, Cushendall
William McAllister, Glens
Hugh McCampbell, Dunloy
Pat McCann, Cushendall

Armagh:
James Murphy, Silverbridge
Donal Murray, Lurgan
James Smith, Forkhill
James Tobin, 76 Edwards Street,
    Lurgan

Belfast:
Patrick Ashe
Peter Burns, 20 Linden Street
John Dillon, 49 Gibson Street
Edward Kelly, 289 Falls Road
Denis McCullough, Killowen,
    Falls Road
Éamon McDaniel, 26 Clonard
    Gardens
P.J. McLernon, 50 York Street
Pat Nash, 52 Gibson Street
John O'Neill, 75 Springfield Road
Owen Rogan, Springfield Road
Pat Smith, Violet Street

Carlow:
Michael Conway, Farans,

Ballickmogler
John Rice, Clonegal

Cavan:
Patrick Baxter, Gortnacleigh,
    Belturbet
William Bouchier, Arvagh
Thomas Brady, Bawnboy
Thomas Brady, Virginia
Owen Burns, 17 Bridge Street,
    Cavan town
Philip Caffrey
Owen Cahill, Listinigan, Drung
Patrick Cahill, Miltrain, Virginia
Cathal Colum
James Daly, Main Street,
    Arvagh
Matt Fay or Fahy, Straugh, New
    Inn
Joseph Flood
Matt Flood
James Flynn, Virginia
Edward Hart, Ballyhaise
Art Johnston, Railway Road,
    Cavan town
Pat Kiernan, Arvagh
Pat Lee, Tully
Owen McBreen
Patrick J. McCabe, Workhouse,
    Cavan town

Phil McCaffrey, Clinconnor
Peter McGee, Arvagh
Joseph McGovern, Gurteen,
    Arvagh
Joseph McGovern, Swanlinbar
Seán (John) McGrane
John McManus, Swanlinbar
Art McShane
Joseph Mullery, Francis Street,
    Cavan town
Liam Mulligan, Arvagh
Richard O'Connell, Arvagh
James O'Donnell, Main Street,
    Arvagh
Liam O'Donnell, Main Street,
    Arvagh
Hugh O'Reilly, Lahard, Corr
Michael O'Reilly, Lahard, Corr
Eoin Smith, Annaglough
Patrick Smith
John Tully, Drumohan,
    Ballyhaise
Matthew Tully, Castleterra,
    Ballyhaise

Clare:

Nicholas Carmody, Clarecastle
John Cassidy
Patrick Comer, Garraunboy,
    Killaloe
Joseph Connole, Ennistymon
Michael Connolly, Tulla
Michael Considine, Feakle
Michael Cummins Jnr,
    Newmarket-on-Fergus
Patrick Gleeson, Bodyke
Éamonn Grace, O'Callaghan's
    Mills
John Hamilton, Bodyke
John Hayes, Tulla

Seán Hughes
James M. Keane, Sixmilebridge
Joseph Keane
Matthew Lynch, Scariff
Patrick McMahon, Scariff
Dan McMenamin, Feakle
Donal McNamara
Michael McNamee
Daniel Minogue, Tulla,
    Killuran
Thomas Moroney, Feakle
Con O'Halloran, Ennis
Martin Rodgers, Feakle
Patrick Rodgers, Tulla

Cork:

Thomas Aherne, Ballineen
Richard Barrett, Tullyglass,
    Enniskeane
Edward Barry, Rochestown
Tadhg Barry, 54 Blarney Street,
    Cork city
Thomas Bennett, Clonakilty
John Breen, Ballineen
Frank Brennan, Ballinadee,
    Bandon
Dermot Buckley
Joseph Buckley, Annamore,
    Ballinhassig
Jerome Bushy, 14 Longford
    Row, Cork city
David Callaghan
John Calnan, Clonakilty
Lar Calnan, Clonakilty
Owen Caulfield, Blarney
Edward Colbert, Rathcormack
James Coleman, Carrigtwohill
Thomas Coleman, Carrigtwohill
Connor Collins
Michael Collins, Kilbrittain

Richard Collins, Courtmacsherry

Con Connolly, Kilbrittain

James Cooney, Coachford

Edward Cotter, Rathcormack

James Cotter, Innishannon

John Cotter, 41 Market Street, Bantry

Charles Coughlan, 14 Barrack Street, Cork city

J. Coughlan, Timoleague

Pat Coughlan, Fermoy

John Cronin, Macroom

Pat Cronin, Crossbarry, Upton

Dermot Crowley, Bandon

Jeremiah Crowley, Bandon

Larry Cullinane

Patrick Cunniffe, Bandon

Joseph Daly

Pat Daly, Watergrasshill

Simon Daly, John Street, Cork city

Thomas Daly, 4 Kearney's Lane, Cork city

J. Deasy, Bandon

William Deenehy, Kanturk

John Devereux, Passage West

Charles Dineen, Clonakilty

Connie Dineen

Martin Dolphin, Kilmeen

Con Donovan, Bandon

Denis Donovan, Bandon

J. P. Donovan, Ballineen

Frank Drew, Upton

William Duggan, Bandon

James Egan, Fermoy

Pat Egan, Kilbrittain

Augustine Farrelly

Dónal Finn

Dan Fitzgerald, Kilbrittain

Dermot Fitzgerald

Jeremiah Fitzgerald, Kilbrittain

John Flavin, Blackrock, Cork city

Donald Flynn, Bandon

Michael Flynn, Bandon

Thomas Foot, Ballintemple, Cork city

Gus Frawley, 19 Bandon Road, Cork city

Dan Griffin, Bandon

Dónal Hallahan, Ballinspittle, Kinsale

Art Hallinan, Fermoy

Dermot Hallinan

Jeremiah Hallinan, Clondulane, Fermoy

Pat Hallinan, Fermoy

Michael Hallissy, Kilbrittain

Dónal Hart, Bandon

William Hart, Bandon

Jeremiah Harte, Bandon

Jeremiah Hayes, Passage West

Patrick Hayes, Bandon

Dermot Healy, Harbour View Road, Cork city

Jeremiah Healy, 4 Coburg Street, Cork city

Dermot Hughes

Patrick Hughes

Pat Ivors, 136 Lee Road, Cork city

William Ivors, 136 Lee Road, Cork city

Owen Jackson, Victoria Cross, Cork city

Robert Jackson, Victoria Cross, Cork city

D. Keane, Bandon

R. Kelly

Michael Kenny, Mayfield, Cork

Raphael P. Keyes, 4 Market Street, Bantry

Denis Kiely, Kinsale

Thomas Kiely, Kinsale

D. Kingston, Clonakilty

Patrick Lane, Mallow

William Lombard, Ballineen

Batt Loughlin

Daniel Lynch, Annistown

J. Lynch, Bandon

John Lynch, Bandon

Matt Lynch, Cork

Thomas Lynch, Bandon

A. Lyons, Crookstown

Edward MacSweeney, Macroom

Batt Mahony

John Mahony, Ahiohill, Enniskean

Laurence Mahony

Michael Marshfield, Fermoy

James McCabe, 21 James Street, Cork city

Leo McCann

Daniel McCarthy, Ballinadee

Thomas McCarthy, Ballydehob

Thomas McCarthy, Bandon

Thomas McCarthy, Ballinadee, Bandon

Raphael McGee, Timoleague

Liam McKeever

Patrick McKeever

Robert McKeown

Patrick McLean

Thomas McMullen, Timoleague

Seán McSparran, Blarney

Patrick Minihane, Timoleague

Jeremiah Moloney, Timoleague

Stephen Moore, Upton

James Mulcahy, Mallow

Dermot Muldowney

Patrick Muldowney

Thomas Mullins, 6 Main Street, Kinsale

Denis Murphy, Ballinascarthy

Dónal Murphy

Pat Murphy, Fermoy

Richard Murphy, Cobh

William Murphy, 8 St Mary's Terrace, Fairhill

John Neehan, Pearse Street, Clonakilty

J. Nook, 9 Victoria Terrace, Passage West

James Nultey, MacCurtain Street, Fermoy

D. O'Brien, Drimoleague

J. O'Brien, Cloyne

John O'Brien, Courtmacsherry

Michael O'Brien, Timoleague

William O'Brien, Conna

David O'Callaghan, Castletownroche

Pat O'Callaghan, Upton

Seán O'Connell, 9 Langford Row, Cork city

William O'Connell, Passage West

R. O'Connor, Kanturk

Thomas O'Connor, Watergrasshill

Denis O'Cuill, 5 Red Abbey Street, Cork city

Michael O'Cuill, 5 Red Abbey Street, Cork city

J. O'Donnell, Church Place, Araglin

Seán Pól O'Donovan, Clonakilty

Seán O'Leary, 3 Ashburton Hill, Cork city

Batt O'Mahoney, Rathcormack
John O'Mahony
Lee O'Mahony, Macroom
Stephen O'Neill, Ashe Street,
    Clonakilty
James O'Regan, Shanballymore
J. O'Riordan, Lisgoold,
    Midleton
Stephen O'Riordan, 16 High
    Street, Cork city
Daniel Joseph O'Sullivan,
    Castletown, Rath
J. O'Sullivan, Castletown, Rath
Pat O'Sullivan, Clonakilty
Pat O'Sullivan, James Street,
    Mitchelstown
Denis Quill
Michael Quill
Michael Quinn, Kinsale
Joseph Richardson
Pat Roberts, Cork city
Batt Russell, Bandon
Dermot Scanlon
John Scannell, Macroom
John Sexton, Blarney
John Sheehan, Ardnagreena,
    Cape Clear
William Sheehan, St Brigid's
    Villas, Cork city
William Sheehan, Evergreen
    Road, Cork city
Michael Sinnott
Pat Spillane, Passage West
Edmund Stack,
    Templenacurriga, Midleton
Jeremiah Sullivan, Ballinhassig
Leo Sullivan, Glengarriff
Pat Sullivan, Timoleague
Thomas Swaine, Station Road,
    Fermoy

John Sweeney, Clondulane,
    Fermoy
Charles Tewksbury, Blackrock,
    Cork city
Thomas Troy
Edward Walsh, Fermoy
J. Walsh, Iniskeen
Jeremiah Walsh, Bandon
Maurice L. Walsh, 1.2 Frenches
    Quay, Cork city

Derry:

William Cullen, 222 Lecky
    Road, Derry city
Austin Doherty
D. Doherty, Rosemount
Derek Doherty, 1 Eglington
    Place, Derry city
V. Doherty, Creggan Street
John Fox, 25 Howard Street,
    Derry city
Patrick Frill, 41 Nelson Street,
    Derry city
James Hannon, Ballyrory
John Kennedy, 136 Bogside,
    Derry city
John McDaid, Creggan Road,
    Derry city
A. V. O'Doherty, 61 Beechwood
    Avenue, Derry city
Joseph O'Doherty, Clarendon
    Street, Derry city
Neil St John, Criterion Hotel,
    Derry city

Donegal:

John Boyle, Lettermacaward
Patrick J. Brennan, Ardara
Seán Brennan, Bundoran
Hugh Byrne, Bogagh, Kilcar

Prisoners of War

Patrick Cassidy, Leghowney
Joseph Crawford, Ballybofey
Seán Crawford
Charles Cunningham, Killybegs
Thomas Devine, Castlefin
Charles Doherty, Killygordan
Hugh Farren, Malin
Michael Forker, Burtonport
Hugh Gallagher, Ballindrait,
  Lifford
James Gallagher, Glenties
Joe Gallagher, Ardara
Charles Gordan, Ballybofey
D. Green, Glenties
James Hannigan, Ballybofey
Patrick Hannigan, Killygordan
Edward McBrearty, Killygordan
James McBride, Annagry
Joseph McBride, Annagry
J. McCormack, Ballybofey
Owen McElhinney, Cardonagh
John McGoldrick
William McGoldrick, Buncrana
Henry McGowan, Ballybofey
Patrick McGowan, Ballybofey
J. J. McIntyre, Kilcar
Hugh McLoughlin,
  Carndonagh
John D. McLoughlin,
  Carrowmenagh, Moville
Dan Meehan, Inver
F. J. Morgan, Ballyshannon
John O'Gara, Kilcar
Michael O'Carroll, Bundoran
David Quigley, Malin
James Quinn, Ballybofey
John Quinn, Convoy
Bernard Ryan, Bundoran
James S. Ward, Ballyshannon

Down:

Thomas Brannigan, Annadown,
  Loughinisland
Hugh Halpenny, Loughinisland
J. Keanan, Rathfriland
Pat Lavery, 4 Water Street,
  Newry
J. Woods, Ardglass

Dublin:

Frederick J. Allan, 2 Brighton
  Vale, Monkstown
Richard Baxter, 44 Sitric Road
J. Bohan, 36 Blackhall Place
Seán Bohan
John Bowden, 43 Hammond
  Street
Robert Boyd, 34 Lower Stephen
  Street
Joseph Brabazon, Mountjoy
  Street
Joseph Bracken, 73 Fitzroy
  Avenue, Drumcondra
William Bracken, 73 Fitzroy
  Avenue, Drumcondra
Joseph Bradley
James Brangan, Swords, Co.
  Dublin
Séamas Brannigan
James Brennan, North Circular
  Road
John Breslin, 43 Ushers Quay
Dan Brophy, Lusk, Co. Dublin
James Brown, South Dublin
  Union, c/o Mrs Lynch,
  Meath Street
John Brown, 95 Talbot Street
Seán Brown
William Brown, 34 Denzille
  Street

Liam Bruagha

James J. Burke, 9 Claremont Road, Sandymount, Co. Dublin

Thomas Butler, 44 Church Street

Dan Byrne, 5 Sir John Rogerson's Quay

E. Byrne, 9 Melrose Avenue, Fairview

James Byrne, 7 Barrow Street

Joseph M. Byrne

Michael Byrne, 7 Whitworth Place

Pat Byrne, 21 Aungier Street

Peter J. Byrne, 1 Barrow Street

Pat Caddell, Collintown

Harold Cahill, North Circular Road

Patrick Cahill, Co. Dublin

Edward Campbell, Chapel Street, Balbriggan, Co. Dublin

John Carney, Raheny, Co. Dublin

F. Carr, 63 Ranelagh Road

John Carroll, Dublin city

Joseph Clarke, 6 Convent Street

Michael Clarke, 18 Hollyfield Buildings, Rathmines

Patrick Colgan, North Circular Road

John Connolly, 9 Brabazon Row, Newmarket

John Connolly, Raymond Street, South Circular Road

John Connolly, North Circular Road

Seán Connolly, 109 Amiens Street

Joseph Corcoran, 5 Montague Street

William Crean, 5 Carnew Street

Thomas Croke

Michael Croke, Drumcondra

John Crowe, 43 Eugene Street

Michael Cullen, 131 North King Street

William Cullen, 6 Whitworth Place

Patrick Cunny

Joseph Curran, Stella Gardens, Irishtown

James Daly, 3 Roe Terrace, Wharf Road

James Deegan, 25 Richmond Hill

Aloy Demange, 4 Townsend Street

Dan Dempsey, 23 Lower Mount Street

James Denham, Balbriggan, Co. Dublin

Edward Devitt, 32 Denzille Street

Pat Dillon, 107 Marlboro Street

James Dolan, Rose Cottage, Malahide, Co. Dublin

Pat Domican, Kill, Sallins, Co. Kildare

Thomas Domican, Kill, Sallins, Co. Kildare

James Donnelly, Clanbrassil Street

Patrick Donovan

Liam Doran

Michael Douglas, 6 Granby Place

John Dumphy, 5 Phoenix Terrace, Blackrock, Co. Dublin

Richard Dumphy, 33 Mary Street

Alfred Dunne, 12 James Street

John Dunne, 13 South Dock Street

Peter Durnin, Kinsealy, Malahide, Co. Dublin

Patrick Dusie/Ducie, 6 Upper Mountain, Dún Laoghaire

Chris Ennis, 27 Temple Street

Leo Ferns, 82 Ranelagh Road

Theo Fitzgerald, 173 Great Brunswick Street

Michael Flanaghan

Thomas Fullam, 54 Denzille Street

D. Golden, 2 Victoria Street, South Circular Road

William Greene, 35 Aungier Street

John Gregory, Cadogen Road

James Hanlon, 52 Mountjoy Street

Michael Hanlon

Matthew Hayden, 8 Donnellan Avenue

Matthew Hayes, 15 Augustine Street

Professor Michael Hayes, 49 Longwood Avenue

Leo Henderson, 5 Windsor Villas, Fairview

John Hennessy, 43 Avondale Avenue

James Heron, 30 Upper Wellington Street

James Heron, 23A Bessborough Avenue, North Strand

John Hickey, St Nicholas Place

Richard Hickey, 2 Wharton Terrace, Harold's Cross

George Hogan, 106 Lower Clanbrassil Street

Joseph Hogan

Matthew Honan, 27 Synge Street

J. Hopper, 12 Upper Clanbrassil Street

Michael Hopper, 12 Upper Clanbrassil Street

James Howard, Swords, Co. Dublin

Joseph Jackson, 26 South King Street

Peter Jones, Kilcarrig Street, Bagnalstown, Co. Dublin

John V. Joyce, St Vincent's Hospital

Edward Keane, 29 De Courcy Square, Glasnevin

P. J. Keane, 83 Clare Terrace, Harold's Cross

Ben Kelly, 10 Vernon Avenue, Clontarf, Co. Dublin

Joseph Kelly, 4 Mount Pleasant Parade, Ranelagh

Peter Kelly, Swords, Co. Dublin

Richard Kelly, Corduff, Lusk, Co. Dublin

William Kelly, 13 Caledon Road

P. Kenefrick, North Strand Road, Co. Dublin

Pat Kenny, 2 Bolton Street

John Keogh, 53 Aungier Street

Pat Lalor, 65 Nash Street, Inchicore

Patrick Landers, 151 North King Street

Brendan Lawless, Saucerstown, Swords, Co. Dublin

Colm Lawless, Saucerstown, Swords, Co. Dublin

Frank Lawless, Saucerstown, Swords, Co. Dublin

J. V. Lawless, Botanic Avenue

Michael Leamy

John Leary, Baskin, Raheny

R. Ledwidge, 30 Royal Canal Bank

Patrick Loughlin

M. Love, Bessborough Avenue

Fionán Lynch, 98 Pembroke Street

James Lynch, 1 Berkeley Street

Michael Lynch, 24 Reuben Street

Patrick Mackin, 34 Sherrard Avenue, South Circular Road

Frank Magill

James Mallin, 8 Georges Quay

George Managan, 7 Fitzgerald Street

Louis Mangan

James Markey, 35 Wellington Street

Thomas Martin, 11 Ballsbridge Terrace

John McAllister, Malahide, Co. Dublin

M. McAllister, Donabate, Co. Dublin

Richard McAllister, Co. Dublin

William McAllister, Glens, Co. Dublin

James McAuley, 26 Martin Street, Dublin

Séamas McAuliffe

Patrick McCann

L. McDermott, 16 Oaklands Terrace, Terenure

Éamonn McDevitt

Seán McEleany

Thomas McGauley, 59 Caledon Road

Conor McGinley, Drumcondra Road

Maurice McGonigal, Ranelagh

James McGuigan, 19 St James Terrace, Dolphin's Barn

John McGuigan, 19 St James Terrace, Dolphin's Barn

Joseph McGuinness, 27 Lower Dorset Street

Pat McKenna, Kinsealy, Malahide, Co. Dublin

James McLernon, Kinsealy, Malahide, Co. Dublin

William McLernon, Kinsealy, Malahide, Co. Dublin

Liam McQuillan

Seamus Mers

Joseph Molloy, 106 Lower George's Street

Joseph Molloy, Dún Laoghaire

Richard Mooney, 41 Rialto Cottages

Éamonn Moore

James Moore, 34 Marlboro Street

Peter Moran, Forrest Little, Cloghan, Swords, Co. Dublin

James Mulkerns, 21 Royal Canal Bank, Phibsboro

Seamus Mullen

Chris Mullins, 3 Spencer Terrace, Ringsend Road

Peter Mulvey, 9 St John Street, Blackpitts

Martin Murphy, 13 Maples Street, South Circular Road

Henry S. Murray, 31 Effra Road, Rathmines

James Myers, 49 Queen's Square, Great Brunswick Street

Oscar Nevin, 16 St Nicholas Place

James Nolan, 106 Cork Street

James Nolan, 3 Castle View, Rathfarnham

M. L. Nolan, 9 Marlboro Place

Pat Nolan, 97 Harold's Cross Cottages

Thomas Nolan, 45 York Street

Thomas Noonon, 58 Blackhall Place

J. Noud, 13 Harold's Cross Road

John Nugent, 11 Bishop Street

Thomas J. O'Brien, 6 Tivoli Avenue, Harold's Cross

William O'Brien, 6 Tivoli Avenue, Harold's Cross

Pat O'Connor, 3 Tivoli Avenue, Harold's Cross

Donncha Ó Driscoll, 16 Whitworth Row, Seville Place

Patrick Ó Duibhir, Dún Laoghaire

Seán O'Dea, 46 Upper Rathmines

Eoin O'Donnell

Harry O'Donnell, 86 South Circular Road

Con O'Donovan, Brittas, Co. Dublin

Pat O'Donovan, 39 City Quay

M. O'Flanaghan, 14A Wexford Street

John O'Hanlon, 12 Queen's Square, Great Brunswick Street

Séamas Ó hUaghaigh, County Dublin

Patrick O'Kane

Pat O'Loughlin, 39 Lower Kevin Street

E. O'Moore, 6 Lower St Columba's Road, Drumcondra

Thomas O'Reilly, 6 Lower Gardiner Street

William O'Reilly, Grosvenor Gardens, Harold's Cross

Philip O'Shea, 92 Upper Dorset Street

John Parker, 23 Phoenix Street

Alfred Power, 20 Hollis Street

Cathal Price

Oscar Rankin

James Reilly, 3 Wallsley Place

Tom Ronan, St John's Avenue, Pimlico

Terence Rooney, Dublin

James Rosshorough, 16 Capel Street

Chris Ryan, 15 Wentworth Place

John Ryan, 7 Parkgate Street

Martin Ryan, 26 Killan Road

Pat Ryan, 41 Mountjoy Street

Richard Saunders, Waterpark, Kimmage

Charles Saurin, 3 Seafield Road, Dollymount, Clontarf, Co. Dublin

Arthur Scale, 4 Montague Street

Thomas Scully, 2 Glenmine Terrace, Anna Villa, Ranelagh

Thomas Scully, Baggott Court

William Sears, 74 Leinster Road, Rathmines

Pat Sheehan, The Bungalow, Chapelizod, Co. Dublin

Paul Shanahan, 8 Moore Street

J. Sheridan, 53 Carters Lane, Arran Quay

William Spillane, 51 Parnell Square

Frank Stapelton, 52 Marlboro Street

John Stephenson

William Stewart, Drummond Place

John Stynes, Bedles Hill, Clondalkin, Co. Dubln

Richard K. Sweetman, 44 Hardwicke Street

Joseph Taylor, Main Street, Swords, Co. Dublin

William Tierney, The Cottage, St Teresa's Terrace, Glasnevin

Stephen Treacy, 44 Upper Wellington Street

John Walsh, 22 Mary's Abbey

Nicholas Ward, 3 St Teresa's Place, Glasnevin

John Watkins, Tallaght, Co. Dublin

Michael Weddick, Ard Rí Road

B. Whelan, 7 Elm Grove, Ranelagh

George Whelan, Russell Street

Dara Wilson

Mark Wilson, 27 North Frederick Street

William Wilson, 120 North Strand Road

James Woods, Swords, Co. Dublin

Fermanagh:

Philip Carey, Kilmackbrack, Newtownbutler

James Foster, Newtownbutler

Alex Lynch, Newtownbutler

James Lynch, Newtownbutler

Thomas McElhinney, Irvinestown

Galway:

John Alberton, Abbey Lane, Loughrea

Michael Bannerton, Mountbellew

James Barrett, Athenry

Thomas Barrett, Abbey Row, Athenry

Michael Broderick, Loughrea

John J. Burke, Abbey Lane, Loughrea

Thomas Burke

Pat Callanan, Craughwell, Athenry

Michael Carroll, Tubber

Thomas Cleary, Athenry

Dan Connelly, Loughrea

John Costelloe, Belclare, Corofin

C. Coughlin, Loughrea

Martin Crowe, Bohermore

Patrick Cullen

John Cunniffe, Athenry

James Curran/Curreen, Spiddal

Joseph Curran/Curreen, Bayhill, Athenry

Patrick Deegan

Thomas Delaney, Ballinakill

Michael Doyle, Mountbellew

Patrick Faherty, Freeport, Barna
Patrick Fahy
Peter Fogarty, Gort
M. Fuery, Craughwell
Bernard Gibbs, Gort
Brian Giblin
Seán Goodman
Frank Hardiman, Galway
Thomas Haverty, Springlawn,
    Moylough
Michael Healy, Kingsland,
    Athenry
Frank Henry, Market Street,
    Galway
Thomas Hobart
John Hosty, Galway
Joseph Houlihan, Abbey,
    Loughrea
William Hussey, Kilcolgan
Joseph Keane, Loughrea
James Keavney, Shannagh,
    Glenamaddy
Pat Kennedy, Athenry
John Killeen, Abbeyland, Eyre
    Court
John Lahey, Springlawn,
    Moylough
John Loughnane, Castlefrench
Seán MacCotter
Michael Mahon, Moonbrook,
    Loughrea
John Malloney, Clonlee, Tynagh,
    Loughrea
Michael A. Martyn, Portumna
    (Tuam)
Seán Meany
Richard Moore, Ballinasloe
James Moran, Cloon, Gort
Pat Moran, Cloon, Gort
John Muldowney

Michael O'Connell, Duniry,
    Loughrea
Arthur B. O'Connor,
    Caherlistrane
Pat O'Connor, Galway
Michael O'Dea, Stradbally,
    Kilcolgan
Patrick O'Dea, Stradbally,
    Kilcolgan
James Quinn, Craughwell
Joseph (O') Rourke, Coxtown,
    Ardrahan
Martin Ryan, Loughrea
Michael Smith, Loughrea
M. Staunton, Ballinasloe
Michael Trayers, Gort
John Wade, Ballinasloe
Joseph Walsh, Portumna
Michael Ward
Joseph Weldon

Kerry:

Christopher Cannon
James Coffey, Gortre, Killarney
Chris Courtney, Killarney
Denis Donovan, Ballybrack,
    Killarney
John Fitzgerald
Pat Fitzgibbons, Listowel
John Guerin, Tullig, Killarney
Seán Hallissy
Pat Hassett, Caragh Lake,
    Killorglin
Patrick Hogan, Killorglin
John Hussey, Ballyheigue
John Lynch, Kilgarvan
Henry McCarthy, 4 Walshes
    Terrace, Tralee
Seán McCarthy, 4 Walshes
    Terrace, Tralee

James Mullins, Tralee
Dermot Murphy, Ballydaly,
    Rathmore
J. Murphy, Tullaree,
    Castlegregory
Michael J. O'Brien, Listowel
David O'Connor, Milltown
David O'Connor, Rushbrook
    Cove, Killarney
Gerry O'Connor, Tralee
Dr Michael O'Connor, The
    Square, Listowel
Thomas O'Grady,
    Newtownsandes
James O'Leary, Killarney
Con O'Leary, Killarney
Michael O'Sullivan, 1 Bridge
    Street, Killarney
Michael Reidy, Killarney
Daniel Riordan, Rangue,
    Killanglin
Liam Spillane
Eugene Sugrue, Castlegregory
Dónal Sullivan
Seán Sullivan, Killarney
Thomas Talbot, Tralee
D. Treacy, Abbeydorney, Tralee

Kildare:

Patrick Colgan, Maynooth
Patrick Davern
Thomas Davern
Patrick Domincan, Kill, Straffan
Thomas Domincan, Kill,
    Straffan
Thomas Dunne, Eyre Street,
    Newbridge
Michael Fay, Celbridge
Pat Fullam, Riverside,
    Newbridge

Michael Kelly, Williamstown,
    Carbury
John B. Maher, 23 Leinster
    Street, Athy
Joseph A. May, Woodstock
    South, Athy
William (Liam) McGrath,
    Kilgowan
Joseph Merrick
Joseph Milroy
Richard Murphy, Athy
John O'Sullivan
Thomas Patterson, 11 South
    Main Street, Naas
Joseph Reidy
Peter Shanahan
Thomas Trainor
James Whyte, 18.1 South Main
    Street, Naas

Kilkenny:

Edward Comerford, 6
    Wellington Square,
    Kilkenny
Patrick Dempsey, Paulstown
Richard Donaghy
Seán Donaghy
Michael Loughinan, New
    Street, Kilkenny
James Merenagh, Glenmore
Joseph Rice, Outrath
James Roughan, Athenure,
    Callan
Seán Ruane
Éamon Walsh
James Walsh, Glenmore

Laois:

Seán Barrett, Coolkerry Road,
    Rathdowney

Peter Brennan, Boley, Ballylinan

Stephen Carroll, Errill, Ballybrophy

Liam Carthy, Coolkerry Road, Rathdowney

Joe Conroy, Clonaslee

Michael Croghan

Thomas Delaney

James Donagher, Droughill, Portarlington

Stephen Lynch, Mountmellick

Thomas Maher, Luggacurran, Stradbally

Joseph L. Meehan, Maryborough

Dan Moore, Garryglass, Timahoe

Donal Moore

Thomas Morris, Clonaslee

Pat Muldowney, Mountrath

James O'Neill, Spire Hill House, Portarlington

Patrick J. O'Neill, 9 Market Square, Maryborough

Martin Pierce, Chapel Street, Portarlington

Pat Pierce, Chapel Street, Portarlington

P. J. Ramsbottom, 28 Main Street, Maryborough

Michael J. Sheridan, 6 Coote Street, Maryborough

Frank Ward, Main Street, Portarlington

Leitrim:

Peter Connolly, Carrigallen

Thomas Devaney, Carrick-on-Shannon

Pat Dunne, Carrick-on-Shannon

Pat Flood, Cloverhill, Ballinamore

Patrick McGeohan, Kilbracken, Carrigallen

John Mitchel, Manorhamilton

P. Pinkman, Kilclare, Carrick-on-Shannon

Patrick Sweeney, Drumkeeran

Limerick:

Éamonn MacAuliffe

Pat Brandon, Ballingarry

Michael Daly, Holycross

Jerome Driscoll, Bruree

John Driscoll, Bruree

Michael Fitzgerald, Castle-Erkin

William Landers, Lisard, Galbally

Edmond McAuliffe, 6 Tullabracky, Bruff

James McInerney, Broad Street, Limerick

D. Neville, Kilmallock

Michael Noonan, Ardnamoher, Galbally

Longford:

P. Bannon, Ballymahon

D. Cosgrove, Granard

John Coughlan, Ballymahon

Joe Farrell, Keenagh

Frank Flynn, Newtownforbes

John Joseph Geraghty, 42 Main Street, Granard

Lee Kiernan, Granard

John Macken, Milltown, Castlepollard

D. Maguire, Keenagh

A. McCormack, Ballymacken
Michael Rooney, Granard
Michael Ross, 16 Main Street,
    Edgeworthstown

Louth:

J. Agnew, Wynne's Terrace,
    Parnell Park, Dundalk
Hugh Bellew
Michael Bellew, Castletown
    Road, Dundalk
Joseph Clarke, Moorland,
    Dundalk
Gerard Coburn, 94 Castletown
    Road, Dundalk
Andrew Connor, Castlering,
    Chandon Rock
Joseph Cotter, Ballybarrack,
    Dundalk
Philip Cullen
James Cunningham, 23 John's
    Street, Dundalk
Andrew Curran, Carrickaneena,
    Ballymascanlon
Thomas Devine, Dyer Street,
    Drogheda
Patrick Donnelly, Jocelyn Street,
    Dundalk
Bernard Farrell, 11 Rope Walk,
    Drogheda
John Fearon, Carrickaneena,
    Ballymascanlon
Owen Fearon, Carrickaneena,
    Mount Pleasant
Patrick Flynn, Quay Street,
    Dundalk
Arthur Greene, 40 Mary Street,
    Dundalk
Larry Grogan, Mornington,
    Drogheda

John Hughes, Marsh Road,
    Drogheda
James Kelly
Barney Lennon, 54
    Dowdallshill, Dundalk
John Mandeville, Castletown
    Road, Dundalk
Joseph Markey, Lower Faughart
    Terrace, Dundalk
Frank Martin, Dundalk
Patrick McAvaney
Laurence McCooey, Bridge
    Street, Dundalk
Pat McCraney, The Mall,
    Drogheda
Owen McGough, 18 Emer
    Terrace, Dundalk
Michael McGowan
John McKeown, Castletown
    Road, Dundalk
Michael McLoughlin, 8 Roden
    Place, Dundalk
Thomas McNamara, Fair Street,
    Drogheda
Phil McQuillan, Maxwell's Row,
    Dundalk
Peter Melia, 2 Bridge Street,
    Dundalk
Owen Miller, 17 Trinity Street,
    Drogheda
James Moran, 23 Barrack Street,
    Dundalk
James Morgan, Abbey Grange,
    Drogheda
Owen Morris, Castletown Road,
    Dundalk
Gerard Mulherne, 16 New
    Street, Dundalk
Corneluis Mulholland, 24
    Williamson's Place, Dundalk

Owen Mullen
Peter Murphy, Silverbridge, Dundalk
Andrew O'Connor, Castlering, Channonrock
Bernard O'Hare, Maxwell's Row, Dundalk
James O'Kelly, Grangebellow/ Dunleer
James O'Neill, Dowdallshill, Dundalk
Joseph O'Neill, Trinity Street, Drogheda
James Rowan, Callan
Séamas Sáirséal
Joseph M. Smith, 79 Bridge Street, Dundalk

Mayo:

Cathal Barrett
John Biggins, Ballinrobe
John Breslin
Andrew Burke, Ballindine
Thomas Burke, Cloongowla, Ballinrobe
Michael Cafferty, Kilkelly
Michael Collins, Geesala, Ballina
John Comer, Swinford
Andrew Flatley, Swinford
James Gallagher, Claremorris
Michael Gallagher
Thomas Gleeson, Claremorris
Pat Goonan, Geesala, Ballina
Martin Groonell, Cloongowla, Ballinrobe
Martin Haire, The Neale
Thomas Hand
Aloysius Heaney, James Street, Claremorris

Michael Heaney, James Street, Claremorris
John Hoban, Castlebar
Thomas Kane
William Kenny, James Street, Claremorris
Seán Lonegan
Charles Lydon, Kilkelly
William Mackin, Claremorris
Edward Mangan, Geesala, Ballina
Thomas McCague
Donal McCusker
Andrew McTighe, Kiltimagh
P. Melvin, Swinford
Pat Nielan, Ballycastle
Mat O'Byrne, St Muredock's Terrace, Ballina
John O'Dea, Claremorris
Patrick O'Malley, Ardaley, Westport
John Peyton, Charlestown
William Quinn, Hollymount
Thomas Reidy
Peadar Roland
Séamas Roland
Michael Rooney, Charlestown
James Rowley, Swinford
Patrick Rushe
Michael Ryan, Ballinrobe
Patrick Stanton
Joe Toohey
John Tucker, Claremorris
Pat Tucker, Claremorris
A. Walsh, Charlestown
Harry Watters, Castlebar

Meath:

Éamonn Arthurs
Joseph Bailey, Navan

George Beggan, Kells
Owen Clarke, Oldcastle
Pat Clarke, Carrick Street,
  Kells
Thomas Clarke, Navan
Patrick Cunnings
J. Fagan, Oldcastle
Nick Farrelly, Seymourstown,
  Crossakiel
Phil Farrelly, Carnaross/
  Crossakiel, Kells
Michael Finamore
Andrew Finnerty, Trimgate
  Street, Navan
Pat Flynn, Carrick, Kells
P. Garrigan, Oldcastle
J. Gavin, Oldcastle
Michael Gaynor, Navan
Nick Gaynor, Ballinlough, Kells
Matthew Gibney, Oldcastle
James Ginnitty, College Hill,
  Slane
Joseph Gleeson, Church View,
  Navan
Joseph Goodfellow
William Grace, Castle Street,
  Oldcastle
Pat Hand, Kilskyre, Kells
Edward Harte, Bohermeen,
  Navan
John Husband, Oldcastle
Patrick Keelan, Kells
Pat Loughran, Market Square,
  Navan
Richard Lynch, Castle Street,
  Oldcastle
John Maguire, Bective Street,
  Kells
Christopher McCabe, Maudlin
  Street, Kells

James McGinn, Castle Street,
  Oldcastle
Michael McGinn, Castle Street,
  Oldcastle
Leo McKenna, Trimgate Street,
  Navan
Bernard McKeown, Crossakeel
Patrick McKeown, Crossakeel
Patrick McMahon, Nobber
John Mitchell, Tankardstown,
  Navan
John Morris, Cannon Street,
  Kells
Joseph Morris, Cannon Street,
  Kells
Robert Mullen, Bective Street,
  Kells
Robert Mullins, Bective Street,
  Kells
D. O'Sullivan, Kells
William Sheridan, Oldcastle
Michael Skelly, Kells
Patrick Smith, Maudlin Street,
  Kells
Pat Timmons, Oldcastle
John Tuite, Ardcath
Leo Twomey, Oldcastle
Hugh Ward, Nobber
Patrick Woods, Clonee

Monaghan:

Frank Boylan, Clontibret
Michael Boylan, Clontibret
Pat Boylan, Clontibret
Pat Boylan, Carrickmacross
Pat Boyle, Newbliss
James Brady, Tydavnet
Alastar Bradley, Claslough
  Street, Monaghan town
Patrick Brennan, Castleblayney

Luke Cassidy, Carrickmacross
Charles Carragher, Ballybay
Michael Carragher,
    Carrickmacross
Arthur Cavanagh, Drumlish,
    Tydavnet
James Christy, Thomas Street,
    Castleblayney
Thomas Clarke, Canal Street,
    Monaghan town
John J. Conlon, Ballybay
Peter Conlon, Main Street,
    Ballybay
James Connolly, Tydavnet
Oliver Coogen Glasslough
    Street, Monaghan town
Phil Corr, Stranooden
Patrick Cosgrove, Tullyglass,
    Shantonagh
Frank Deery, Castleblayney
James Downey, Carrickmacross
Pat Finn, Inishkeen
A. Furlong, Carrickmacross
Phil Garther, Castleblayney
Thomas Gillanders, Old Cross
    Square, Monaghan town
Patrick Greenan, Newbliss
Art Kavanagh
Dan Keelan, Corduff,
    Carrickmacross
James Keely, Stranooden
Liam Kielty
Peter King
Edward Leanagh, Laragh
Patrick Macklin, Dublin Street,
    Monaghan town
John Mahony, Inishkeen
Hugh McAdam, Park Street,
    Monaghan town
Michael McArdle,
    Tullynahinera
Thomas McArdle, Castleblayney
Peter McAree, Mullyera,
    Tydavnet
Brian McBride, Broomfield,
    Castleblayney
John McCabe, The Diamond,
    Clones
Michael McCann
Leo McCarron, Clarna,
    Tydavnet
Seán McCaughey
Edward McCormack, Emyvale
Oliver McCrudden, Clarna,
    Tydavnet
Edward McDermott, Sheetrim
Frank McDonald, Ardaghey
John McDonald, Belgium
    Square, Monaghan town
Richard McDonald, Ardaghey
Pat McDonnell, Newbliss
P. McEntee, Old Cross Square,
    Monaghan town
Patrick McFlynn
James McGough, Monaghan
    town
James McKenna, Tydavnet
M. McKenna, Emyvale
P. McKenna, Pound Hill,
    Monaghan town
Pat McKenna
Owen McKenney, Glasslough
F. McMahon, Latnamard PO
Patrick McNally, Castleblayney
Edward Meehan, Emyvale
James Merron, Carrickmacross
Maurice Moen, Ballybay
James Mullan, Market Street
James Mulligan, Kilnacloy
Seán Mulligan

John O'Connor, Carrickmacross
Eoghan Ó Curragúin
James O'Donoghue, Newbliss
William P. Quinn, Inishkeen
Henry Sherlock, Tydavnet
Oliver Sherlock, Clarna,
　Tydavnet
Dr Leo Reynolds, Scotstown
P. Traynor, Kilnamaddy,
　Braddocks
Brian Ward
James Ward, Emyvale

Offaly:

Fr Thomas Burbage, Geashill
Ben Cash, Rathrobin, Tullamore
James Clarke, Columcille Street,
　Tullamore
Laurence Cocoman, Clonbrown,
　Clonbulloge
John Daly, Molloy Street,
　Tullamore
John Duffy
Denis Finlay, Colehill,
　Tullamore
Joseph Gallagher, O'Carroll
　Street, Tullamore
Michael Gibson, Geashill
Larry Guegan
B. Halpenny, Coolderry
Alf Johnson, Harbour Street,
　Tullamore
Liam Johnson, Harbour Street,
　Tullamore
Seán Kelly
Pat Lawlor, Geashill
James Long
Pat Loyd, Cormac Street,
　Tullamore
James Mahon, Ballycommon

Michael McBride
Patrick McCullough
Denis McGinley
Thomas McIntyre, Cloghan
Patrick J. McNally, Claremont,
　Banagher
Liam McKeown
John O'Kelly, Thomas Street,
　Tullamore
James O'Neill
Martin Pearse
Patrick Pearse
Michael Sheehy, Coolemount
　House, Rhode

Roscommon:

Michael Beatty, Castlerea
Patrick Cannon
Patrick Crawley, Loughglinn
　Town, Loughglinn
John Cummins, Croghan
Thomas Devaney, Croghan
T. Donoghue, Scramoge,
　Strokestown
George Duignan, Scalta, Roosky
James Duignan, Scalta, Roosky
Joseph Duignan
Seán Gilmartin
J.P. Hallissey, Caher, Castlerea
John Kilmartin, Kilteevan
Pat Lannon, Ballagh, Kilrooskey
Denis Maguire/McGuire,
　Scramoge
Martin Maguire, Longford,
　Castlerea
Turlach McDonagh
Michael J. McNamara,
　Scramoge
Micheal J. Noone, 4 Ballyfarnan
　Town, Ballyfarnan

Vincent A. Ryan, Knockranny
House, Keadue
Patrick Roddy, Ballymore,
Boyle
Bernard Scanlon, Stralbragan,
Aghafin

Sligo:
Henry Benson, Sligo Town
James Doory, Adelaide Street,
Sligo
Seán Duffy, Cloghan, Banagher
M. J. Gallagher, Clonlora
Nicholas J. Gallagher, Bridge
Street, Sligo
John Ginty, Carns, Aclare
Charles Hargadon, Colgagh
Patrick Madigan
James Marren, Collooney
Edward Masterson, Tobercurry
Seán McGinty
Henry Morohan
Patrick Mulligan, Gurteen
Michael O'Hara, Kilmacteige
John Pilkington, 10 Abbey
Street, Sligo
James Scanlon, Cairns View

Tyrone:
Michael Daly, Aghanereagh,
Athenree
Patrick Daly, Aghanereagh,
Athenree
James Ferris, Omagh
Dan Fraher, Dungannon
William Joseph Kelly,
Charlemont Street,
Dungannon
Joe McGrane, Main Street,
Dromore

Joe McGuckien, Dungannon
Brian McKenna, Railway Street,
Strabane
John Shields, Lisnacroy,
Benburb

Tipperary:
James Boyle
William Brosnan, Greenore
Joe Burns
P. J. Christian, Carhue,
Dundrum
Denis Costelloe, Cloughjordan
Michael Curry
Pat Donoghue, Patrick Street,
Templemore
A. Grady, Ballinure
Liam Graney
William Grant, Templemore
James Hayes, Grangebarry,
Fethard
Desmond Hughes
Pat Keating, Wolfe Tone Street,
Nenagh
Dave Kelly
Jeremiah Kelly, Nenagh
Pat Kennedy, Bansha
Denis Kindlon
Michael Kirby, Tipperary (at
time of arrest was living in
Ballyconnell, Co. Cavan)
William Leahy, Martlestown,
Cahir
John Marken, Patrick Street,
Templemore
Edward McGrath, Templemore
Maurice McGrath
John Morhan
Joe Mulcahy, Cashel
John Murphy, Scart

Liam Murphy
Andrew O'Grady
Frank O'Meara
Michael O'Meara, Main Street,
Borrisokane
John O'Sullivan, Church
Avenue, Templemore
Michael Phelan, Borrisokane
P. Prendergast, Bohernagore,
Cloghenn
Michael Quish, Emly
John Ryan, Dualla, Cashel
John Ryan, 4 Fianna Road,
Thurles
J. F. Ryan, Bohernarnane
Michael Ryan, Annacarthy
Thomas Ryan
John Sheehan, Dualla, Cashel
Edward Treacy, Ivy House,
Holycross

Waterford:

James Aherne, Knockboy,
Ballinamult
Patrick Brassill (Brazil), 4
Lombard Street, Waterford
Michael Brennock, Dungarvan
James V. Butler, Knockboy,
Ballinamult
John Cashin, Ballyduff
P. Cashin, Dungarvan
Laurence Condon, Dungarvan
Patrick Condon, Dungarvan
Thomas Crowe, Villierstown
Pat Cullinane, Kilmacthomas
Tadhg Doogan
Frank Drohan, Kilmacthomas
Daniel Fraher, Dungarven
Maurice Galvin, Tallow
Patrick Halloran

M. Hassett, Dungarvan
Edward Healy
Edward Higgins, Ballyduff
John Keyes, Lismore
Thomas Kirwan, Johnstown
P. Lynch, Dungarvan
Felix Mallow, Dungarvan
Charles Mansfield, Dungarvan
Thomas McCarthy, Dungarvan
Joseph McRickland, Rossduff,
Woodstown
Thomas Mooney, Ballinamona,
Old Parish, Dungarvan
Pat Mulcahy, Dungarvan
Patrick Ormonde, Mitchell
Street, Dungarvan
Pat O'Bragil, 4 Lombard Street,
Waterford
Patrick C. O'Mahony, 2 Western
Terrace, Dungarvan
Edward Power, Dunmore East
Nicholas Power, Rossduff,
Woodstown
Seán Quirke
John Riordan, Dungarvan
Michael Ronayne, Villierstown,
Dromana
N. Troy, Dungarvan
Michael Ward, 12 New Street,
Lismore
Pat Whelan, Dungarvan

Westmeath:

Kieran Aspill, Athlone
Patrick Bannon
Christopher Bennett, Milltown
Pass, Mullingar
Edward Bertles, Walterstown,
Athlone
James J. Boyle, Horseleap

Prisoners of War

John Claffey, Moate
Pat Claffey, Tully, Moate
J. Conlon, Athlone
Pat Donlon, Delvin
William Donlon, Littletown,
    The Pigeons
Christopher Duffy, Milltown
    Pass, Mullingar
Joe Duffy, Athlone
Chris Fitzsimons, Austin, Friars
    Street, Mullingar
John Gallagher, Killucan
Joseph Gilsenan, Fore,
    Castlepollard
Lee Ginnell, Delvin
L. Hannavey, Athlone
William Kelly, Castlepollard
J. Kennedy, Castlepollard
Patrick Killian, Glasson,
    Athlone
Edward Leonard, Delvin
Patrick Leonard, Delvin
James McAuley, Moate
Joseph McElhnney
Laurence McGinley
Thomas McGuire, Green Street,
    Castlepollard
Owen McLoughlin, Newbrook,
    Mullingar
J. McManus, Clonyegan, Mount
    Temple
Dan Murray, Fearmore, Moate
Pat Nestor, Gorteen, Tubber
Michael Nugent, Mount
    Temple, Moate
James Quinn, Mount Temple,
    Moate
Thomas Quinn, Milltown,
    Mullingar
Michael Scanlon, Athlone

John Scott, Ballybnahowen
J. Tiernan, Inchmore Island,
    Glasson
Ciarán Walsh, Curries, Moate

Wexford:

John Atkins, King's Street,
    Wexford
William Cullinmore, Main
    Street, Wexford
James (Seamus) Doyle,
    Enniscorthy
Robert Duggan, Wexford town,
    arrested in England
Seán Kelly, South Main Street,
    Wexford
A. F. McGown
Pat Morris, Swan View, The
    Folly, Wexford
Nick Newport, Main Street,
    Wexford
Denis O'Brien, Weafer Street,
    Enniscorthy
John O'Curry, Ferns
James Quinn, Camolin
James Quinn, Enniscorthy
P. Redmond, Kildavin, Ferns
Michael Rossiter, Ramsgrange
Albert Sinnott, Enniscorthy
Thomas D. Sinnott, Rafter
    Street, Enniscorthy
Albert F. Smith, Enniscorthy
Thomas Traynor, Parnell Street,
    Wexford
Seán Walsh
John Warner, Swan View, The
    Faythe, Wexford

Wicklow:

Christopher Cullen, Delgany

Thomas Murphy, Roundwood
James Tyre/Tier, Greenport
      Road, Bray
Richard B. Whelan

Notes

BMH   = Bureau of Military History
BNA   = British National Archives, Kew, London
HC   = House of Commons
MA   = Military Archives, Dublin
NLI   = National Library of Ireland, Dublin
UCD AD = University College Dublin Archive Department

Introduction

1   *The Freeman's Journal*, 19 May 1921.

1 Internment – 1916 to 1920

1   *Sinn Féin Rebellion Handbook*, 1917.
2   Seán O'Mahony, *Frongoch, University of Revolution*, FDR Teoranta, 1987, p. 18.
3   BNA, CAB 23/6 – IR 0017.
4   *Derry Journal*, 20 May 1918.
5   BMH, MA, WS 1280, Éamon Broy, p. 71.
6   Seán Ó Lúing, 'The German Plot 1918', *Capuchin Annual*, 1968, p. 378.
7   BNA, CAB 23/9 – IR 0014.
8   Michael Hopkinson, *The Irish War of Independence*, Gill & Macmillan, 2004, p. 39.
9   *Ibid.*, p. 28.
10   BNA, CAB 24/98 – IR 0080.
11   *Ibid.*
12   Major-General Joseph A. Sweeney, 'Donegal and the War of In-

dependence', *The Capuchin Annual*, 1970, pp. 433–4; Hansard, HC debate 21 June 1921, Vol. 143, cc 1106–7; http://hansard. millbanksystem.com.

2 Bloody Sunday

1   T. Ryle Dwyer, *The Squad and the Intelligence Operations of Michael Collins*, Mercier Press, 2005, p. 165.
2   BMH, MA, WS 1,280, Éamon Broy, pp. 80–1.
3   BMH, MA, WS 445, James J. Slattery, pp. 13–14.
4   BMH, MA, WS 1,762, J. V. Joyce, p. 2.
5   BMH, MA, WS 413, Patrick McCrea, p. 17.
6   BMH, MA, WS 663, Joseph Dolan, p. 10.
7   Dwyer, *The Squad*, p. 166.
8   BMH, MA, WS 434, Charles Dalton, p. 20.
9   BMH, MA, WS 668, Gerald (Garry) Byrne, p. 11.
10 *Ibid.*
11 BMH, MA, WS 445, James J. Slattery, pp. 13–14.
12 *The New York Times*, 24 November 1920.
13 Dwyer, *The Squad*, p. 170.
14 BMH, MA, WS 380, David Neligan, p. 9.
15 BMH, MA, WS 413, Patrick McCrea, p. 18.
16 *Ibid.*, p. 19.
17 Hansard, HC debate, 22 November 1920, Vol. 135 cc 34–8, http://hansard.millbanksystems.com.
18 *Ibid.*; BMH, MA, WS 445, James J. Slattery, pp. 14–15.
19 Hopkinson, *The Irish War of Independence*, p. 90; BMH, MA, WS 663, Joseph Dolan, p. 10.
20 Hansard, HC debate, 22 November 1920, Vol. 135 c 37, http://hansard.millbanksystems.com.
21 *Ibid.*, Vol. 135 c 38.
22 *Ibid.*
23 *Ibid.*
24 *The Freeman's Journal*, 22 November 1920.

25 Tim Carey and Marcus de Búrca, 'Bloody Sunday 1920 – New Evidence', *History Ireland*, Issue 2 (Summer 2003), Vol. 11, www. historyireland.com.

26 BMH, MA, WS 631, Bernard C. Byrne, p. 20.

27 Dwyer, *The Squad*, p. 193.

28 BMH, MA, WS 380, David Neligan, p. 12.

29 *The New York Times*, 24 November 1920.

3 The Internment Round-Up

1 UCD AD, P80/136 (73), Desmond Fitzgerald Collection.

2 William Sheehan, *Hearts and Mines*, Collins Press, 2009, p. 52; *The New York Times*, 24 November 1920.

3 UCD AD, P80/137 (1–5), Desmond Fitzgerald Collection.

4 BMH, MA, WS 1322, Art O'Donnell, pp. 58–9.

5 UCD AD, P80/136 (22), Desmond Fitzgerald Collection.

6 BMH, MA, WS 1093, Thomas Treacy, pp. 75–6.

7 BMH, MA, WS 707, Michael Noyk, p. 49.

8 BMH, MA, WS 668, Gerald (Garry) Byrne, pp. 11–12.

9 UCD AD, P80/136 (87), Desmond Fitzgerald Collection.

10 UCD AD, P80/136 (123), Desmond Fitzgerald Collection.

11 UCD AD, P80/136 (46), Desmond Fitzgerald Collection.

12 *The Freeman's Journal*, 9 December 1920.

13 UCD AD, P80/136, Desmond Fitzgerald Collection.

14 BMH, MA, WS 639, Maurice Donegan, pp. 6–7.

15 BMH, MA, WS 633, Michael Joseph Ryan, pp. 26–7.

16 BMH, MA, WS 885, Seán Kennedy, p. 25.

17 BMH, MA, WS 1385, James McMonagle, pp. 12–13.

18 BMH, MA, WS 1583, Michael Doherty, pp. 13–14.

19 BMH, MA, WS 1385, James McMonagle, p. 13.

20 P. J. Dunne, 'Ballykinlar Internement Camp', www.butlersbridge. net.

21 *The Irish Times*, 18 December 1920.

22 BNA, CAB 24/116 – IR 0066.

23 BNA, CAB 23/23 – IR 0013.

24 *The Freeman's Journal*, 11 December 1920.

25 BNA, CAB 23/23 – IR 0027.

26 *The Irish Times*, 4 December 1920.

27 *Irish Independent*, 6 December 1920.

28 *The Irish Times*, 18 December 1920.

29 UCD AD, P80/135, Desmond Fitzgerald Collection.

30 BMH, MA, WS 1322, Art O'Donnell, p. 59; BMH, MA, WS 639, Maurice Donegan, p. 7.

31 Louis J. Walsh, *On My Keeping and in Theirs*, The Talbot Press, 1921, p. 42.

32 *The Freeman's Journal*, 19 March 1921.

33 Hansard, HC debate 21 June 1921, Vol. 143, cc 1106–8 W, http://hansard.millbanksystems.com.

34 BNA, CAB 24/123 – IR 0103.

4 Ballykinlar Camp

1 *The Freeman's Journal*, 26 January 1921.

2 *The Irish Times*, 4 December 1920.

3 UCD AD, P53/117 (12), Michael Hayes Collection.

4 UCD AD, P80/137 (1–5), Desmond Fitzgerald Collection.

5 *Irish Independent*, 19 November 1921.

6 UCD AD, P80/137 (1–5) Desmond Fitzgerald Collection.

7 Walsh, *On My Keeping and in Theirs*, p. 43.

8 *Ibid.*

9 Hansard, HC debate 21 June 1921, Vol. 143, cc 1106–7 W, http://hansard.millbanksystems.com.

10 BMH, MA, WS 1093, Thomas Treacy, pp. 77–8; UCD AD, P80/137 (1–5), Desmond Fitzgerald Collection.

11 UCD AD, P80/137 (1–5), Desmond Fitzgerald Collection.

12 *The Freeman's Journal*, 21 December 1920.

13 BMH, MA, WS 952, Maurice Horgan, p. 8.

14 BMH, MA, WS 668, Gerald (Garry) Byrne, p. 12.

15 Walsh, *On My Keeping and in Theirs*, pp. 48–9.

16   BMH, MA, WS 952, Maurice Horgan, p. 9.
17   Kilmainham Gaol Archives 19FO-1D33-01, Internment Order, Thomas Kerr, 14 April 1921.
18   BMH, MA, WS 850, Patrick Colgan, pp. 76–7.
19   BMH, MA, WS 952, Maurice Horgan, p. 9.
20   Jim Dawson Ballykinlar Papers – Private Collection, Patrick Dawson, Letterkenny, County Donegal.
21   BMH, MA, WS 952, Maurice Horgan, p. 10.
22   Walsh, *On My Keeping and in Theirs*, pp. 65–6; John Graham was not the name of the internee and was changed by Walsh to conceal the true identity of the person.
23   Walsh, *On My Keeping and in Theirs*, p. 49.
24   BNA, CAB 24/118 – IR 0071; *The Freeman's Journal*, 3 February 1921.
25   BMH, MA, WS 1582, Thomas McGlynn, pp. 11–12.
26   BMH, MA, WS 1596, Henry McGowan, p. 6.
27   BNA, CAB 24/118 – IR 054.
28   *The Freeman's Journal*, 19 March 1921.
29   *Ibid.*
30   Walsh, *On My Keeping and in Theirs*, p. 47.
31   Major Lawrence Gordon, *British Battles and Medals*, revised by John Hayward, Diana Birch and Richard Bishop, Spink, 2008.
32   Kilmainham Gaol Archives, Ballykinlar Diary of Ted Donohue. A special thank you to Liz Gillis for this source.
33   *The Freeman's Journal*, 27 October 1921.
34   *Ibid.*, 23 December 1920.
35   Walsh, *On My Keeping and in Theirs*, p. 51.
36   BMH, MA, WS 665, Francis O'Duffy, pp. 19–20.
37   *Irish Independent*, 24 January 1921.
38   Jim Dawson Ballykinlar Papers – Private Collection, Patrick Dawson, Letterkenny, County Donegal.
39   Walsh, *On My Keeping and in Theirs*, pp. 59–60.
40   Kilmainham Gaol Archives, 19MS-1B41-06, Roll of Men in Camp Two.

41   BMH, MA, WS 734, Thomas J. Meldon, pp. 47–8.

42   *The Freeman's Journal*, 21 December 1920.

43   BMH, MA, WS 734, Thomas J. Meldon, pp. 47–8.

44   Hansard, HC debate 21 June 1921, Vol. 143, cc 1106–7 W, http://hansard.millbanksystems.com.

45   UCD AD, P80/137 (1–5), Desmond Fitzgerald Collection.

46   *The Freeman's Journal*, 13 October 1921.

47   *Ibid.*, 2 March 1921.

48   UCD AD, P80/137 (1–5), Desmond Fitzgerald Collection.

49   UCD AD, P53/117 (3), Michael Hayes Collection.

50   *The Freeman's Journal*, 13 October 1921.

51   UCD AD, P80/137 (1–5), Desmond Fitzgerald Collection.

52   BMH, MA, WS 665, Francis O'Duffy, pp. 12–13.

53   UCD AD, P53/117 (3), Michael Hayes Collection.

54   *Ibid.*

55   Walsh, *On My Keeping and in Theirs*, pp. 59–60.

56   UCD AD, P53/117 (3), Michael Hayes Collection.

57   BMH, MA, WS 665, Francis O'Duffy, pp. 10–13.

58   *Ibid.*, p. 12.

59   *The Freeman's Journal*, 13 October 1921.

60   *Ibid.*

61   *Ibid.*

62   UCD AD, P80/140 (1–2), Desmond Fitzgerald Collection.

63   *Irish Independent*, 20 October 1921.

64   Dr Moore's Report (2), *The Freeman's Journal*, 19 October 1921.

65   *The Freeman's Journal*, 22 September 1921.

66   *Ibid.*, 19 October 1921.

67   *Ibid.*, 13 October 1921.

68   Jim Dawson Ballykinlar Papers.

69   Kilmainham Gaol Archives, Ballykinlar Diary of Ted Donohue.

70   Hansard, HC debate 2 June 1921, Vol. 142, cc 1206, http://hansard.millbanksystems.com.

71   Kilmainham Gaol Archives, Ballykinlar Diary of Ted Donohue.

72 Dr Moore's Report, *The Freeman's Journal*, 5 October 1921.
73 *Ibid.*
74 BMH, MA, WS 1322, Art O'Donnell, p. 61.
75 *Irish Independent*, 2 May 1921.
76 *The Freeman's Journal*, 14 November 1921.
77 UCD AD, P80/ 140 (1–2), Desmond Fitzgerald Collection.
78 *The Freeman's Journal*, 20 July 1921.
79 BMH, MA, WS 665, Francis O'Duffy, p. 5.
80 Walsh, *On My Keeping and in Theirs*, p. 45.
81 *Ibid.*
82 *Evening Herald*, 19 February 1962.
83 Comdt Owen Quinn, 'The Books of Ballykinlar', *An Cosantóir*, December 1983, p. 402; *Evening Herald*, 19 February 1962.
84 *Ibid.*
85 Walsh, *On My Keeping and in Theirs*, p. 45.
86 Seán McConnell, 'De Valera, priest ponder the morality of taxation', *The Irish Times*, 2 March 2000.
87 BMH, MA, WS 1387, Patrick O'Daly, p. 58.
88 BMH, MA, WS 665, Francis O'Duffy, p. 2.
89 Quinn, 'The Books of Ballykinlar', p. 402.
90 Walsh, *On My Keeping and in Theirs*, p. 46.
91 *The Freeman's Journal*, 16 August 1921.
92 National Archive, Dublin, P/A 98/25 (3).
93 *The Freeman's Journal*, 8 January 1921.
94 UCD AD, P80/137 (1–5), Desmond Fitzgerald Collection.
95 *The Freeman's Journal*, 13 October 1921.
96 UCD AD, P80/137 (1–5), Desmond Fitzgerald Collection.
97 Kilmainham Gaol Archives, 19MS-1B41-17.
98 *The Freeman's Journal*, 4 November 1921.
99 UCD AD, P53/117 (12), Michael Hayes Collection.
100 Hansard, HC debate, 21 April 1921, Vol. 140, cc 2047, http://hansard.millbanksystems.com.
101 *Ibid.*, 22 June 1921, Vol. 143, cc 1377, http://hansard.millbanksystems.com.

102 *Ibid.*, 14 April 1921, Vol. 140, cc 1270, http://hansard.millbank-systems.com.

103 BNA CAB 24/123 – IR 0103.

5 Protecting Wanted Men

1 BMH, MA, WS 1385, James McMonagle, pp. 14–15.

2 BMH, MA, WS 665, Francis O'Duffy, p. 5.

3 BMH, MA, WS 850, Patrick Colgan, p. 84.

4 BMH, MA, WS 1596, Henry McGowan, p. 8.

5 BMH, MA, WS 850, Patrick Colgan, pp. 84–7.

6 BMH, MA, WS 707, Michael Noyk, p. 49.

7 BMH, MA, WS 850, Patrick Colgan, pp. 84–7.

8 UCD AD, P53/117 (10), Michael Hayes Collection.

9 BMH, MA, WS 850, Patrick Colgan, p. 87.

6 The Murders of Joseph Tormey and Patrick Sloane

1 Walsh, *On My Keeping and in Theirs*, p. 75; UCD AD, P53/117 (2), Michael Hayes Collection.

2 BMH, MA, WS 1093, Thomas Treacy, p. 79.

3 *Ibid.*

4 BMH, MA, WS 952, Maurice Horgan, pp. 11–12.

5 BMH, MA, WS 850, Patrick Colgan, p. 79.

6 BMH, MA, WS 1582, Thomas McGlynn, p. 11.

7 BMH, MA, WS 850, Patrick Colgan, p. 79; UCD AD, P53/117 (2), Michael Hayes Collection.

8 *Westmeath Examiner*, 22 January 1921.

9 Kilmainham Gaol Archives, Ballykinlar Diary of Ted Donohue.

10 *Irish Independent*, 24 January 1921.

11 *Ibid.*

12 BMH, MA, WS 850, Patrick Colgan, p. 80.

13 *Irish Independent*, 9 February 1921.

14   Hansard, HC debate 16 February 1921, Vol. 138 cc 93–4, http://hansard.millbanksystems.com.
15   Hansard, HC debate 24 February 1921, Vol. 138 cc 1113–5, http://hansard.millbanksystems.com.
16   UCD AD, P53/117 (2), Michael Hayes Collection.
17   BMH, MA, WS 850, Patrick Colgan, p. 80.
18   UCD AD, P80/138, Desmond Fitzgerald Collection.

7 Camp Intelligence and Communications

1   UCD AD, P80/139 (1), Desmond Fitzgerald Collection.
2   BMH, MA, WS 1093, Thomas Treacy, pp. 82–5.
3   *The Freeman's Journal*, 20 October 1921.
4   BMH, MA, WS 850, Patrick Colgan, pp. 87–9.
5   BMH, MA, WS 665, Francis O'Duffy, p. 8.
6   BMH, MA, WS 850, Patrick Colgan, p. 88.
7   BMH, MA, WS 665, Francis O'Duffy, p. 9.
8   BMH, MA, WS 639, Maurice Donegan, p. 8.
9   BMH, MA, WS 1093, Thomas Treacy, p. 82.
10   *Ibid.*, p. 81.

8 Letters, Parcels and the Ballykinlar Post Office

1   UCD AD, P53/117 (11), Michael Hayes Collection.
2   *The Freeman's Journal*, 8 January 1921.
3   UCD AD, P53/117 (11), Michael Hayes Collection.
4   *Ibid.*
5   UCD AD, P80/137 (1–5), Desmond Fitzgerald Collection.
6   Jim Dawson Ballykinlar Papers.
7   UCD AD, P53/117 (1), Michael Hayes Collection.
8   *Ibid.*

9 Education, GAA, Drama and Other Recreation

1   UCD AD, P53/117 (5), Michael Hayes Collection.

2   Walsh, *On My Keeping and in Theirs*, 1921, p. 71.

3   BMH, MA, WS 1322, Art O'Donnell, p. 65.

4   UCD AD, P53/88, Michael Hayes Collection.

5   *Irish Independent*, 3 September 1921.

6   BMH, MA, WS 665, Francis O'Duffy, p. 18.

7   NLI, Ms 26,763, Frederick Allan Collection.

8   BMH, MA, WS 665, Francis O'Duffy, pp. 24–5.

9   UCD AD, P53/117 (12), Michael Hayes Collection.

10   BMH, MA, WS 665, Francis O'Duffy, pp. 23–4.

11   NLI, Ms 26,763, Frederick Allan Collection.

12   *The Freeman's Journal*, 19 October 1921.

13   Kilmainham Gaol Archives, 19N-1D23-28, *The Barbed Wire*, August 1921.

14   *Ibid.*

15   Kilmainham Gaol Archives, 19NW-1E11-06, *Ná Bac Leis*.

16   *Ibid.*

17   Jim Dawson Ballykinlar Papers.

18   Kilmainham Gaol Archives, 19NW-1D22-15, *Ná Bac Leis*.

19   Kilmainham Gaol Archives, 19NW-1E11-06, *Ná Bac Leis*.

20   BMH, MA, WS 665, Francis O'Duffy, pp. 24–5.

21   Walsh, *On My Keeping and in Theirs*, pp. 95–6.

22   *Ibid.*

23   UCD AD, P53/117 (8), Michael Hayes Collection.

24   *The Freeman's Journal*, 22 September 1921.

25   UCD AD, P53 /117 (8), Michael Hayes Collection.

26   Kilmainham Gaol Archives, 19NW-1E11-06, *Ná Bac Leis*.

27   *Ibid.*

28   NLI, Ms 26,763, Frederick Allan Papers.

10 Disputes between the Internees and British Military

1   BMH, MA, WS 665, Francis O'Duffy, p. 21.

2   BNA, CAB 24/125 – IR 0084.

3   Walsh, *On My Keeping and in Theirs*, pp. 50–1.

4   BMH, MA, WS 850, Patrick Colgan, pp. 81–3.

5   Walsh, *On My Keeping and in Theirs*, pp. 83–6.

6   BMH, MA, WS 850, Patrick Colgan, pp. 81–2.

7   UCD AD, P53/117 (8), Michael Hayes Collection.

8   BMH, MA, WS 850, Patrick Colgan, pp. 82–3.

9   Walsh, *On My Keeping and in Theirs*, pp. 87–92.

10   NLI, Ms 10,972 (2).

11   *Ibid.*

12   UCD AD, P53/117 (7), Michael Hayes Collection.

13   Kilmainham Gaol Archives, Ballykinlar Diary of Ted Donohue.

14   Letter by Thomas Fitzpatrick (Maurice 'Mossie' Donegan), *The Freeman's Journal*, 13 October 1921.

15   NLI, Ms 10,972 (2).

16   Letter by Thomas Fitzpatrick (Maurice 'Mossie' Donegan), *The Freeman's Journal*, 13 October 1921.

17   *Ibid.*

18   *Ibid.*

19   *Ibid.*, 4 November 1921.

20   *Ibid.*, 13 October 1921.

21   *Ibid.*, 4 November 1921.

22   BMH, MA, WS 668, Gerald (Garry) Byrne, pp. 13–14.

11 The Irish Products League

1   UCD AD, P53/117 (6), Michael Hayes Collection.

2   Kilmainham Gaol Archives, 19N-1D23-28, *The Barbed Wire*.

3   NLI, Ms 26,763, Frederick Allan Papers.

12 Escape Attempts

1   BMH, MA, WS 665, Francis O'Duffy, p. 14.

2   BMH, MA, WS 1093, Thomas Treacy, p. 86.

3   BMH, MA, WS 1582, Thomas McGlynn, p. 9.

4   BMH, MA, WS 1322, Art O'Donnell, p. 62.

5   BMH, MA, WS 1582, Thomas McGlynn, p. 10.

6   *Irish Independent*, 30 December 1924.

7   BMH, MA, WS 639, Maurice Donegan, p. 7.

8   *Ibid.*, p. 8.

9   BMH, MA, WS 1322, Art O'Donnell, p. 63.

10   BMH, MA, WS 850, Patrick Colgan, pp. 88–9.

11   *Irish Independent*, 30 December 1924.

12   BMH, MA, WS 1322, Art O'Donnell, p. 63.

13   BMH, MA, WS 1322, Art O'Donnell & WS 1582, Thomas McGlynn; *Irish Independent*, 30 December 1924.

14   BMH, MA, WS 639, Maurice Donegan, p. 8.

15   BNA, CAB 24/126 – IR 0098.

16   Kilmainham Gaol Archives, Ballykinlar Diary of Ted Donohue.

17   BMH, MA, WS 1093, Thomas Treacy, pp. 86–7.

18   *The Freeman's Journal*, 19 November 1921.

19   UCD AD P17 b/104, Ernie O'Malley Notebooks, Michael Sheehy interview. Thank you to Margaret Carton, Rathmullan for this source.

20   *Irish Independent*, 30 December 1924.

21   UCD AD, P17b/104, Ernie O'Malley Notebooks, Michael Sheehy interview.

22   *Irish Independent*, 14 October 1921.

23   UCD AD, P17b/104, Ernie O'Malley Notebooks, Michael Sheehy interview.

24   BMH, MA, WS 639, Maurice Donegan, pp. 8–10.

25   BMH, MA, WS 850, Patrick Colgan, p. 89.

26   *Ibid.*

27   Letter by Thomas Treacy, *The Freeman's Journal*, 24 October 1921.

28   BMH, MA, WS 387, Patrick O'Daly, pp. 60–1.

29   BMH, MA, WS 1582, Thomas McGlynn, pp. 11–12.

30   BMH, MA, WS 1581, Seán D. MacLoughlin, pp. 6–7.

31   *Derry Journal*, 6 June 1921.

13 The Ballykinlar Newsletters and Photography

1   BMH, MA, WS 1322, Art O'Donnell, pp. 67–8.
2   Kilmainham Gaol Archives, 19N-1D23-28, *The Barbed Wire*.
3   Kilmainham Gaol Archives, 19NW-1E11-06, *Ná Bac Leis*.
4   *Ibid*.
5   *Ibid*.
6   Kilmainham Gaol Archives, 19NW-1D22-15, *Ná Bac Leis*.
7   Kilmainham Gaol Archives, 19NW-1E11-06, *Ná Bac Leis*.
8   *Ibid*.
9   *Ibid*.
10 Kilmainham Gaol Archives, 19NW-1E11-01, *Ná Bac Leis*.
11 Kilmainham Gaol Archives, 19NW-1E11-06, *Ná Bac Leis*.
12 Kilmainham Gaol Archives, 19MS-1B41-10, 'Barbed-Wire Photography. How it was done in Ballykinlar.'
13 Ballykinlar Diary of Ted Donoghue, Kilmainham Gaol Archives.

14 Ballykinlar and the 1921 Elections

1   BNA, CAB 24/94 – IR 0069.
2   BNA, CAB 24/117 – IR 0027.
3   *Irish Independent*, 12 May 1921.
4   *Ibid*., 13 May 1921.
5   *Ibid*.; Walsh, *On My Keeping and in Theirs*, p. 103.
6   *Irish Independent*, 12 May 1921.
7   www.oireachtas.ie/parliament/about/history/parliamentinireland/
8   *The Irish Times*, 25 May 1921.
9   Dorothy Macardle, *The Irish Republic*, Wolfhound Press, 1999.

15 The IRA and British Truce – July 1921

1   BNA, CAB 24/126 – IR 0066.
2   *Irish Independent*, 2 May 1921.
3   *Ibid*., 25 July 1921.

4 *The Freeman's Journal*, 12 August 1921.
5 *The Irish Times*, 8 August 1921.
6 BNA, CAB 24/127 – IR 0024.
7 Jim Dawson Ballykinlar Papers.
8 *The Freeman's Journal*, 22 September 1921.
9 BMH, MA, WS 665, Francis O'Duffy (Addendum).
10 *The Freeman's Journal*, 4 November 1921.
11 *Ibid.*, 7 November 1921.
12 *Irish Independent*, 7 October 1921.
13 *Ibid.*, 12 October 1921.
14 Reported in the *Westmeath Examiner*, 29 October 1921.
15 Reported in the *Irish Independent*, 12 October 1921.
16 *The Freeman's Journal*, 18 November 1921.
17 *Ibid.*, 19 October 1921.
18 *Irish Independent*, 14 October 1921.
19 *The Freeman's Journal*, 17 October 1921.
20 *Ibid.*, 15 October 1921.
21 *Ibid.*, 15 October 1921, 17 October 1921.
22 *Ibid.*, 27 October 1921.
23 *Irish Independent*, 1 December 1921.

16 The Murder of Tadhg Barry

1 BMH, MA, WS 665, Francis O'Duffy, p. 25.
2 BMH, MA, WS 1093, Thomas Treacy, p. 88.
3 UCD AD, 17b/104, Ernie O'Malley Notebooks, Michael Sheehy interview.
4 BMH, MA, WS 944, Michael Staines, pp. 31–2.
5 UCD AD, P17b/104, Ernie O'Malley Notebooks, Michael Sheehy interview.
6 *The Freeman's Journal*, 17 November 1921.
7 BMH, MA, WS 1581, Seán D. MacLoughlin, p. 6; BMH, MA, WS 952, Maurice Horgan, p. 11.
8 *The Freeman's Journal*, 17 November 1921.
9 BMH, MA, WS 665, Francis O'Duffy, pp. 25–6.

10 Donal Ó Drisceoil, *Tadhg Barry (1880–1921) The Story of an Irish Revolutionary* (pamphlet), Trade Union Labour, 2011, p. 26.

11 BMH, MA, WS 665, Francis O'Duffy, pp. 25–6.

12 *The Freeman's Journal*, 19 November 1921.

13 BMH, MA, WS 665, Francis O'Duffy, p. 26.

14 *The Freeman's Journal*, 16 November 1921.

15 Ó Drisceoil, *Tadhg Barry*, pp. 7, 11, 14.

16 UCD AD, P80/136, Desmond Fitzgerald Collection.

17 BMH, MA, WS 665, Francis O'Duffy, p. 26.

18 *The Freeman's Journal*, 17 November 1921.

19 *Ibid.*

20 *Irish Independent*, 19 November 1921.

21 *The Freeman's Journal*, 19 November 1921.

22 *Ibid.*, 18 November 1921; *The Irish Times*, 21 November 1921; Ó Drisceoil, *Tadhg Barry*, p. 28.

23 Ó Drisceoil, *Tadhg Barry*, p. 28.

24 *The Irish Times*, 21 November 1921.

25 *The Freeman's Journal*, 28 November 1921.

26 BMH, MA, WS 665, Francis O'Duffy, p. 27.

27 BMH, MA, WS 1322, Art O'Donnell, pp. 65–6.

28 *Irish Independent*, 14 December 1921.

29 *Ibid.*

30 *Ibid.*

17 The Treaty and Release

1 BNA, CAB 23/27 – IR 0018.

2 BNA, CAB 23/39 – IR 0019.

3 BNA, CAB 23/27 – IR 0018.

4 BMH, MA, WS 1322, Art O'Donnell, pp. 66.

5 UCD AD, 17b/104, Ernie O'Malley Notebooks.

6 *Irish Independent*, 10 December 1921.

7 BMH, MA, WS 1093, Thomas Treacy, p. 89.

8 BMH, MA, WS 1322, Art O'Donnell, pp. 66–7.

9   *The Freeman's Journal*, 10 December 1921.

10   *Irish Independent*, 10 December 1921.

11   *The Freeman's Journal*, 10 December 1921.

12   *The New York Times*, 10 December 1921.

13   BMH, MA, WS 1093, Thomas Treacy, p. 90.

14   *Ibid.*, pp. 91–4.

15   *The Freeman's Journal*, 10 December 1921.

16   NLI, CAB 24/131 – IR 0065.

17   BMH, MA, WS 1322, Art O'Donnell, pp. 66–7.

18   NLI, Ms 10,972, Ballykinlar and Miscellaneous; BMH, MA, WS 1322 Art O'Donnell, pp. 66–7.

19   *Derry Journal*, 14 December 1921.

20   *The Freeman's Journal*, 15 December 1921.

21   BNA CAB 24/131 – IR 0065.

22   BMH, MA, WS 665, Francis O'Duffy, pp. 27–8.

Postscript

1   BNA, CAB 24/125 –IR 0084.

2   *Ibid.*

3   BNA, CAB 24/126 – IR 0066.

Bibliography

Primary Sources

Kilmainham Gaol Museum
Ballykinlar Collection
Diary of Ted Donohue

University College Dublin Archives
Desmond Fitzgerald Collection
Michael Hayes Collection
Ernie O'Malley Notebooks

National Library of Ireland
Frederick Allan Papers
Owen Quinn Papers
Seán O'Mahony Papers
Ballykinlar Miscellaneous Collection
Book of Ballykinlar (Microfilm)

Bureau of Military History
Witness Statements 1913–1921

National Archives of Ireland
Accession Number: 98/25 (Photographic Collection)

British Parliamentary Records
(accessible at http://hansard.millbanksystems.com)
Contains parliamentary information licensed under the Open
    Parliament Licence v1.0

Private Collections
Patrick Dawson, *Jim Dawson Ballykinlar Papers*

Kathleen McKenna, *Stephen Carroll Ballykinlar Collection*

Newspapers

Derry Journal
Evening Herald
Freeman's Journal, The
Irish Independent
Irish Times, The
New York Times, The
Westmeath Examiner

Secondary Sources

Carey, Tim & de Búrca, Marcus, 'Bloody Sunday 1920 – New Evidence', *History Ireland*, Issue 2 (Summer 2003), Vol. 11 (www.historyireland.com)

Dwyer, T. Ryle, *The Squad and the Intelligence Operations of Michael Collins*, Mercier Press, 2005

Gleeson, James, *Bloody Sunday*, First Four Square Edition, 1963

Gordon, Major Lawrence, *British Battles and Medals*, revised by John Hayward, Diana Birch and Richard Bishop, Spink, 2008

Hopkinson, Michael, *The Irish War of Independence*, Gill and Macmillan, 2004

Macardle, Dorothy, *The Irish Republic*, Wolfhound Press, 1999

Ó Drisceoil, Donal, *Tadhg Barry (1880–1921) The Story of an Irish Revolutionary* (pamphlet), Trade Union Labour, 2011

Ó Lúing, Seán, 'The German Plot 1918', *Capuchin Annual*, 1968

O'Mahony, Seán, *Frongoch, University of Revolution*, FDR Teoranta, 1987

Quinn, Comdt Owen, 'The Books of Ballykinlar', *An Cosantóir*, December 1983, p. 402

Sheehan, William, *Hearts and Mines*, Collins Press, 2009

Sinn Féin Rebellion Handbook, 1917 (Private collection Liam MacElhinney)

Sweeney, Major-General Joseph A., 'Donegal and the War of Independence', *The Capuchin Annual*, 1970

Walsh, Louis J., *On My Keeping and in Theirs: a record of experiences 'on the run', in Derry Gaol, and in Ballykinlar Interment Camp*, Talbot Press, 1921 (Private Collection, Liam MacElhinney)

Index